QUALITY ASSURANCE IN CONTINUING PROFESSIONAL EDUCATION

Higher education in the 1990s is characterised by a pre-occupation with quality assurance. This book provides an examination of what that means for the academic speciality of continuing professional education. As well as working towards a practical strategy for quality CPE, the author considers a number of issues which emerge from discussions of quality and of educating professionals – recurrent themes include the problems associated with the adoption of customer ideology and the relationship between pedagogic aims and prevailing assumptions about quality.

Based on research conducted in and around UK universities, the book is divided into two parts. Part one deals with context, looking at theoretical developments and practical strategies used for quality assurance in other areas, such as the construction industry, health care and welfare provision. This section also includes a detailed review of BS5750, and its relevance to CPE. Part two explores the range of attitudes and existing practice in CPE. And identifying CPE as a distinct subject area, it is argued that solutions cannot simply be brought in, but must be developed in relation to setting.

Philip Tovey is Senior Research Fellow in the Department of Continuing Professional Education at the University of Leeds.

QUALITY ASSURANCE IN CONTINUING PROFESSIONAL EDUCATION

An analysis

Philip Tovey

London and New York

First published 1994
by Routledge
11 New Fetter Lane, London EC4P 4EE

Simultaneously published in the USA and Canada
by Routledge
29 West 35th Street, New York, NY 10001

Typeset in Garamond by LaserScript, Mitcham, Surrey
Printed and bound in Great Britain by
Biddles Ltd, Guildford and King's Lynn

British Library Cataloguing in Publication Data
A catalogue record for this book is available from the British Library

Library of Congress Cataloging in Publication Data
Tovey, Philip, 1963–
Quality assurance in continuing professional education:
an analysis/Philip Tovey.
p. cm.
Includes bibliographical references and index.
1. Professional education – Great Britain – Evaluation.
2. Continuing education – Great Britain – Evaluation.
3. Quality assurance – Great Britain. I. Title.
LC1059.T68   1994
378′.013′0941 – dc20   93-40798
CIP

ISBN 0-415-09831-9

CONTENTS

ILLUSTRATIONS

TABLES

FIGURES

ACKNOWLEDGEMENTS

The research on which this book is based was supported by the Universities Funding Council (UFC). Chapter 4 is a revised version of a paper previously published in *Studies in the Education of Adults* (Tovey 1992).

Turning to individuals, my initial thanks go to the wide range of people – in universities, the National Health Service, commercial companies and professional institutions – who completed questionnaires, gave forthright interviews and contributed numerous valuable documents. Of course, all of the above participants must remain anonymous.

Thanks are also due to: James Armstrong, Heather Dickie, Pauline Neale, and Reg Wright (all – now or recently – of the Department of Continuing Professional Education, University of Leeds); Ray Pawson (Department of Sociology, University of Leeds); and Liam Murphy (Leeds Metropolitan University). Lynda McStay provided exceptional support work throughout the project, including the typing of the manuscript.

I would also like to acknowledge the role of: Frankie Todd, especially for her comments on an earlier draft of the text; Rudi Taylor for similarly ploughing through the book and offering constructive comment on it; and Keith Hurst for looking at the health section of chapter 1 and for providing access to unpublished material.

INTRODUCTION

Both quality assurance (QA) and continuing professional education (CPE) have a high profile in contemporary UK universities. One is not reliant on the other, each has an impact in its own right. But it is the integration of the two that is the concern of this book. The following analysis – of QA in CPE – addresses issues raised by this fusion; it is also directed towards the identification of a framework within which practical strategies can emerge.

Such a project is in many ways a challenging one. For, to date, there has been a tendency to conceptualise both of these elements in limited and restrictive terms: QA as a matter of organisation; CPE as technical updating. Frequently both have been treated as isolated phenomena, devoid of context. In considering the interaction of these two strands, the appropriateness of such a foundation will be questioned.

The book draws heavily on my own research into quality in CPE, carried out during the early 1990s. In keeping with the need to open up discussion – to move beyond limits implied by the restrictive interpretations of the main concepts – the research was approached from a number of angles: the contextual (a review of the complexities of working towards quality in various settings); the analytical (a detailed critique of a favoured system frequently discussed at the level of generality); and the empirical (qualitative and quantitative analyses of the key figures of CPE in and around UK universities). Considered separately, each offers insight into aspects of the current trend towards quality assurance; taken together they can help to shape the direction and composition of future action.

QUALITY IN CONTEXT

On the face of it there could hardly be a more suitable match than the pursuit of quality and the provision of education. Indeed, it might well be argued that the link has (in ways more or less tightly defined) existed consistently almost at the level of assumption, as a rule of pedagogic practice. But to talk of quality in the late twentieth century – and certainly to talk of quality assurance in the same period – is to refer to a specific phenomenon. Quality is not just a concept of education, it is a linchpin of wider society: of consumer society.

Thus while academics and commentators attempt to come to grips with the 'new' idea, its existence as an essential feature of commercial planning, as a near clichéd component of advertising, as a regular feature of countless marketing strategies continues unabated. Quality in the commercial world is a means to an end, and that end is viability and profit.

So from the outset there is something of a paradox: that while quality enhancement as a principle will rarely be questioned, quality assurance as a practice has a meaning embedded in the non-educational. It could certainly be argued – and not without a good degree of justification – that the use of such terminology is fundamentally inappropriate for CPE. And, as will be seen, there is every reason to expect that an uncritical adoption of dominant perceptions of QA would only magnify the tendency for a trivialisation of CPE. However, the case for the development of entirely fresh concepts might have held rather more potential at an earlier juncture. For while education was not the first sector to incorporate the concept of quality assurance, the phrase is now firmly established as part of the general discourse. Significantly, funding bodies and other influential institutions have adopted this terminology. Thus, as a matter of pragmatic realism, an acceptance of the faint possibility of a complete and successful replacement of such language is necessary. Yet, this does not negate the need to actively pursue approaches which reflect the character and purposes of the setting to which they will eventually relate. In other words, the task is to engage with the concepts of quality and quality assurance to produce modes of practice which satisfy the (varying current) requirements of external bodies, but which also – with this being the crucial point – provide the basis from which CPE can develop (bearing in mind the full range of influences and restrictions) in its own right. As such, an educational and social agenda takes precedence over a purely managerial one.

Thus the following sections of this introduction are more than a mere preamble to the main chapters of the text. A closer look at the terms quality and quality assurance, and continuing professional education provide a basis on which subsequent discussions build. The introduction of a broadly based perspective on CPE, alongside a discussion of some of the main problems in the dominant understanding of quality, mark a necessary opening stage for an analysis of the topic.

PROFESSIONS, PROFESSIONALS AND CONTINUING PROFESSIONAL EDUCATION

The initial task to be given some attention is a clarification of the area, a look at the character of the subject matter of CPE. Although this can be undertaken by highlighting usual and expected features of provision, an attempt to impose an overly strict definition on the area might prove to be counter-productive. This is because the range and limits of CPE are to some extent pragmatically determined. Both the subjects covered, and the nature of participants, are influenced by instrumental demands as well as a clear sense of area demarcation. The potentially wide catchment area of CPE is reflected in the definition provided by Jarvis: 'Those learning opportunities which are taken up after the completion of basic vocational preparation' (1990: 78).

The inherent pragmatism of CPE is evident in the type of 'professional' which it embraces. The use of the term in this context perhaps owes rather more to flexibility on the part of universities, and status aspiration on the part of clients, than to an adherence to historically developed identities; or, indeed, to academic definitions of the term. (I will return to the scholastic discussions of professions shortly). It is certainly true that university CPE incorporates elements directed specifically towards those occupational groups which have traditionally been seen to embody 'professional status', for instance, law and medicine. However, it also includes, as a matter of course, many beyond this clique. Indeed this latter group incorporates those whose character has been identified (by writers adhering to a 'trait' centred analysis) as the antithesis of a profession (see Witz 1990: 40–1). For instance, managers, and business personnel in general, are heavily represented amongst CPE participants, despite being

3

frequently (not least by the high status professions themselves) presented as exemplifying the very opposite of a profession (defined in terms of possession of specialist knowledge, holding public service principles and the like).

Where then does such flexibility leave the concept of profession for our concerns? Clearly, at the level of practice the whole issue is frequently side-stepped. Whether or not a particular group constitutes a profession, a semi-profession, an emerging profession or, indeed, not a profession at all tends to be submerged under a consideration of whether the group in question has a particular need which can be met by the institution. But to say that pragmatism governs (or at least heavily influences) day to day action is not to imply the absence of consistencies across client groups. While the search for a tight and unaltering definition of participants may not be appropriate, some similarities between them can be identified. This will help to provide an indication of the make-up of the professions, and the professionals, of university CPE.

These frequently exhibited tendencies (expressed in relation to individuals but clearly describing groups of individuals as well) can be described as follows. First of all, attending clients are usually actively practising in their particular field. This practice is almost invariably made possible by the possession of existing qualifications. Secondly, participants are frequently already educated to at least graduate level. Thirdly, they are in occupations which, as a consequence of the structure of modern societies, almost without exception contain the potential to influence the lives of others. This influence can be direct or indirect; it can lead to an impact at a personal level; or, indeed, at an environmental, social or legal level. Such influence is frequently integral to practice. Fourthly, because of qualifications obtained, and because of the occupational label which goes with those qualifications, such individuals are operating from a basis of legitimate expertise.

Due to the pragmatic entry requirements for involvement in CPE, not every participant will possess each of these characteristics. However, those who hold neither recognised qualifications, nor authority and influence of some kind, will be very few.

Such an appreciation establishes an important basis to the discussion. Although the precise limits of professional status may be debated – and indeed fought over because of the positive connotations it holds – university CPE has a particular niche; an approach to its quality should evolve from an understanding of that.

Once beyond the nature of participants, there are perhaps four further areas which help to clarify the shape of CPE. These are, in the main, essentially practical matters.

1 The short course has been, and to a large extent remains, the usual form of provision. Given the employment responsibilities of attenders this is to be expected. The entire programme may be completed in just one or two days rather than say an academic year. This leaves little room for error. The situation is not, however, a static one. An interest in longer term and/or accredited and/or qualification-based courses is real enough. And while changes in funding arrangements for universities may or may not encourage this, the desire for confirmation of status amongst individuals and occupational groups is certainly very likely to.

2 This leads on to the second of these areas – the reasons for participation. Whilst these are undoubtedly manifold, certain benefits (which act as a spur to involvement) are identifiable. For instance, employers can expect informed or more highly skilled staff; and individuals achieve a higher level of expertise, perhaps confirmed by 'credentials'. Meanwhile, professions are able to point to high levels of education amongst members in order to secure or advance their combined case. CPE, then, fits into the needs structure in a variety of ways. In each case, though, there is a direct line to individuals, communities and societal forms. Whether this is in terms of the confirmation of occupational status, the influence on the practice of individual practitioners or whatever, the link is noted.

3 There is a feature of contemporary CPE which has not yet been included in the discussion, but is one which represents a major constraining, if not determining, influence on its character. It is that probably more so than any other aspect of higher education, CPE (despite the availability of various forms of state input, such as development funds) is, essentially, a self-financing activity. This point will be taken further in due course.

4 Finally, despite the focus of this text, the temptation to regard CPE and university CPE as synonymous should be avoided. Courses in other forms of educational institutions; and the in-house provision of companies and organisations in the public and private sectors, professional bodies, and specialist private companies all contribute to what is currently available. Such an acknowledgement is primarily a question of appropriate

contextualisation. Each source of provision will have its own character and priorities. These will frequently be distinct from those of other providers.

Broadly speaking, then, the above is a summary of the main characteristics of CPE. Clarifying the nature of the professional was an essential part of this. At this point, that theme can be developed somewhat through a brief dip into what can loosely be described as the sociology of the professions. This is, of course, not the place for a comprehensive review of recent developments in this field. However, reference to certain important contributions is of some value. From the start it should be re-affirmed that the relationship between those occupations discussed by the cited authors and those involved in CPE may not always constitute a perfect match. But the point is that there is enough crossover (in terms of the qualification basis, the potential to exercise influence and the other factors listed above) to suggest a definite relevance.

Perhaps the most important of all the theoretical insights of the last two decades or so has been the break with the cosy, uncomplicated, public service idea of a professional (Johnson 1972). Writings earlier in the twentieth century (Carr-Saunders and Wilson 1933; Parsons 1954) frequently emphasised what was apparently special about the professional. The accepted wisdom – of an occupation wedded to distinctive characteristics – was (and is) one that such occupational groups were happy to cling to. An altruistic outlook, the possession of a highly specialised body of knowledge somehow inaccessible to the general public, self-regulation and a professional code were all integral to this. An Anglo-American ethnocentrism (Burrage and Thorstendahl 1990) was characteristic of much of the early work.

Once beyond the interpretation of a profession as a simple, given category, writers were able to discuss professions on a rather different basis. So, for instance, the importance of power struggles in the historical development and evolution to desired status became as much a part of the discussion as any occupational peculiarities (Saks 1983: 2).

Although it is not necessary to extend this discussion too far, it is certainly worth drawing attention to one aspect of the critical re-appraisal of the professions. Whilst itself the subject of much debate, the concept of social closure (see Parkin 1979; Murphy 1988; Collins 1990; Witz 1990) has frequently held centre stage in discussions. In essence, the concept is used as a means of analysing the way in which social groups (of which professions might well be primary examples) manipulate situations in order to secure or enhance their own positions. Restricting access to a defined status by means of establishing and/or confirming the nature of the valid credentials needed to practise is one such means. While the process of closure may relate to securing upward social mobility for the occupation as a whole, or maintaining advantages already secured, the importance of defining and acquiring expertise as a basis for legitimate practice is considerable.

How then do such writings feed the task of understanding the nature of professions and, not unrelatedly, the nature of those people participating in university CPE? On this, there are several points which can be made. First, professional status has been, and continues to be, highly prized. Moreover, these categories are not fixed but are influenced by competition and struggles between various interested parties. The quest for professional status goes on.

Second, the understanding of a profession based primarily on an image of selflessness and community interest has been seen to be dubious. As complexities beyond this image are characteristic of the traditional professions which formed the basis of sociological analyses, the need to take a realistic view of CPE's less traditional professions is apparent. This is not to suggest an across-the-board disregard for the 'community good', but rather that as a defining characteristic of the particular population, it is not particularly informative.

Third, that their place in the social structure is almost invariably one which contains some level of power and/or influence. Now to the crux of the matter: in this ongoing pursuit of, or attempt to maintain, professional status, both at an institutional and individual level, education plays a vital 'credentialing role'. It provides one means by which claims to professional status can be objectively supported. And, as a part of this educative process, CPE is inextricably linked with the ongoing operations of professions.

This theme can be developed further. CPE, then, as a component of the education system, has a bearing on status protection and even (in so far as the context permits) status acquisition. An understanding of its particular impact requires the separation and distinct acknowledgement of two elements. To begin with there is the legitimation function already alluded to. CPE does not, and cannot, satisfy this need on its own. However, as part of the overall educational system (by definition, its ongoing element) it clearly contributes to a perception of knowledgeable professions – with skilled professionals – competent to practise. Attendance may be required by professional bodies as part of their attempt to maintain credibility; proof of that attendance may be the only resulting credential. Elsewhere, recognised qualifications may result. Thus, the essence of this is that CPE fits into an overall system of provision which (on this level) *irrespective of content* (i.e. merely by its existence) has an impact on the nature of occupations: on the shape of professions; and on continuing membership of them.

This could be described as a structural characteristic – an almost built-in consequence of the interplay between expertise, (continuing) education and the occupational structure. The other source of influence relates to a point raised earlier – that it is in the nature of the clientele of CPE that their actions affect, in one form or another, the lives of individuals in a wider society. So, what is of significance is that while the form of education may equate with a function of legitimisation and thereby impinge on reality at a structural level, the content will often provide the basis for practical application – it will be utilised in the execution of professional duties. As a result, it may well influence the lives of a broad sweep of non-professionals (and, in fact, professionals of other specialisms). This is, of course, not to argue that such learned material would be applied in a non-mediated singular form. It is instead to make explicit the realisation that such occupations are in part defined by their potential to affect the lives of others: it therefore brings the *ultimate recipient* (of applied professional expertise) into the CPE equation.

To summarise, there is a need to acknowledge that: professions and professionals are socially constructed and contested statuses; and that education plays a key role in achieving and securing that status and in marking off lines of differentiation from non-professionals. Also, professionals are able to exert influence (as legitimate purveyors of expertise) over others; the content of expert knowledge evolves and is modifiable; and the CPE provision does not reach its end point with the professional. It is interpreted by him or her, and is subsequently developed and applied in numerous local settings.

What then are the implications of all this for our understanding of, and approach to, CPE? Probably the most pressing question which evolves from such discussions relates to the breadth of concerns which are identifiably those of CPE. The issue is whether it is appropriate to treat CPE as merely an isolated process of short-course provision, of technical updating – a matter to be tackled in relation to a straightforward relationship between the buyer and seller, or to borrow the terminology currently sweeping through another public sector, the purchaser and the provider. It is my view that such conceptual relegation of CPE is not helpful. Indeed, to persist with this would be to disregard the actual importance of ongoing education for wider social processes. Furthermore, it would actually serve to direct discussions of quality away from those matters which go some way towards defining the territory.

As an activity traditionally at the margins of university life, and one exposed to the market, it is not too difficult to see how such a limited perception may become institutionalised. The requirement to address quality in CPE does though provide an opportunity for a closer examination of the subject matter.

Despite the institutional pressures which exist on providers of CPE, support for a more demanding understanding of CPE does exist. Houle (1980, 1983, 1984) has, of course, done much to consider this area of education. One feature of his work has been an argument that the history of CPE can be divided into eras. It is proposed that there is currently a shift under way from an era in which CPE has been all about establishing minimum permissible standards towards an era defined by the pursuit of the highest attainable level (1983: 257). This aim of ultimate professional effectiveness clearly requires that the ongoing source of professional education be conceptualised rather differently than as provision-in-a-vacuum. For ultimate effectiveness can only be considered in relation to activity beyond the university.

Implications of a similar form can be drawn from the following quotation from another well-known commentator.

> Being an effective continuing professional education practitioner requires a clear and explicit recognition of the place of the professions in society. Without this understanding, educators are left without an important tool for making decisions in their daily practice and ultimately for improving their practice.
>
> (Cervero 1988: 18)

New technology is often a mainstay of CPE provision. It can secure an impersonal and apolitical image which contributes to a technical orientation for education. But as has been pointed out by several writers, such innovations are applied by professionals and, therefore, have direct social consequences. These same writers note the implications of this for practice. For instance, McIlroy (1988: 13) has argued that a practical and vocational continuing education requires a balance which considers the social setting into which – for example – new technologies might be applied. Although the argument is essentially one couched in terms of the problems facing liberal adult education, the implications for CPE remain intact. And on a similar theme, it has been argued that

> education for the professions must not only involve some conscious attention to the technical component of the professional service (physiology, circuit analysis, operational research etc) but also to the fundamentally moral issue of who is controlling what knowledge for whose benefit.
>
> (Goodlad 1984: 9)

Such a perspective is evident in the socio-technical approach to CPE of Hartley (1990). Here again, the centrality of the technical dimension to education is not denied. Instead, the stated intention is for an integration of it with an awareness of the policy context, and of the consciousness of the professionals themselves.

And lastly, a non-isolationist approach finds support in the writings of a major international institution. Although there is only a partial overlap with our concerns, the emphasis in the writing is clear enough. For while the practical concerns of the European Commission see to it that the demands induced by technological change figure prominently in thinking, it is stated that 'the social role of continuing education should not be overlooked' (Commission of the European Communities 1991: 25).

As part of the approach which attempts to extend the conceptualisation of CPE, the notion of an activity *existing at a point of tension* can be introduced. By this I am suggesting that the influences on CPE interact to form a situation of potential conflict. This is a distillation of some of the issues introduced earlier: for the potentially conflicting elements are the market location of provision; and the underlying character of that same provision as a socially located form of education. To a large extent a simple understanding of the subject matter – one which focuses heavily on the market and the provision of a technical correct product – avoids this tension. However, the inevitable consequence is that a sense of the complexities of the nature and role of professionals, their reliance on education and their place in the social whole are lost. Thus, opening up discussions about the nature of CPE does not, in the initial stages at least, make life easier. But without it, a very one-dimensional and distorted image of the subject matter is produced.

The whole subject area of professions, professionals and their continuing education is thus far from unproblematic. Matching skills and knowledge with those who want to acquire them is but one facet of CPE. It might be the all-important one for certain individuals, but for those concerned with the direction and significance of CPE, it is unable to offer more than a partial expression of the totality. A clarification of the nature of CPE is a necessary stage in the development of an approach to its quality.

QUALITY AND QUALITY ASSURANCE

Something of a consensus has emerged alongside the increased use of the above terms. In many and varied settings, a degree of harmony has developed about their meaning and about the range of events which it is appropriate for them to embrace. Some measure of continuity with these assumptions can be maintained for the analysis of CPE. There is, though, a problem. Having moved towards an interpretation of CPE which reaches beyond the technical, the chosen conception of quality must be able to tie into that. Those which dominate proceedings currently tend to have rather different emphases.

In simple terms quality assurance can be described as the means of 'getting it right first time' (Muller and Funnell 1991: 3); or as the attempt 'to ensure that high quality is achieved first time, without costly repetitions . . . or slow learning curves. It is concerned with the prevention of error, not with the discovery of errors, its aim is assurance, not the checking of finished products' (Armstrong 1991: 8). Quality assurance, then, is all about putting in place a framework which is designed to maximise the chances of achieving particular goals, as a matter of course.

On the face of it all this seems well and good. There seems little reason to question such a principle, whatever the context. But once past this initial stage, difficulties associated with the use of the term quality assurance become somewhat clearer. The immediate problem of incorporation relates to both the origin and orientation of the recent quality assurance phenomenon in the UK; and to the understanding of quality which is brought with it.

The difficulty lies in the commercial basis of much of the writings in this field and the assumptions which are carried forward from these. The pivotal issue is whether the way in which quality is defined is amenable to the task of tackling a complex activity like CPE. Quality has come to be understood in a very limited way, as if no other interpretation of greater breadth were possible. A closer look at the concept will reveal some of the problems faced.

Taken in isolation, currently favoured definitions of quality can be seen to range from the essentially bland and uncontroversial – 'fitness for purpose' – to the rather more troublesome – 'conformance to specification' – (see Ruston 1992: 86). In themselves, they do not tell us too much. There is a need to gain an idea of what lies behind them.

By looking one step beyond the headline definition, what is arguably the real centrepiece of the current trend is revealed. For example, in a recent text directly concerned with the integration of quality into vocational education, the reader is told, 'Quality is conforming to customer requirements. . . . Quality is customer driven and is the total of all those things which combine to satisfy the needs of the market place' (Muller and Funnell 1991: 34). In the preceding discussion, doubt was expressed about the value of re-stricting an interpretation of CPE to an interplay between attending professionals and providers. Quality expressed in the way detailed above – with the customer and the market as the major reference points – would induce just such a narrowness of perspective, and a denial of the location and impact of CPE. It is a realisation of this that has led to the introduction of a theme to be developed at various points in the text: the questioning of whether broad approaches to quality (and relatedly its assurance) make sense; or whether in contrast, context-specific formulations should be pursued. With this in mind, the *critique of the customer* can be advanced a little further.

As a cornerstone of the new wave of interest in QA, the concept of the customer fulfils a range of criteria essential to a market-based approach. At once, it gives high priority to 'responsiveness'; to meeting 'real' needs; it is straightforward; and has more than a liberal sprinkling of populist appeal. In much the same way as a critic would be on dangerous territory if s/he failed to embrace the idea of 'getting it right first time', to fail to adhere to the primacy of the customer is to court the charge of unresponsiveness, and there-fore the charge of an absence of quality.

It is, though, the idea that everything hangs on the customer that is the problem. One point should be made clear: in no sense am I rejecting the importance of producing provision which satisfies client need. But what I am arguing is that to rely on the concept of the customer (satisfaction) as the only indicator, as *the* measure of quality, *is to encourage precisely the limited notion of CPE already rejected.* This is because – following commercial rationale – it is only suited to dealing with one aspect of provision, its immediate and observable face. The bi-party customer satisfaction model has no need, and no capacity, for anything which does not directly relate to discrete aspects of provision. Quality becomes confined to one level.

Just as the introduction of the customer as the key term has practical implications, so too it has symbolic importance. It draws in an acceptance of the principles of a market philosophy. There is a sense in which the high profile given to the concept of the customer is symptomatic of a belief that all significant institutions – be they public or private – are essentially operating within the same terms of reference.

Following this line of thought the only difference is that the commercial world is significantly further advanced in the pursuit of the desired goal than the public services. The task for the latter is to emulate the 'successes' of the commercial world. By challenging this assumption, the first steps can be taken towards drawing into the quality debate those characteristics which help define the specific character of CPE. Moreover, this works to mark out lines of distinction from purely commercial enterprises. Measures of quality based on repeat business, institutional survival and related matters have a particularly damaging corollary. It is to reduce the discussion of quality in CPE to a level which has little meaning beyond the ability of a given unit, centre or department to present an acceptable image: it takes on a marketing rationale.

The above can be used to clarify the most appropriate starting point for an engagement with the nature of QA in CPE. My contention is that although it may be appropriate to acknowledge the potential relevance of features of QA as practised elsewhere, the frameworks within which they operate should be treated with considerable caution. There is a need to question perceptions of quality borne of the commercial, and to consider whether an approach to a quality CPE can build on the experiences of other sectors, but develop a strategy distinct from them. A crucial task is to query the pursuit of quality as customer satisfaction; to ask whether an understanding of quality more suited to the actual character of CPE is required.

Neither these comments (on quality and quality assurance), nor the earlier ones on professions and professionals, are of academic interest alone: they go to the heart of discussions. Both yield practical implications. Moreover these analyses are closely connected. The concerns of CPE as an entity are broad: they involve questions about forms of knowledge; about the impact of techniques and skills; and about the role and influence of clients in broader society. It would be hard to justify a claim for quality – in anything but the most instrumental sense – which had not included a consideration of the same issues.

ABOUT THE BOOK

The topic of quality assurance is quite clearly a practice-related matter; the implications of what is discussed are looked at in terms of shifts in policy at departmental and institutional levels. That much is self-evident and not specific to CPE.

Indeed, by and large, discussions of QA are accompanied by a step by step guide to system utilisation – writings focus on the how-to dimension. But a consequence of this understandable pre-occupation with policy is that other issues remain untouched. In this text, whilst retaining a hold on the need to work towards a practical solution, matters relating to quality, to the nature of CPE, or both – matters of interest in their own right – are also developed (in fact, implications for action are rarely far away).

QA is not treated in a way which confines it to the level of organisation. It is seen as a challenge requiring a creative solution in the context of many layers of influence and interest. Thus, there is an attempt to open up a wide range of information sources. Details of practices and systems are included for sure, but so too are analyses of attitudes and motivations.

So, a major consequence of the employed rationale and emphasis is that the book does not spoon-feed intricate details of procedure from the outset. Instead, the aim is to offer access to, and an active engagement with, evidence of particular relevance to the subject matter.

The resultant framework for action is precisely that – a frame-work, a model within which there is a possibility of, or even a requirement for, individual interpretation. Consequently, while elements of the framework are laid out in some detail, this does not close off options. It identifies those areas which an educationally centred approach to quality would do well to address, without dictating every nuance of eventual application. The priorities of the author, not least in relation to favoured components and rejected systems, will though become clear in the course of the text.

The book is divided into two parts. Part I deals with context: it looks at potential concerns, influences and systems. The practical relevance of this section for CPE will become clear. However, because it provides details on, and analysis of, a range of new information, it will also be of value to those interested in the nature of quality as a generalised feature of modern societies. For in the course of identifying work of value to CPE, the first three chapters bring together commentaries, research and reviews – frequently from the 1990s – which have, to date, remained largely confined to their own specialist audience.

Part II presents the findings of my empirical research with the key figures of CPE in and around UK universities. It should be noted that as UFC funded research, conducted immediately prior to the end of the binary divide, the focus is on the 'old' universities. As with part I this section is of value on two levels: it can be read as contributing to the basis of knowledge from which approaches to quality can be considered, and it can be seen to provide stand-alone analyses – providing hitherto unavailable data, and discussion on the basis of that data.

Chapter 1 is based on the recognition that QA is not an education-specific concept or practice, but instead constitutes a widely based trend. The examples of the construction industry, health care and welfare provision are employed to illustrate the kinds of practical strategies utilised in other sectors and – perhaps in many ways more importantly – to highlight the kinds of analyses and commentaries which have accompanied the quality process. The themes of the chapter are therefore: to provide a focused review of these areas as part of the general process of context establishment; to consider the potential for cross-sectoral deployment of strategies; and to consider what there has been in the experience of these sectors which may hold implications for CPE.

Chapter 2 concentrates solely on BS5750 – or to be more specific – on a critical review of its form and requirements. The issue involved is a simple one: whether or not this standard provides a sound basis for the institutionalisation of quality in CPE.

Chapter 3 can be read as a link between parts I and II. For whilst still very much a review chapter, it brings discussions 'closer to home'. It is concerned with quality and post-compulsory education. In this relatively short chapter evidence on activity in further education, higher education and, indeed, UK and US university continuing education is presented. There is also a brief clarification of the national setting within which quality issues in CPE must be addressed.

Part II opens with chapter 4. This is a discussion of a survey-based investigation of existing activity and prevailing attitudes amongst the co-ordinators and central providers of CPE in UK universities. Included in this chapter is an analysis of definitions of quality; aims for provision; ongoing practice; valued procedures; and perceived barriers to the development of quality.

In chapter 5 the empirical analysis is extended to the second main group of CPE providers in UK universities – those located beyond the centre in non-CE departments. This is also based largely on the quantitative data of a questionnaire-based survey. The nature of the data allowed for consideration of results independently, and comparatively – with the evidence from chapter 4. The terms 'CPE specialists' (for respondents from central units), and 'non-CPE specialists' (for those respondents from other departments) are used. Such terms should be taken as descriptive of major activity and not, of course, as a judgement of any sort. As contributors to professional education, the providers of chapter 5 are specialists in their own fields.

For chapter 6, attention shifts beyond universities into the realm of interest groups: specifically professional bodies and employers. Through a qualitative review of selected cases, issues relating to the relevance of non-university practice are considered. The role and impact of the customer are discussed.

In the concluding chapter, a framework for quality is proposed. The chapter begins with a re-assessment of the main themes (and questions pertaining to them) of the book. The task is to gather together the practical relevance of the discussions. As a consequence, the framework draws on evidence from each part of the analysis. It is a strategy devised to allow for a proper consideration of the main concepts – QA and CPE – and to thereby avoid the over-simplifications to which they have tended to be exposed. It embraces both procedures which are found to be currently operating effectively, and those which are presently under-used. But crucially it works towards the removal of the assumption of neutrality from the operation of those procedures, and from associated conceptions of quality. Thus, the framework draws on the contextual, analytical and empirical phases of the book to establish a practical, yet broadly based, approach.

Part I

QUALITY AND
QUALITY ASSURANCE

1

THEORY AND PRACTICE
BEYOND EDUCATION

With all the hullabaloo surrounding quality issues in higher education
it is easy enough to overlook the point that the process which is under
way is actually being mirrored, and in some cases has been preceded,
by similar attempts to pin down and operationalise the term in a range
of contexts. It is seemingly becoming an institutional ever present, the
first item to be confirmed on the agenda in both the public and private
sectors. But that is only a part of the story. For while a review of many
sectors will reveal a consistency of terminology, the courting of the
same managerialist rationale and even pressures for the adoption of the
same systems, a closer examination will reveal points of divergence
which are helping to shape the trends in particular sectors.

Given the range of options available, selecting three sectors – the
construction industry, health and welfare – inevitably involved a
degree of subjective assessment. Despite this the selection was not
purely arbitrary. Each case offers details of theory, practice or of
continuing evolution which should prove to be of interest to these
beyond the immediate specialism.

In a sense the rationale of this chapter is consistent with that for
part I and, indeed, for the book as a whole. For it acts as both a
discrete source of information; and it provides implications for
developing approaches. The resource role emerges against a
background of patchy and uneven knowledge about QA activity
amongst CPE practitioners. This situation is quantified in part II.

The potential applications of this review extend beyond the overt
search for usable practices. This review offers insight into varying
interpretations of quality, and identifies how quality emerged as an
issue in particular locations. Also, it provides access to aspects of
practice, isolated cases of theoretical development, and the main
lines of emerging critical discourse.

21

Although there is some similarity in the themes discussed in each example, the production of a strict comparative analysis is not the aim. Instead, each sector is approached in a manner specific to it; one designed to maximise the value of each illustration. For example, the inclusion of the construction industry is a deliberate attempt to provide some detail on the way in which quality is understood and applied in one branch of the private sector. The emphasis here is on detailing the kind of system which operates in construction, and on revealing the interpretation of quality which provides the foundation for this. The discussions of health and welfare are structured rather differently. Priority is given to commentators on the process, to those whose input helps uncover the frequently complex and contentious nature of the quality issue. Whether or not the human/social character of health and welfare have encouraged context-specific discussions and solutions is a dominant theme.

QUALITY ASSURANCE AND THE CONSTRUCTION INDUSTRY

In introducing a discussion of construction industry practice we are, by any definition, a considerable distance from CPE. This is where the demands of the market are matched with the technical skills of the engineer. This is where the concepts of quality and quality assurance are clearly understood and equally clearly operationalised.

So why an interest in construction? Plainly, such an interest does not lie in the potential for a step by step utilisation of exactly the same procedures that this sector employs. The very real differences between the titles and responsibilities of key participants, and the obvious differences in content, see to that. However, once immediate expressions of inappropriateness have been put to one side, there are features of the situation which help to clarify why an interest in this area is a legitimate one.

To begin with, it contributes to the process of information acquisition already alluded to. Thus, if for no other reason than to gain an understanding of how the concept is institutionalised in this sector, one far removed from the life of higher education institutions, our attention is valid. But interest is grounded in something more substantial than inquisitiveness and a standard collation of background knowledge alone. We are, in fact, forced to take notice of what practice entails in settings like construction because the principles employed frequently re-appear in other settings: managerialism and complying with pre-identified schema are recurrent examples of this. This is an opportunity to reach beyond the rhetoric – of lessons to be learned – to see whether the style of approach utilised in industry is compatible with the requirements of education.

There is one feature of the construction industry which ensures that it is of particular interest to educationalists. For while the quality process is in part directed by the nature of standards developed within the relevant professions, much of what takes place does so within the limits of British Standards. While there are numerous standards involved, the co-ordinating role is reserved for BS5750.

Thus the example of the construction industry is able to provide an illustration of the kind of formalised approach – including the use of BS5750 – that is currently sweeping organisations in modern Britain. It cannot, of course, be taken as representing each and every one of these. It does, though, provide an indication of what may regularly be involved.

To pull this discussion together, it is possible to distinguish two issues which the review should properly address, and which will require comment subsequent to it. The first goes to the centre of the debate. It is whether the quality that is being worked towards in construction can be conceptualised in the same terms as that which is relevant to CPE. This is not a matter of content, but form: orientation and structure. The second issue develops from the first. It is a consideration of whether approaches to assuring quality (systems, procedures) can be developed in the same terms in sectors as diverse as education and construction. To consider these issues, I will begin with a brief overview of the industry and continue with a presentation of the typical QA requirements placed on its main professionals and other participants. A recent article by Armstrong (1991) is the source of much of the technical information.

NATURE OF THE CONSTRUCTION INDUSTRY

The construction industry usually deals with large-scale projects. It is not unusual for these to take several years to complete. It is in the nature of the work that once finished no future project will be conducted in quite the same terms again. These one-off projects, virtually without exception, require substantial financial backing.

23

They also require the co-ordination of a range of participants, each contributing specific skills or the provision of particular materials. The importance ascribed to ensuring that the construction meets specific quality requirements first time is – even to those of us beyond the industry – recognisably appropriate.

CPE provision rarely takes the form of a non-repeated event; although as Armstrong (1991) points out, the repeated units are frequently the subject of only minor modification. In both the construction and the educational setting the institutionalisation of quality would seem to make practical as well as professional sense. However, perhaps the identification of a basis of similarity between the two processes does not take us too far. The recognition that each of the projects needs to be performed in a way which can be designated as high quality is unlikely to be challenged in any quarter; that it facilitates or offers support for any kind of mutual compatibility of approach is perhaps less apparent. For, as will be suggested, it is questionable whether the understanding of quality which underlies the production of procedures is able to meet the multi-faceted requirements of CPE.

In the business of construction there is a clear, identifiable goal. While the pre-construction phase may be one characterised by debate, once a given design has been accepted the quality objective is plain enough: a project conforming to strictly laid-out technical and financial specification. While beyond the confines of the site, arguments may rage about the relative merits of a particular construction, what faces those directly involved is the performance of a specific task – to construct in a manner which complies with best practice.

Of course, there will be few professional undertakings which are not started with an idea of the achievement of a positive end product. In those occupations where people are the immediate concern, such end products are, though not always, as simply identified. In these human/social professions good practice, it can be argued, is characterised by a degree of flexibility. While in each professional setting a broad notion of a desired end result will be present, it is frequently the interaction between professional and client (or range of clients) which helps to shape (more or less tightly defined) objectives.

For construction, the unequivocal nature of the desired end product allows a definite sense of formality and order to be applied to procedural requirements. The contribution of all those involved can be pre-defined and documented in great detail. It is within this context of apparent certainty the QA system is developed. An idea of what this might typically involve can be gleaned from the following examples.

PARTICIPANTS, PROFESSIONALS AND QUALITY ASSURANCE

The earliest point of the quality process is concerned with translating ideas on what is necessary into straightforward workable instructions. Instilled in practice from the beginning is the idea that there is one correct way of going about things; conformity to which is the essential requirement. Such clearly defined responsibilities begin with the project owner (who will draw on specialist help from a number of sources).

According to Armstrong (1991), before the various construction professionals are introduced into the process the owner has clear roles to perform. S/he will be required to provide the necessary finance, clarify exactly what is required from the project, select those professionals on which the job will eventually rest, and establish all necessary lines of contact with these on-site workers as well. S/he will also liaise with those involved in the supply of materials.

Such a level of involvement brings with it a place in the QA system; mechanisms exist which aim to ensure that the groundwork is done appropriately. Thus, there may well be a requirement to check on the skills and experience of those lined up to perform specific tasks; and, in order to prevent delays later, a requirement to ensure that all those involved are clear about the meaning and implications of the contract documents. Whether or not the eventual applicability of an industry-based system is accepted, there is certainly something of importance here: the inclusion of an error-exclusion procedure in the earliest stages of an event.

The task of job managers is to perform those functions – be they organisational or administrative – necessary to ensure the appropriate interaction of all the members of the team, at whatever level. The procedures used by the various members of such a team will relate to the phase of the project, and to the particular personnel, with which they are concerned. The need to ensure that tasks are being completed within a pre-established time and cost framework is the main determinant of the work schedule of such managers.

A clear indication of the very formalised way in which task lists are demarcated is revealed by a check through the typical responsibilities of job managers. These can be split into four phases.

1 Setting up the job entails: establishing a team; obtaining the brief from the client; obtaining services and fee agreements; preparing the office brief and completing the relevant job records.
2 During the planning phase, preparation of the job quality plan takes centre stage. In this, management diagrams, quality objectives, and professional, review, and administrative procedures are all formally documented.
3 This phase is all about working to the plan. It involves ensuring that each of the specifications are met. This is managed through reviews – both managerial and technical – through meetings and through audits.
4 During the final stage, responsibilities include archiving, completing records, establishing feedback and handing over the project.

This is manifestly the outline of a very elaborate process and quite possibly one with real value to a construction project. Without wishing to decry the value of an agreed-upon approach to the organisation of CPE events, just how far such inevitably time-consuming approaches would be welcomed – within a context of increasing calls on time in universities – has to be raised. And this is to leave aside any doubts surrounding the 'managerialist' tone of the process. For now, though, I will continue with the descriptive process.

While managers of a project are concerned with matters of overall organisation, more specific aspects of the work are the domain of the construction professionals. One group of such professionals are those that contribute to the design process in one way or another. Included here are architects, structural and service engineers, and quantity surveyors. Consistent with the need for a detailed system, the activity of these professionals is the subject of rigorously prepared procedures. A brief summary of the requirements prepared for architects can be used to illustrate those demanded of the design professionals as a whole.

The activity of the architect draws on a plan of work produced by their professional association: Royal Institute of British Architects (RIBA). The architect's quality plan is usually made up of a set of procedures which makes clear the precise stages, checks, and confirmations needed to secure objectives. Such components of a job-specific quality plan then fit into the aforementioned plan of action promoted by RIBA. Before reaching the stage of procedural detail such a plan would address and highlight all related responsibilities. This might include, for instance, the demarcation of points of authority, and details of established line management structures. Each element of the following list is operationalised via a detailed procedure. Compliance with the relevant National Standards is an integral part of this.

The standard procedures for a given project would begin with attention to initial briefing and the co-ordination of information. It would go on to embrace those matters directly related to professional activity such as drawing practice, the establishment of a specification system, and a review of design. Beyond this, procedures would be concerned with the inspection and monitoring of action on site, keeping appropriate records, sampling the procedures, and eventually with completion and the collection of feedback.

Such a set of procedures will bring with it a detailed task list. This would of course relate closely to the stages outlined above. Tasks would be identified in relation to matters of design, operations on site and the rest. As mentioned, as well as roles relating to professional activity, a management role may also be adopted. In such cases the expectation would be for this to be integrated into the system and for tasks relating to it to be specified in the regular way. This kind of detail is certainly not specific to the architects: what is required of engineers or surveyors is very similar.

Construction work is, of course, as much dependent on materials as the people who utilise them. As such, it comes as little surprise that formalised procedures are in place to deal with the manufacture, delivery and installation of the necessary equipment and components.

It is not only the systems of those involved at the purchasing and constructing end that are of concern, but also those of the suppliers. Details of the systems and procedures adopted by suppliers may well be requested for inspection and approval prior to their selection. The process of selection will include reference to the ability of a supplier to deliver on time as well as to the nature of the product concerned. There may even be a need for an independent review of the QA system of suppliers to be established. Similar specifications and controls are stressed for delivery of materials and their acceptance on site.

27

Armstrong (1991) identifies one further arm of the QA process in the construction industry: the contractors. In the early stages of a given project the collection and review of bids is followed by the selection of contractors. Setting QA procedures in place is an immediate concern. Such procedures are distinguished by membership of one of two categories: contractor activity and the monitoring of that activity. The requirements laid down for the former are no less rigorous than those required of on-site professionals. At the level of management, procedures are found concerning the establishment of a construction management team, concerning the personnel management section, and relating to all aspects of the management of sub-contractors (thereby extending the reach of the system one stage further). Beyond this, mechanisms will be in place to deal with payments, safety, gaining all necessary permissions, procurements and so on. All this is subject to monitoring procedures which themselves produce a quite substantial list of activities.

While the above provides an overview of the main focuses of attention in an approach to QA in the construction industry, without almost book-length description it can only ever give an indication of which is involved. In fact, for a major construction project the quality documents will run to a gruelling catalogue of some several hundred pages.

TECHNICAL ACCURACY AND COMMERCIAL VIABILITY

I do not think that the limits of interpretation are being crossed if QA practice in the construction industry is described as both formalised and rather complex. This is apparent despite the inevitable omission of the intricate details of procedural action. Moreover, that such activity is geared towards establishing and maintaining technical accuracy and commercial viability seems readily apparent. That the definition of quality relates closely to such criteria is also evident.

One of the purposes of including the construction industry in this chapter has been to detail an example of a non-educational sector which has wholeheartedly embraced and institutionalised QA and done so in relation to its commercial basis. QA in the construction industry is not just about ensuring the quality of a technical product, it is also about ensuring that it satisfies market criteria: that it achieves customer satisfaction.

So, what of the relevance of all this for the provision of a quality university-based CPE? The answer to such a question is inevitably determined by the level at which detail is drawn from construction industry practice and, indeed, by how aims and definition of quality in CPE are understood and operationalised. It would perhaps be a little harsh to fail to acknowledge a degree of compatibility – at a fundamental level – between the two sectors. The undoubted benefit of establishing something (be it a bridge or a course) on a successful footing from the earliest point to avoid messy and damaging correction; the value of some form of written documentation to provide readily accessible information to all concerned; and the need to ensure appropriate organisation of equipment and interaction between staff are all clear examples. However, it seems unlikely that the value or even necessity of any of these will come as much of a surprise to CPE specialists. There is every reason to expect that procedures dealing with these organisational matters would be a part of any system which evolves from within CPE itself. These are signs of a certain level of affinity, not legitimation for the transfer of practice.

Once beyond these immediate expressions of compatibility, others are less easy to find. Of course, it could be argued that the straightforward certainty offered, not least by the identification of an unambiguous end product, is appropriate for CPE. Indeed, it is not difficult to see how the principles of the above system could be employed to develop a quality approach of sorts. But this is to deny a quality which relates to the more ambitious agenda for CPE raised earlier.

Technical effectiveness and commercial viability are possible (and comfortable) dimensions on which to assess quality; they are though hardly the most challenging.

In essence the discussion revolves around the issues of aims and definitions. This is a suitable point at which to reintroduce the first of the two issues identified as central to this discussion: whether the quality being worked towards in construction can be seen as being of some order – at a fundamental level – as that in education. Now, quality in construction is all about the achievement of a technically correct, financially viable product: they construct for commercial success; quality depends on, and is defined by, these factors. If the intention to develop quality CPE on the basis of its social location and societal impact is a serious one, there is a fundamental discrepancy of purpose and a fundamental discrepancy between

29

what can be taken to constitute quality in two sectors. This gap is also evident in relation to the second issue: the potential compatibility of systems and procedures. This is because systems are developed to meet the quality requirements of particular settings. Quality defined as technical accuracy and commercial viability requires assurance systems so oriented. This theoretical difficulty is borne out in practice. Descriptions throughout this section have revealed this association. Moreover, problems not only relate to the general shaping of practice to conform to these two principles, but also to latent consequences of employing this approach. These latter difficulties (such as excessive time commitments and inappropriate organisational forms, to be dealt with in more detail in chapter 2) are also confirmed by the evidence. The major role assigned to clarifying each of the many management structures and accompanying levels of authority is a case in point.

Overall, then, in the construction industry quality is defined in relation to its particular concerns and objectives. Modes of QA are devised in relation to that understanding of quality. To employ a definition of quality based on financial success and technical accuracy in CPE would be to deny the more complex character of CPE, and to overlook the implications of that for the development of a strategy for quality.

Once a feel for the very real differences between sectors is achieved, the adequacy of a generic understanding of QA is brought into question. This is not to question the value of the approach of the construction industry in relation to its own tasks; it is only to offer critique of it as a directly relevant example to the concerns of CPE. Within its own context it is performing the function required: matching objectives with a definition of quality, and providing procedures to facilitate the achievement of that quality. The argument is that CPE needs to be afforded the same respect: conceptions of quality and systems of QA need to evolve together.

What is being questioned is the value of context-neutral approaches. Thus, by implication, the potential offered by the principle of context-specificity is noted. This is an issue which runs through the following presentation of evidence from health and welfare.

QUALITY ASSURANCE AND HEALTH

From the construction industry to the health services is a fairly substantial leap; the significance ascribed to quality assurance, however, remains unaltered by this change of content. Much of the following discussion will deal with the British National Health Service (NHS), although perspectives developed and applied beyond that structure are included, as are references to international trends.

A noticeably different emphasis is to be adopted in the coverage of health in comparison with that used for the case of construction. This section will scale down the cataloguing of the component parts of systems in favour of a review of a broader range of features and issues which a look at this sector reveals. The rationale behind this is to bring forward aspects of this presently dynamic context which might well feed deliberations on QA in CPE. The elements of interest go well beyond the level of technical implementation.

The opening phase of the review is one which briefly presents the reasons for the (re)emergence of QA as an issue in the field of health. Its evolution is seen to have been one which occurred within a context of discernible social and political trends.

Given my preference for the formulation of context-specific approaches to QA, the existence of two conceptual (or theoretical) models which have been developed to deal with the particular character of health provision is welcomed. This is especially so when the prominence they have achieved is acknowledged. Details of both their pure form and practical examples of their utilisation are given.

The presence of such frameworks should not be taken to imply the exclusion of systems and ideologies nurtured in commercial settings. This is far from the case. Examples of this crossover will be given, and these will be followed by a review of the small (but nonetheless astute) range of critiques offered of parts of this process. The final phase of this section will advance evidence on the somewhat less than perfect state of play in the field as a whole.

Although the point is frequently made that an involvement with QA in the health field is not actually new (Black 1990: 97; Carr-Hill and Dalley 1992: 10) – means of producing a quality service in a more or less formalised way have arguably been a part of the ethos and practice of orthodox medicine (embracing nursing and professions supplementary to medicine) since it emerged as institutionally pre-eminent – this has in the recent past developed a new primacy in thinking and action. Indeed, some indication of the contemporary nature of this phenomenon can be seen by the fact that as recently as 1985 one commentator was able to make a call for

31

incorporation which would be largely superfluous today. Mason stated: 'I believe that quality assurance should be an essential part of the health care services of this country [UK]' (1985: 7). While the new interest may have begun in the years preceding this point, it clearly had not become fully ingrained in practice.

One of the characteristic (though not unique) features of QA in health care has been its capacity to transcend national boundaries. This is apparent from even a cursory glance at the journals which are explicitly devoted to this topic (see for instance, *Quality Assurance in Health Care*, the journal of the International Society for Quality Assurance in Health Care). Despite the relatively longer histories of interest which frequently prevail in countries beyond the UK, developments remain patchy. For example, a recent review of the situation in Sweden (Allsop *et al.* 1989) concluded that while a number of structures and practices are well ingrained, the 1990s will nonetheless be a period in which attention to many features of the health system will mirror activity in the UK. Elsewhere a discussion of the experience of Finland – despite noting the very early introduction of the topic to that country (the early 1970s) – takes as one of its initial questions 'why did it fail?' (Vuori 1992: 162). Thus confirmation that the project is far from complete in that country as well is provided.

However, despite the realisation that the path to assuring quality has brought with it many difficulties, the tendency has certainly been for programmes to be up and running well before their counterparts in the UK. Indeed Hurst and Ball (1990) identify the UK as 'the only western nation which has not developed a formal mechanism of quality in its health service' (1990: 120).

Not only is the broad base of QA apparent in its geography but it is also illustrated by the range of health care to which it is being applied. For instance, examples can be found relating to work on hernia surgery (Kald and Nilsson 1991); radiotherapy (Mijnheer 1992); and even urine analysis (Larsson and Ötiman 1992). Beyond institutional confines, quality in community psychiatric care has been addressed (Smylie *et al.* 1991) and discussions have extended beyond the first world (Reerink 1989).

In part, then, the question of why quality assurance has attained such a position of importance in UK health provision can be understood in terms of the imperatives of a world dynamic. While Carr-Hill and Dalley (1992) certainly note this international dimension, they also identify a number of home-grown factors to explain the current level of attention. In total, they point out six influences.

1 The introduction of general management and the importance ascribed to customer satisfaction in the Griffiths Report (1983). This is an influence also regarded as crucial by Hunt (1989).
2 The ever-present concern about financial restrictions and the accompanying emphases on value for money.
3 The increasing interest of professional institutions in the quality issue (a trend we will see mirrored in non-medical professions in chapter 6).
4 The growth of the consumer lobby.
5 The international dimension is recognised in terms of the UK's commitment to World Health Organisation (WHO) targets.
6 The need to include a quality component in the contracts between purchasers and providers which underpin current changes within the health service as a whole.

We are clearly dealing with a set of interacting influences: that they are as politically as well as medically grounded is evident. This link actually becomes quite explicit in certain instances. For instance, Griffiths – the then head of the Department of Health's NHS trust unit – has stated 'I am convinced NHS trusts will lead to a significantly greater preoccupation with the quality of service provided' (1989: 1466). Quality developments and political ones are thus inextricably linked.

The importance of the political dimension has certainly not been lost on Pollitt (1990). His discussion is particularly pertinent, for in it he draws a justifiable comparison between trends in health and in education, most notably in the priority ascribed to establishing competition, efficiency and the ethos of the consumer to pivotal status. In an attempt to support the validity of such changes 'quality is high on the political and professional agendas, and the government is anxious to show that quality assurance mechanisms are in place' (Pollitt 1990: 447).

The underlying point here must not be lost: for health, and for education (including CPE), quality has to be regarded as a constructed, politically influenced concept. Definitions of quality and claims for its achievement are being grounded in particular perspectives about valid institutional arrangements and objectives. Such an awareness is a necessary component of future attempts to shape the nature of that construction in ways which can embrace alternate social, pedagogic and, indeed, political ends. For to appreciate that the priorities and emphases of a discussion have been shaped and created (rather than being in some way pre-established) is to imply that a re-orientation is at least theoretically possible.

CONCEPTUAL MODELS IN THEORY AND PRACTICE

The two context-specific QA models which I will cover at this point not only perform the useful service of theoretical clarification, but they have actually both been picked up by those with a QA remit in contemporary health settings.

The model of Maxwell was presented in its original form in a short article in the *British Medical Journal* in 1984. Although it has since been updated slightly (Maxwell 1992), the basis of the perspective presented has remained fairly stable. Whilst pointing out that mechanisms of various sorts had been in place in various sections of the NHS for a considerable time, he consciously stressed the need for objective evidence to be established. One important reason for an increased formalisation was that positive future responses from the treasury (for health service funding) were seen to be dependent on establishing a position in which claims of quality could be based on something more than anecdotal self-assessment.

Putting political considerations to one side, a fundamental building block of Maxwell's approach can be identified. It is the differentiation that is made between the task of health services (to secure a quality of care) and the task of business (to secure a profit). (This issue is also discussed by Ellis (1988), Lynch (1984), Shaw (1986).) Maxwell argued that while quality in commercial settings can indeed be legitimately discussed on a single dimension (profit), quality in health care cannot possibly be reduced to such a simple notion. The implication is that if the points of ultimate reference are different, the approach taken must also be different.

As a consequence, Maxwell proposed a six-element schema – six dimensions of quality – which need to be understood as distinct features in their own right and in turn need to be given differing means of development and assessment. This really is a very important stage in the discussion of quality assurance. Whilst it cannot be expected that the particular features of the Maxwellian model will be applicable to the demands of CPE – indeed that would be to go against the principle of context-specificity of which it provides such an important illustration – we can see from the features of the model both the way in which the notion of quality has an organic unity with the subject area; and more, that the component parts actually veer towards acceptance of social criteria. And, by implication, it fosters a recognition that the activity is socially located and must make sense within that location.

The six dimensions of health care quality are: access to services; relevance to need (for the whole community); effectiveness (for individual patients); equity (fairness); social acceptability, and efficiency and economy. Clearly, this is a good deal more far-reaching and detailed as a means of understanding quality than one limited to a simple business-oriented buzz-word. It should certainly be noted that the way in which this model has been applied in practice may not always be pushing it to its potential limits (due to its integration with particular ongoing institutional and sectoral dynamics). But this does not detract from the impetus to discussion that its original composition presents.

The application of such criteria to the development of standards/procedures for direct medical care is one which can be seen to hold great potential. A clearly stated belief in notions of equity, and of provision that is relevant to the community as a whole is both welcome and potentially rewarding. It is also worth pointing out, however, that the model has been applied to the support services – the non-clinical features – of hospital life. For example, a district general hospital's works department has interpreted the dimensions in relation to their regular tasks (Hurst and Ball n.d.). The 'access' criteria was accompanied by a standard unequivocally stating that a suitable staff member would be available to deal with requests, 24 hours a day, 7 days a week. On the equity dimension, a clear statement was employed to the effect that requests would be dealt with in terms of priority, a decision which would be grounded in agreed-upon criteria.

Returning to the model in its pure form, it can be reiterated that what we have is not only a practical basis for action in numerous clinical and non-clinical settings but one which evolves from an awareness of context. It is not that the notion of customer satisfaction is distanced from such an approach, on the contrary it forms an essential part of it; it is rather that it is accompanied by a recognition that appealingly common sense, narrow, perceptions of quality are simply not enough.

The implications of choosing between competing definitions of quality are clear enough in the health setting. For instance, if customer satisfaction is the sole indicator of quality, an individual patient's view on the treatment received is adequate. But if that same treatment, however clinically effective, is limited to a small section of the community, whilst measures of 'meeting the needs of the customer' would be satisfied, Maxwellian notions of, for instance, equity, would not. To provide treatment which solves the immediate problem of an individual is crucial; as a measure of overall quality provision, though, it is partial.

When looking at this issue of perceptions of quality in CPE we would do well to address a similarly grounded question: is customer satisfaction and repeat business really a solid enough basis from which to proceed; or, should we be looking to construct a multi-dimensional understanding of quality which extends beyond the opinions of those directly involved to include an appreciation of the (possible) impact (at whatever level) the work is having in specific communities and/or the society at large. For in the theoretical developments and practical applications of the health sector there is evidence which helps to substantiate the concern about what might be termed 'prevailing customer reductionism' which I outlined as an issue in the introduction. In short, there seems little reason to suggest that an attempt to socially locate both practice and the initial understanding of quality is any less relevant to CPE than to health care provision. And, consequently, this is a theme which will be developed later.

The second model to be introduced is that of Donabedian (1980). It is drawn from experience of the US health system. In chronological terms this precedes Maxwell's contribution and is – at least at first sight – more simple. For Donabedian, the approach to medical quality assurance rests on the utilisation of three broad headings: structure, process, outcome. Perhaps the best way to illustrate this is by reference to an example taken from the draft documents of a UK health authority in relation to its nursing care. (The name of the health authority is omitted for reasons of confidentiality.)

The document discusses action surrounding several elements of care. An accurate illustration of what is involved can be gained by looking at the standards for one of these – the physical comfort of patients. At the level of structure, there is a requirement for the availability of adequate resources to ensure patient comfort and competence in the carers responsible for that comfort. The process component is interpreted in relation to the use of assessment-based care plans and in relation to the presence of staff of proven competence working towards patient comfort (the latter is also open to a classification as structure). And at the level of outcome, the guiding standard is that both patients and carers will be satisfied that full efforts have been made to secure their comfort. A part of this is a clinical audit incorporating assessment of factors on each of these levels. So, for instance, questions to be answered may relate to the acceptability of the furnishings as well as to the correct administrating of oxygen.

With such a flexible model as a starting point, interpretation will inevitably play a key role in determining eventual formats. Donabedian's position on at least one feature of such applications has been made clear in a recent article. It is certainly one which finds accord with one of the recurrent themes of this text. It is stated:

> It is essential not to regard clinical performance monitoring as primarily a policing activity imposed by external agencies for their own purposes. It should be regarded, rather, as a requirement for the conduct and management of practice, so that trustees, administrators and clinicians can achieve their own legitimate, compelling objectives. If this total change in orientation does not take place, performance monitoring is in danger of becoming a repressive form of policing, something of a club to be used to beat health care providers and practitioners into submission.
>
> (Donabedian 1989: 8-9)

I have already noted the point that models such as the above are interpreted for various features of the health care set-up. One such extension beyond the immediately obvious is of some relevance: it is an application to the education of those within the system (see table 1.1), taken from a UK university. It shows how educational quality is amenable to assessment in a way which takes account of rather more than financial criteria. Such dimensions need not be restricted to those drawn from the frameworks of Maxwell and Donabedian. The requirements of differing settings will suggest alternatives.

Here then, drawing on the detail of the two frameworks, educational quality is being treated as a multi-faceted matter. In the sphere of medical education, exposure to such models has opened up the possibility of employing policies which relate to more than just one level.

Table 1.1 Existing application of theoretical models to pedagogic provision

| | Quality grid for school of nursing education | | |
Basis: Maxwell	Standards of practice	Standards of performance	Basis: Donabedian
Access to service	Flexible schedules; part-time courses; warm welcome to all enquirers	Uptake; no. and % of suitable enquirers recruited	Structure process
Acceptability	Teaching style; personal support; smooth schedule; courtesy	No. and % of students retained	Process
Efficiency	Communications to students/hospital etc.; exam arrangements on target; costs per student	Lack of hassle; good working relationships	Process
Effectiveness	Teaching and practice; produce skills knowledge and competency in students; research published	Students get good interim reports; pass rate; number appointed to available posts within authority	Outcomes
Relevance to needs	Different emphases; arrangements for different groups of students e.g. mature students, men, part-timers	Adequate numbers produced for different services e.g. mental health, paediatrics etc.	Structure process
Equity	Available resources shared fairly across all disciplines	Success rate similar for all groups	Outcome

CONTEXT-NEUTRAL APPROACHES TO QUALITY IN HEALTH

Despite the very real influence which the context-specific models have been able to exert, some understanding of the situation into which they fit is necessary. This has three principal features. First,

that belief in, and importation of, well-known approaches of commercial origin is widespread. Second, that in practice these can be
used alongside rather than as an alternative to the kinds of models
detailed above. This is noticeable, for instance, in the co-ordinating
activity of quality assurance managers within the health service.
Third, that although most voices to be heard in this field have been
facilitating this trend, some informative dissent does exist.

The intent in the following pages is to provide some illustrations
of these trends, rather than an exhaustive review of every instance
of practice. The point worth re-emphasising is that despite the
existence of a small but significant body of thinking specific to
health, the sector has not developed a wholly distinct means of
tackling the quality issue. The same management forms which are
making a play for the educational domain are also active in this field.
The lesson is apparent: in themselves context-specific bases of
action do not exclude the commercially based approaches. The
extent to which they may, or may not, do so in the future, in this or
other contexts, is dependent upon attention to their organisational
forms. It also depends on the intentions of those shaping the process
through institutional lines of power. At present, an interaction of
approaches is frequently characteristic of the situation.

A review of the writings of commentators on health reveals a not
infrequent tendency towards adoration for the way in which the
business world has seemingly grasped the nettle of quality. For
instance, it has been claimed that, 'quality techniques and
philosophies . . . have enabled commercial organisations to improve
customer satisfaction and reduce costs at the same time' and that
'they can be applied with benefit within health services' (Øvretviet
1990: 132). Similarly, though at an earlier juncture, Mickevicius and
Stoughton stated 'well proven business concepts applied in
industrial and corporate environments can have practical and
valuable applications for health care providers' (1984: 5).

A short paper by Griffiths (1989) is based on just such a belief and
it is through a closer look at the examples he uses that we can get to
grips with what it is that such philosophies are all about. The
perspective seems grounded in a feeling that parts of the commercial world can provide the inspiration for the task of securing
quality in health. The reported recent shift to a quality emphasis in
the retail food chains is perceived as appropriate information.
Developing his position Griffiths quotes Bechard and Harris (1987),
presumably again in the hope of establishing an affinity between the

situations involved. The selection of the following statement from that source seems to bring with it two implications. One is a willingness to see such industries as providing either role models or at least as offering definite lessons to be learnt. The other is that concentration on image is a valid, satisfactory and complete way in which to understand quality. In writing – as an insider on the NHS – Griffiths also focuses on questions of waiting times, acceptability of food and other matters relating to the medical scene which need to be addressed. However, he is doing so within a framework which is at least partially defined by a positive perception of life in the quality-oriented commercial world. The quotation in question is:

> which of two airlines one uses has to do with service and customer orientation rather than whether aeroplane one is different from aeroplane two. The decision about hotels is made by a client after he or she arrives, depending on the treatment given by reception clerks or the bell boy.
>
> (Bechard and Harris 1987, quoted in Griffiths 1989: 1466)

If the commercial success of a hotel and the subsequent assessment of quality is dependent upon the level of ingratiation adopted by those in poorly paid positions, then that is one thing; but does it really offer a promising start for health or education? Of course, proponents of such a strategy would rightly point out that there is far more to these approaches than could be covered in such illustrations. This is conceded. But it is an essential part of these approaches that a particular 'culture' or 'philosophy' is adopted. The all-smiling, attentive, bell boy is perhaps a reasonable representative of this. This nature of intended practice is, of course, one step on from these broad statements of perspective. They do, though, offer a clear idea of the framework within which that action will need to be justified.

It is, as might be expected, BS5750 and total quality management (TQM) which are at the forefront of those approaches of commercial origin which have some degree of support in the health context. At the time of writing the first health authority had first been awarded BS5750 for effective purchasing (*Health Service Journal* 11 June 1992: 39); and other areas within the NHS, for instance, ambulance services, were similarly pursuing this goal (Hopkinson 1991).

As with education and training the BSI has published guidelines on the application of BS5750 to services (BSI 1990a). This has found favour in certain quarters. For Dickens and Horne (1991), the situation is clear-cut: 'The direct relevance of the new version of BS5750 to the NHS is obvious' (1991: 25). To support this view they cite four items in the make-up of the standard identified by Ellis (1988) as particularly pertinent. These are: the need for a documented system; the requirement of regular review; the need for corrective action; and the appropriate training for staff. There can be little doubt that each of these needs to be considered in some way; whether BS5750 provides the best forum for this is another matter.

TQM is an altogether broader approach than BS5750. Whereas the latter is all about gaining third party validation for a quality system, TQM is claimed to be concerned with a fundamental re-assessment and re-organisation of institutional practice. Writers such as Deming (1986) and Peters and Waterman (1983) have been closely involved with these developments. Practice in post-war Japanese industry is frequently advanced as something near the operating proof of the benefits involved. The near religious enthusiasm which TQM engenders across the board is perhaps most graphically illustrated by the description of its key proponents as 'gurus'. The almost universal adoption of the term is to say the least a little curious, and one cannot help but produce a wry smile at the thought of mass ranks of sober profit-motivated business personnel offering worship in this way! The terminology is though doubtless indicative of the very wide impact TQM has had, and continues to have.

Drawing on Brooks's (1992) interpretation of a management guide to the issue (PA Consulting Group 1989), the following is a précis of the key features of TQM. Of overriding importance is the notion of a deep shift in the 'culture' of an institution, a move designed to ensure a concern with quality at every level. Thus, consistent reference tends to be made to ideas such as each and every individual having a responsibility for quality, whatever their location in the company. Despite this, TQM is understood as management-led. In keeping with a general principle of QA the idea is to produce a quality result/product first time, and not to operate a system of quality control to detect faults. There is also a commitment to continuous improvement.

Whether manifested as a broad affinity with new wave quality philosophy, or represented by an affinity with BS5750 or TQM, the co-existence of the context-neutral with the context-specific is a genuine feature of the UK quality impetus in health services. However, as will now be shown, acceptance of this is not universal.

41

CRITICAL PERSPECTIVES ON ASPECTS OF POLICY AND PRACTICE

Nick Freemantle (1992) has produced an incisive critique of TQM or, to be more accurate, of TQM and its potential for utilisation in the NHS. Early in the discussion he notes an apparent contradiction in the terms used to describe TQM – in particular the use of both 'bottom up' and 'top led'. This is worth considering briefly. It is not too difficult to see how such a situation has evolved. From the brief outline of the character of TQM above, the affinity with the idea of a management-led process is plain enough to see. But this is matched by the attractive notion of quality as the responsibility of everyone, regardless of occupational position. Perhaps what is being seen here is the marrying of rhetoric (e.g. of general responsibility) with a persistence of organisational structure (i.e. of hierarchy endemic to contemporary business structures). We should be wary, indeed, of accepting, without examination, ideas that TQM brings with it non-traditional occupational relationships.

It is becoming apparent that issues surrounding the customer are never far from discussions of quality. For Freemantle the difficulty in the health context is deciding who that is. Although, he argues, this is ultimately the patient, the structure of service provision dictates that the general practitioner (GP) could, with equal justification, be described in this way in certain circumstances.

Such difficulties can be extrapolated to the context of CPE context; and it must be said with rather significant consequences. This can be done by bringing forward the concept of the 'ultimate recipient' first cited in my review of the nature of contemporary professions and professionals (see introduction). For if it is accepted that the patient (in Freemantle's illustration) is seen as the ultimate client (even for instance when it is the GP who is getting a service for the patient from a specialist), the application of a similar rationale poses questions about the assumption of the attender (or payer) as customer in CPE. At one level the case for 'the attender as client' is acceptable. Yet a case can be made for drawing a parallel between the 'client-one-step-removed' of CPE, i.e. the recipient of professional 'knowledge', and the medical patient/customer: the eventual beneficiaries of expertise. In cases where the sole determinants of the nature of CPE are the wishes of the paying and/or attending client, any potential for acknowledging the interests of, or input from, the 'ultimate client' is lost. The validity of ascribing a determining influence to customer-power (as generally interpreted) thereby takes another knock unless providers are happy to see CPE as an essentially limited activity.

In the commercially pure form, customers buy a product and use it for their own needs and gratification; their judgements on its success or failure, its value, or its irrelevance therefore attains a certain legitimacy. The extensions of knowledge which apply here underline just how different the social professions are from their commercial counterparts. Trying to identify who the customer is in any given situation seems to be a perennial pastime of the quality enthusiast. The complications that this introduces to an activity such as CPE must inevitably give rise to questioning whether 'the customer' is a detailed and responsive enough construct to satisfy the demands made of it.

In the previous section, I raised doubts over the value of a concentration on image; a tendency which often accompanies commercial systems. Freemantle raises similar concerns in relation to TQM. He states,

> the emphasis on appearances in the US [health] system, advocated by many TQM enthusiasts, has more to do with financial success in a different environment than it does with meaningful quality improvement. The business of health care does not resemble the cosy commercialism of the car showroom. Quality in health care cannot be represented by shallow and simplistic measurement of patient satisfaction.
>
> (1992: 23)

The question of just how substantial or superficial the commercially based systems are has to be a major concern. A concern which will be re-affirmed by the examination of BS5750 (chapter 2), to be presented in due course.

Even if questions of definition, purpose and range are put to one side, TQM is currently facing a potentially crippling form of critique; one which even the most pragmatic and commercially oriented of providers will find difficult to ignore. It is that for the first time there is real doubt being expressed about whether TQM is actually doing what it claims – even in its industrial heartlands. It is worth quoting Freemantle again at this point.

> The paradox about the current fashion for TQM in the service sector is that it comes at a time when TQM is facing increasing

criticism from the manufacturing industries. As *The Economist* reported: 'Many western managers believe that TQM is a powerful weapon, especially against the Japanese. The trouble is, most of their quality programmes are not delivering the goods.'

(1992: 23)

Its application to health, Freemantle argues, would be most likely to be characterised by a drain on resources and a short-sighted definition of quality inspired by cost reduction and superficial consumer orientation. The financial consequences implied here should certainly not be overlooked. As Brooks (1992) rightly highlights, the notion that 'quality is free' (derived from Crosby 1975) is somewhat wide of the mark. In fact, in stark contrast to this assertion the estimate advanced by Brooks is that a 2,000 employee unit might expect to shell out £500,000 over three years. Although Brooks is not led to reject TQM out of hand, a conclusion casting doubt on the idea of a set of underlying principles which can be applied irrespective of context is reached. This is accompanied by the view that however TQM is eventually formulated it makes no sense at anything less than the level of a whole hospital or its equivalent. And while seemingly prepared to employ the terminology of cultural change, Brooks states that any such modification to institutional life cannot be expected in much under a decade.

Judgements about whether the problems of TQM are terminal will, then, vary from commentator to commentator. Such overall perspectives cannot help but be influenced by the broader objectives of those involved. It does though seem fair to state that at the very least the idea of TQM as a guarantee, or as a panacea, has been considerably damaged by recent analyses. From industry to health, real problems are being uncovered. Any attempt to extend this still further should thus be treated with due caution.

Before concluding this section it will be useful to bring the discussion as far up to date as possible. This will serve to clarify whether or not the vast amount of energy expended is producing a valued system or appropriate systems in health care settings. To this end reference can be made to the empirical research of Carr-Hill and Dalley (1992). Their questionnaire-based research attempted to establish just what point had been reached within the NHS on the road to quality. The conclusion which emerged speaks for itself:

It seems then that, in the NHS, our knowledge about our own quality assurance activities is abysmal. The vast majority of activities are not costed: more than half are not evaluated and where they are, the procedures used do not appear to be a model of rigour.

(1992: 17)

Moreover, despite the existence, as was shown earlier, of context-specific models there was found to be a 'tendency to introduce measurement systems based on no conceptual framework and only flimsy empirical evidence [which] only exacerbates the problem of developing a robust quality assurance strategy' (1992: 18).

Concerns about the approaches so far adopted find parallel disquiet elsewhere. For example, despite the existence of the health-specific frameworks detailed above, Hudson (1991) was drawn both to attack, and call for a rejection of, the still prominent 'pseudo-managerialist process and checklist mentality' (1991: 23). As an alternative to this, the adoption of a more widely based quality paradigm is encouraged. Amongst other things this would be constructed around an explicit acceptance that QA is *not* a value-free activity and that a holistic view of a specific situation is essential. Critical perspectives may as yet constitute a minority of total publications, but the issues they are raising seemingly demand the fullest attention.

As an integral part of the public services, the way in which quality issues are being addressed in health has an immediate relevance for the similarly pre-occupied educational sector. The area is multi-faceted and complex; a factor not unrelated to the point – made by a number of writers – that securing quality in health can never be considered in the same (apparently straightforward) way as in the commercial world.

Furthermore, it is apparent that quality cannot be treated as an objective reality: it is a constructed phenomenon and should be acknowledged as such. That there is a political dimension to the process by which its character is formed is evident, as is the realisation that its character need not be unduly restrictive. Although neither universally applied, nor total in their defining role, the context-specific approaches of this sector have served the function of illustrating that the social context and location of action are legitimate and potentially helpful centres of attention. In turn those approaches which have formed the cornerstone of the almost evangelical fervour for quality throughout modern Britain have, in the light of considered reflection, been seen to present significant difficulties. Thus, important social, political and organisational issues have all been thrown up during the evolution of quality assurance in health. It is a development which is as yet far from complete, and given the recent trend towards critical engagement perhaps more relevant contributions can be anticipated.

QUALITY AND SOCIAL/WELFARE SERVICES

The last of the three areas to be looked at are the welfare services, primarily of the UK. Inevitably, the point at which health services become welfare services is in practice somewhat blurred, and, therefore, the distinction between the two is to some extent arbitrary. They share something of the same background influences. Also the theoretical models of quality assurance in the health services are readily applied in some areas of the social services. Developing a line of continuity with the previous section, my review of welfare is weighted towards a presentation of recent critical, yet forward-looking, analyses. I will, though, open with a brief clarification of the origins of interest in QA, and with illustrations of contemporary practice.

Because of the degree of crossover between health and welfare services, some similarity between the factors influencing the rise to prominence of quality might well have been expected. While the list produced by Wistow (1991) confirmed this, it also stresses the impact of issues specific to the area concerned.

For the first, and most fundamental influence, a peculiarly local influence is identified: the perceived and actual poor performance of caring professions in highly visible areas. The inadequacies of life opportunities afforded to people in a variety of social/nurturing institutions, and the growth of child abuse as an area of concern were especially noted. Given the cross-sectoral rise of quality assurance it is perhaps debatable whether determining impact should be ascribed to such developments. It is evidently the case, however, that where such widely agreed-upon deficiencies are raised the calls for quality gain an eminently receptive audience.

The second point – restrictions on expenditure levels – was identified alongside the growing prominence of managerialism. These are themes which have, of course, transcended sectoral boundaries. The third and fourth points – namely the rising assertiveness of active consumers and the trend to the culture of the customer – are also by now familiar themes. For the fifth and final influence there is a return to a welfare-specific issue: an apparent emerging consensus about the development of occupational objectives defined in relation to 'life-style' enhancement. Consequently, here as elsewhere, an understanding of the perceived need for QA is all about bringing together a knowledge of sector-specific dynamics with trends at the national and international levels.

Moving on to some of the work carried out under the welfare services heading, overlap with the field of health is clearly demonstrable. Williams (1990) describes the utilisation of Donabedian's model in an application to community care. Revealing the characteristic influence of context-neutral approaches, practice established in Japanese industry was readily acknowledged as integral to this work. Similarly, Dickens (1990) also drew heavily on Donabedian as well as 'total quality' principles in work on services in the field of mental handicap.

But this is not to discount the potential for rather more original formulations. A paper by Lynch and Eastwood (1991) gives an example of a QA system being developed at a local level. They report on how the introduction of community care – against a backdrop of the closure of long stay hospitals – produced an initial public concern about the appropriateness of replacement services. Following a period of debate, the local authority and social services department instigated a QA system to address the difficulties. Recognising the impractical nature of applying systems developed elsewhere – for instance on the basis of the peripheral role which they permit for many categories of staff – they devised a new approach which was based around the staff directly involved. This built on the subjective knowledge of these workers. Without going into too much detail, the key objectives were: to identify the contrasting views of users, carers and staff; bridge these gaps so as to establish a more widely respected programme; and then to re-measure (or evaluate) the process. Essentially, a small-scale problem is being worked towards resolution through an approach which makes sense in that situation. While an awareness of existing measures was involved, adherence to previously established systems was seen to be inappropriate to the task at hand and were not, therefore, taken up.

As is the case elsewhere, there is a distinct, if as yet fairly small-scale, strand of scepticism emerging on the development of quality assurance in welfare services. These writers are perhaps connected by no more than an unwillingness to see quality assurance as an inevitably unproblematic and/or progressive process.

Earlier I detailed the account of Wistow (1991) concerning the influences on the development of quality assurance. It can be recalled that this included economic constraints. Later in the same article the point is made that in itself cost, or value for money, cannot be taken as the determinant of quality. It is argued that this view brings with it the danger of confusing appropriate use of available resources with the overall adequacy of the service. It is argued that a valuable service requires full funding and that to focus too much on cost effectiveness is to deflect attention from this obvious yet vital factor.

This can be read as a further contribution to discussion on the matter of defining quality and ensuring that the definition makes sense in the context to which it is applied. It will by now be clear that influences on the development of QA as an issue are many (not only in health and welfare but in education as well). Moreover, it is also the case that the ideological origins of individual factors and the practical purposes to which they will be put are disparate. Different individuals representing different interests have different wants from the quality process. While it is inevitable that the interests of some of those involved will be best represented by an interpretation of quality which gives a high priority to cost effectiveness, this will not be the view of all those concerned with the issue, as seen here. The assumption that quality and quality assurance can have consistent and singular interpretations is brought into doubt. To say that the desire for quality has many causes is, therefore, not to say that all these causes will be equally prominent in the context of each actor or group. With consistent pressures on public spending the tendency to combine and confuse quality with effective resource utilisation might well become exacerbated. This can only be countered by a clear sense of where involvement with the quality issue is intended to lead.

Although not directly framed in such terms, the contribution of Johnson (1991) can also be viewed in relation to the need to establish both aims and parameters of aims in such a way as to be in a position to embrace all matters perceived to be of relevance. Specifically, the expressed concern is that new forms of QA and service delivery should take full account of the needs of ethnic minorities. One element of this, it is suggested, should be an involvement in raising awareness of such need amongst providers. Such an emphasis is a timely reminder of the possibilities of a far-sighted approach to QA. The introduction of aspects of the socio-cultural context creates an interesting comparison with the possibility of narrowing QA purely to the financial domain as detailed above.

Challis's (1991) contribution to critique is produced at a wider level: it addresses the whole process of QA in welfare. Questioning this 'miracle cure', five difficulties for QA to overcome are described. Each builds on the notion that barriers which have worked against change over the last two decades are likely to remain untouched by the latest attempt to overcome them: quality assurance. They are:

1 The continuing tendency towards privatisation is seen to diminish the likely effectiveness of public control.
2 That the specification of standards does not ensure their achievement.
3 That the use of non-statutory bodies allows public-sector managers to distance themselves from poor quality care.
4 That the requirement to be seen to be meeting standards might induce a lowering of those standards in order that quality might become demonstrable.
5 That the independence of assessors will be questioned due to their involvement in correction.

For Challis, there is a need to be every bit as aware of the limits to quality assurance as to its possibilities; only then can its potential be assessed. A part of this challenge is to embrace the role and potential of independent research. What is argued is that such research can take discussion substantially further than an isolated adherence to QA. It would consider the evolving causes of individual and social problems. She concludes, 'The effectiveness of quality assurance depends as much upon the development of our understanding of social issues as does the effectiveness of social intervention itself' (1991: 19).

Such a broadly based perspective is certainly evident in the work of the final writers to which I will refer: Pfeffer and Coote (1991) (and in a similar vein, Pfeffer (1992)). Working from the Institute for Public Policy Research, they have developed a perspective which both offers critical appraisal of some of the approaches which impinge on welfare services, and which proposes an alternative grounded in principles which are regularly absent from discussions of quality. Albeit applied to a very different context, the perspective incorporates the kind of emphases which can only enhance debate in CPE. It offers a definite way forward within the welfare services and in so doing provides a practical illustration of the way in which ideas surrounding QA can be extended.

That the approach of Pfeffer and Coote does not allow for an isolated appraisal of quality is immediately apparent. They locate discussions of quality within the ongoing overhaul of the public sector along 'quasi-commercial lines' (1991: i). The statement that there is no consensus on the meaning of quality can sometimes be thrown into such discussions as something of a truism, leading nowhere. However, in tandem with the identification of 'quasi-commercial' subjectivity and the explicit acceptance of alternatives it does provide a promising starting point.

As part of an appraisal of current practice the authors identify a number of approaches to quality. These are frameworks within which quality has come to be defined and understood. Each one is currently in use and each one is derived from the commercial world for application in the public sector. While the authors are not entirely dismissive of these, each is regarded as having very real limitations.

The 'traditional' approach relates to the pursuit of the highest standard within a given field, unfettered by concerns of value for money. Although acknowledging that such an approach has little overt impact on welfare provision, Pfeffer and Coote make a valid point about the image this helps convey. In everyday settings (at least prior to the spread of the 'new meanings' of quality), the term quality is said to bring with it connotations of luxury. What is important is that a hangover from such an interpretation remains with subsequent usages, and that this serves to diminish the force of potentially negative perceptions of a range of activities carried out using the same central term.

An implication of some significance can be developed from this. It is the realisation that to hold the centre ground – the territory within which definitions are made and operationalised – is to hold a position of some power. This idea can be transferred and developed in relation to the now established link between the term quality and the interpretations of that concept based on managerialism, customer orientation etc. For once a definition is established, opponents of a given approach or style of approach have actually to stand in a rather difficult position. This is because on one level at least they are acting *against quality*, they are acting against quality in its appropriated, yet widely accepted sense. Although the critique is of *one interpretation of quality*, once the terms of reference of a discussion have been set, challenge to the orthodoxy may well have to overcome a process of positive association: consumerist interpretations of quality are presented as synonymous with quality and the idea of quality retains its traditional positive dimension. The 'traditional' conception of quality might not, therefore, be a model generally promoted, but the positive connotations which it can bring with it remain a potentially powerful variable.

The scientific approach is based on standards setting and the means of ensuring that such standards are reached. The notion of 'fitness for purpose' is all important here. The principal difficulty identified by Pfeffer and Coote lies with the extent to which quality under this approach tends to be understood in relation to fixed perceptions of the manager or professional: there is little potential for the co-existence of views from different points in the process. As a consequence, the possibility for 'scientific' approaches to establish quality in terms which are satisfactory to all concerned is limited.

The managerial approach with its reliance on the customer is the third approach discussed. As this has been the source of discussion elsewhere in the book, suffice to say that a questioning of the validity of transfer to the public services is at the heart of Pfeffer and Coote's concerns.

The consumerist approach, based on empowering consumers to force change in providers is acknowledged as one which can provide a useful source of pressure in some instances. However, the failure to address differences between the commercial world and aspects of public provision; and the difficulty inherent in such an approach of understanding human action in a restrictive – consumer-grounded – way are again seen to leave the approach wanting.

What is proposed as an alternative is the 'democratic' approach. Why this is so interesting is that it is a real move in the direction of articulating ideas on quality within wider principles – extending the territory regarded as appropriate for this topic. The approach is established around the belief 'that the public has a complex set of relationships with welfare services – not just as customers, but as citizens and providers too' (1991: i). Thus what is promoted is a system which aims to tackle quality issues bearing in mind the complex character of relationships between individuals, groups and

51

providers; rather than on the basis of a pre-defined, perhaps vigorously promoted, perspective. Just as it makes little sense to see the 'education of professionals' as having no life beyond the 'purchaser–provider' interaction, so too a view of individuals as consumers of welfare without reference to how that fits into social, community and societal structures and processes is plainly bankrupt.

Equity is of paramount importance to the democratic approach. Ensuring that each individual has an equal chance in life becomes a concern of quality. The possible complications of such an approach are acknowledged. For instance, it is accepted that other central elements of the approach (responsiveness to the individual and empowerment of the public as citizens as well as customers) may at times conflict with the principle of equity. The answer is not to reject the objective, but instead to use QA procedures in an attempt to reduce foreseeable difficulties. Other central features of the democratic approach are: rights for the public; an open system; public participation; workforce involvement; and relevant modes of professional activity.

Pfeffer and Coote are prepared to accept that features of each of the listed approaches may have a part to play. For example, the concept of fitness for purpose is given a favourable hearing. But as and when use is made of elements of established approaches this only occurs within a structure which embraces and works towards objectives which are as much about positively influencing life chances and life experience as a whole, as about achieving institutional effectiveness, however defined.

The incorporation of principles of democratic participation; the need to look beyond the immediate; the recognition that people enter into public spheres from a range of starting points; and the realisation that they hold various motivations and requirements which cannot be adequately represented by the label 'customer', represent a style of dealing with quality some way removed from the construction site which opened the chapter. In welfare, as in health, the task of assuring quality is increasingly being seen to have a complexity which the quality gurus might not recognise. In the pursuit of context-specific quality perhaps a more explicit assertion of the existence of the gulf between the commercial world and sectors within the public domain is needed. This is something which it is currently all too fashionable to gloss over.

CONCLUSION

In the pursuit of quality, neither CPE nor, indeed, higher education as a whole is alone; that much is readily apparent from a review of activity in the areas of construction, health and welfare. Across this range of sectors many of the same buzz-words are used and many of the same systems are advocated. Indeed, it is an essential part of some (influential) approaches to QA that this is precisely as it should be, i.e. that the principles of QA and (in modified form) the approaches needed to secure quality are seen to be universal. So, for instance, evidence is found concerning the seemingly relentless advance of TQM, the promotion of BS5750 and the underlying ideology of commerce-like responsiveness. Uncomplicated homogeneity is though far from the whole story. Important issues of context and content are being addressed.

A willingness to see the emergence of the quality issue against a background of institutional, sectoral and political factors was a feature of some of the most interesting writers in the sectors reviewed. An appreciation of the environment within which a single policy evolves is essential when trying to clarify precisely why activity is taking place and on what basis that is to occur. No one can have experienced university life – or life in Britain as a whole – over the last decade or so without being aware of the kinds of ideas and perspectives that have been promoted as being most valid. The role of the market as an ideological as well as economic force, and the pressure on public expenditure have been ever-present themes. Moreover, the commercialisation and/or managerialisation of the public sector have been clearly observable. This is one (important) element of the context for the emergence of QA. While there is no single explanation – it is somewhat naïve to separate the move towards QA from the ever more visible trends outlined.

In the light of this, it is perhaps a little surprising that quality has tended to be treated as an apolitical phenomenon, requiring merely organisational and procedural attention. The point is that if the impetus to develop QA comes from various sources, differing and often competing objectives will also exist. One such example – showing the tension between cost reduction and appropriate service provision as potentially conflicting core concerns for quality – was described earlier. There is a clear lesson here. It is in the need to appreciate explicitly that the reasons for the interest in quality are various: some are pedagogic, some pragmatic, some social, some very much political. Different sectors, and different groups within those sectors, will hold affinity to different ideas. There is not one quality, nor one means of achieving it.

Whatever the setting, which tools and whose systems should be used for the job are central questions. The importance of context-specificity as a principle around which mechanisms should be decided upon is an essential lesson to be drawn from the experience of other sectors. One valuable consequence of that link to individual environments has been the explicit acceptance of an extension into the social as a valid component of conceptualising and operationalising quality. When practice does not exist in a social vacuum, the quality of that practice cannot be worked towards as if it does.

Just as the concept of context-specificity is valuable for CPE, so too are the critical perspectives currently being produced in health and welfare. Amongst the most noticeable are those dealing with TQM. The examination of TQM has not only led to a questioning of its value in the public sector, but has actually brought into doubt the validity of claims for its revolutionary impact in industry and commerce.

When attention is turned to activity in sectors which lie beyond education there is a temptation to assume that successful practices will be found and adopted. The strategy adopted here accepts no such assumption – not least because those sectors closest in form and purpose to education are still actively engaged in coming to terms with the issue themselves. Moreover, the situation is increasingly being recognised as an intricate one for which general cross-sectoral solutions are too insensitive. The priority here has been to offer details of action and debate in the various sectors as a means of working towards a position of knowledge. Experience in other sectors is less likely to provide answers to the questions faced in CPE than to assist in formulating those questions in a properly contextualised manner. That does, though, constitute a very real contribution.

2

BS5750: A CRITICAL REVIEW OF A KEY ISSUE

BS5750 has become virtually synonymous with the discussion of quality assurance. Its potential for tackling the quality issue has been raised, and to a lesser extent accepted, across the spectrum of commercial and professional sectors. Indeed, the 1991–2 annual report of the British Standards Institution (BSI) confidently announced the spread of the philosophy to 'solicitors, a general practitioners' surgery, an insurance company and firms in banking and finance' (1992: 13). And to this can be added examples from manufacturing, from those sectors detailed in chapter 1, and, of course, from education. BS5750 has made this advance within the context of a growing focus on managerialism. The standard is often discussed alongside more general programmes of TQM (see chapter 1). It is, though, despite points of affinity, distinct from it. This chapter will concentrate squarely on BS5750 and its present incarnation as a quality strategy for education. The attention that it has drawn dictates that it should be looked at in some detail: the ensuing discussion addresses key aspects of its content and the difficulties thereof. It also examines the setting of institutional priorities within which they need to be considered.

Broadly speaking, there are three parts to this review. The opening section is concerned with an illustration of the way in which the BSI promotes the standard; what they consider to be its virtues; and the reasons they cite why institutions should adopt it. This will provide an indication of the orientation of the approach as a whole. This is followed by an overview of the nature of the standard: its origins, its structure and the process needed to register for it. The final, and largest, phase is devoted to the critical review noted in the chapter title. Drawing on the education-specific documentation of the BSI (rather than the less focused general standards, though as will be seen there is a strong similarity), and an article written on the BS5750–education link from within the BSI, an examination will be made of central issues and difficulties that its move into education raises. An assessment of the assumptions and demands of the standard will be undertaken, as will a review of certain notable features of the evolution of the education–BS5750 relationship.

BRITISH STANDARDS AND QUALITY ASSURANCE: THE SHAPE OF SYSTEM PRESENTATION

To make sense of how BS5750 might interact with education, explicit account needs to be taken of the standard's point of origin beyond education; and, more, that the nature of it is inextricably linked with the structures and orientations of the parent organisation – the BSI. To understand what QA (and BS5750) is all about in its 'natural habitat' is to establish a clear idea of what it may come to mean elsewhere. For while modification for various contexts is an ongoing concern of the BSI, the core principles of the approach remain intact. So, while it is not necessarily the case that proponents would actively pursue every feature of the standard as it exists in the commercial world (the specific features of the transfer are, of course, detailed later) the value of becoming acquainted with the underlying rationale should not be underplayed. For it is precisely because of its assumed value to industry and commerce that it is promoted as relevant to education. It is said to have a proven format. Therefore, to assume the probability of significant change of emphasis during the transfer might well be to court distortion.

How then is the 'purpose' of using BS5750 (in its original environment) articulated? For an answer to this question reference can be made to a guide to the standard published by the BSI. It states that the purpose is to 'demonstrate to your customers that you are committed to quality' (1987: 7). The impetus to quality, the reason for addressing the issue is then clearly to establish an image that will enhance commercial viability. Matters of intrinsic value may or may not be relevant, but they are not the first point of concern. Instead, to give the *appearance* of quality en route to profitability is all important.

The priority given to such an emphasis is found elsewhere in the publications of the BSI. Indeed, the actual title of one of these documents, *The Way to Capture New Markets: a Guide to BSI Quality Assurance* (n.d.), certainly reinforces such a picture. There is both an implicit acceptance and a positive fostering of the primacy of a strategy of commercial competitiveness evident here.

What is more, this is coupled with the notion of the market as the ultimate point of reference for establishing whether or not quality has been attained. It is an emphasis which is in the first instance implied; it is, though, one which obtains more direct prominence within the text itself.

As part of a discussion entitled 'achieving a competitive edge' (BSI n.d.: 1), the reader is told that to satisfy quality needs is to work towards the essential aim of every company – profitability. Furthermore, introduction to the notion of third-party certification comes not on the basis of the contribution it might make to quality as an absolute, but rather, it is promoted in relation to the commercial benefits which might well occur from *being seen* to have addressed quality. It is stated that such an independent review provides 'possibly the single most important factor in the successful marketing of your company' (n.d.: 1) and that it is 'a first class marketing tool' (n.d.: 7). Having been taken through the details of the process involved the final call is to 'consider the commercial benefits' (n.d.: 7), thereby confirming once more the perspective behind this approach.

It could well be argued that the emphasis on competition and market acceptability is inevitable given the roots of BS5750 and its original audience, and that it is a little churlish to make a big issue of this. But it is precisely this inevitability that is the point of significance, especially if the value of the standard and its approach for university CPE is at issue. Whether or not the prescribed purpose and emphases are relevant in non-educational settings is not my direct concern. What needs to be highlighted is that BS5750 is not a free-standing system; instead it fits into a perspective on quality which embraces a particular social and economic orientation. Such a realisation brings forward certain questions which cannot easily be avoided. Amongst these would be: can a system which lives and breathes on the basis of its commercial and competitive credentials really offer a sound approach to quality in the context of educating professionals? Should not an educational approach to quality be wedded to its own aims and purposes (just as commercial quality is built around its goals)? And, if looking for CPE-specific purposes, is the market the appropriate starting point? To see BS5750 as simply a system or set of procedures is inadequate. The individual features only have meaning against a background perspective, a framework which interprets quality. It is one which is interwoven with both the form of the standard and the system which registers and thus legitimises it.

All in all, BS5750 is a system grounded in an approach to quality which – by virtue of its terms of reference – takes commercial viability, competitiveness and market image to be its central focuses. Its understanding of quality is based on a simple notion of satisfying apparent demands. Any question of considering broader notions of quality is really beyond the possibilities offered by the system. For an apparently 'neutral' system it therefore has a surprisingly strong rationale, one which seemingly remains largely intact during the process of modification for its role in education.

BS5750: EMPHASES, REQUIREMENTS, STRUCTURE

Despite the attention it has received in the recent past, BS5750 is, of course, only one of a whole range of British Standards which are formally documented specifications for the provision or production of a whole range of components of modern industrial society. There are currently around ten thousand such standards. Each of these standards has a direct point of focus and BS5750 is no exception – it is the British Standard for 'quality systems'.

There can be little doubt that irrespective of the outcome of the current interest in the new areas (such as health, welfare and education), BS5750 already has a solid foothold in the practice of much UK industry. Indeed, by 1987 at least 9,000 firms had already registered for this or an equivalent standard (BSI 1987: 1) – and this in the relatively short period from its introduction in 1979. Although its close relationship with the manufacturing sector is widely acknowledged, it is less widely recognised that its original formulation owed much to existing standards used in defence procurement (Ruston 1992: 1). It can, then, with some justification be seen to be a part of the established set-up in many areas. Its potential for education is thus argued for from a position of apparent strength in certain respects.

The actual standard is sub-divided into three main strands (putting aside those which are included but deal principally with matters of definition and information). Part 1 is 'specification for design, manufacture and development'. The important feature of this part is the inclusion of the design element. What this means is that it is established on the basis of its relevance to those concerns which design, as well as deliver, their particular product or service. Part 2 – 'Specification for production and installation' – addresses those situations in which the utilisation of an established method is involved. Part 3 – 'Specification for final inspection and testing' – relates to organisations which undertake such inspection solely to confirm the absence of 'non-conformance'. For education and training, the guidance notes (BSI 1991a) inform us that Part 1 or Part 2 are the ones of use: the decision concerning which is appropriate is dependent on the position of 'design' in institutional practice (as detailed above).

These same guidance notes provide a comprehensive list of those features of the standard which are considered relevant to education and training. They are, therefore, those which would need to be addressed by quality systems therein. The close relationship with Parts 1 and 2 of the standard is indicated by the continued use of the same numbering system and the assertion that the notes should be read in conjunction with, rather than as a replacement for, the original. Certain headings have, though, been excluded where deemed necessary.

The following is a brief presentation (devoid of clause numbers and full description) of those matters which require attention under BS5750. The headings and sub-headings (identified by the use of bold type and italics) are quoted directly from the guidance notes (BSI 1991a: 4–10). The brief accompanying statements give an indication of the meaning of each element. Reference to the original document is recommended, although this is itself presented in a fairly terse style.

QUALITY SYSTEM REQUIREMENTS

Management responsibility

– *Quality policy*, a documented policy signed by top management.

Organisation

– *Responsibility and authority*, clear statement and clarification of;
– *Verification resources and personnel*, monitoring the service;

- *Management representative*, i.e. a designated deputy;
- *Management review*, review of the system 'at the top';
- *Quality system*, to include all factors affecting quality;
- *Contract review*, contracts at all levels written or verbal;
- *Design control*, relating to aspects of programme development.

Document control

- *Document approval and issue*, process of approving and distributing documents;
- *Document changes and modifications*, a means of updating.

Purchasing

- *General*, all products to be purchased to clear specifications;
- *Assessment of sub-contracts*, essentially relevant personnel;
- *Purchasing data*, descriptive of item involved;
- *Purchaser supplier product*, including, for example, coursework;
- *Product identification and traceability*, concerned with records.

Process control

- Including everything from the library to attendance-recording procedures.

Inspection

- *Receiving, inspecting, testing*, 'inspecting' new students and equipment;
- *In-process inspection*, ensuring compliance;
- *Final inspection and testing*, for example, assessment;
- *Inspection and test records*, documentation;
- *Inspection, measuring and test equipment*, consistency;
- *Inspection and test status*, records and documentation.

The notes conclude with reference to:

- *Control of non-conforming product or service*, not meeting expectations.
- *Non-conformity review and disposition*, action resulting from non-compliance.
- *Corrective action*, in relation to non-compliance.

- *Handling, storage, packaging and delivery*, student care.
- *Quality records*, the keeping of.
- *Internal quality audits*, to cover all aspects of the system.
- *Training*, of all staff.
- *Servicing*, of contract agreements.
- *Statistical techniques*, analysis of performance indicators.

Attention to the above is certainly pivotal to the whole approach. But this list of requirements does not exist in isolation; it fits into a stage by stage process of assessment and registration. The third-party verification of the system is all important. Thus, 'To be registered by BSI means that your firm has been independently assessed by a team experienced in quality assurance and the technical conditions that apply in your industry' (BSI n.d.: 3). The group of inspectors are agreed upon between the standard-seeking organisation and the BSI, and it forms one of the very real costs to be incurred by that organisation. Registration only becomes operational when the assessors are satisfied that the specified requirements of the particular system have been met.

Ruston (1992) has detailed the process by which an organisation can achieve BS5750 status. A timescale of between 10 and 18 months is identified as necessary for the whole task – one which would include development of the system, the initial running of that system, and the assessment process mentioned above. Following the preliminaries (of which a commitment emanating from the top is an essential part) the first substantive phase is the establishment of the all-important system. Although carried out under the direction of a manager, and a team responsible to that manager, it is very likely that (costly) external consultants will be used in the planning stage. The BSI offers informal comments during this period. After formal agreement between the co-ordinating body and the organisation, the system is operationalised as a necessary step towards assessment. The quality manual is checked against BS5750 to ensure consistency; an assessment undertaken on the basis of whether the organisation is doing in practice that which it claimed it would; corrections are made (which would result in a fresh assessment procedure being undertaken if serious discrepancies were found); and registration is achieved. Once established, a continuing process of assessment is activated, again involving external checks.

The attractiveness which picking up on an apparently tried and tested method has for a number of people can certainly be understood. It apparently provides a ready made solution to quality concerns; pre-established and ready to be locked into. As will now be discussed, however, a critical examination of this situation reveals the matter to be somewhat more complex than that.

BS5750 AND EDUCATION: KEY ISSUES AND THEMES

My discussion in this section will deal primarily with points of concern about various elements and emphases of the standard. However, as a precursor to this, it is useful to draw attention to a couple of features of the process by which BS5750 has taken its place within the educational sector.

Integration and transfer

That the original document, in its initial form, could not be applied to education does not seem to be a point of contention. For proponents this marked not a signal to reject the standard, but rather the point from which to embark on a period of adjustment to make it relevant. This is, no doubt, grounded in that fundamental belief – referred to earlier – that the value of the approach is not merely restricted to the most obviously amenable sectors. All that is required is re-interpretation for each new setting.

It is from that basis that an examination of the consultation process, the phase in which the much cited modifications for education occurred, can take place. There is a need to be absolutely clear about what this period was (and is) all about. Of particular importance is that there should be no temptation to look at an apparently detailed evolutionary period and consider that a fundamental questioning of the merits of BS5750 for education has taken place. On the contrary, it seems an eminently reasonable conclusion that the goal (of an integration between the two) was pre-established, and that the purpose of the debate was to clarify the most effective means by which this could happen. Of course, there is no reason why this should not be the case: if those involved identify an aim, and a means of achieving that aim, that is perfectly valid. What it does mean, however, is that those looking to BS5750 for educational purposes should see the conclusions and modifications in these terms. Such end results cannot be regarded as constituting a fundamental assessment of the value of the approach. I will elaborate further.

The development of 'guidance notes' (BSI 1990, 1991, 1991a) for the new field of education and training was undertaken with the involvement of a sector committee. Plainly, the composition of that committee influences both the type of questions which will be considered and the range of possible conclusions which might be reached. In this instance the committee was made up of representatives from bodies already positively oriented to the transfer or whose societal location might suggest that they would be amenable to it. So, for example, the involvement of 'quality assurance firms' and participants from the 'business community' is noted. Representatives from two further education colleges at the forefront of the move to registration also had a role. Undoubtedly, a committee of like-minded people working towards the utilisation of the standard in a new area is perfectly sensible from a starting perspective of assumed applicability.

But the seeking and consideration of fundamentally critical comments is unlikely to be a priority in these circumstances. This is certainly relevant to a discussion advanced by Ruston (1992). It is stated that the first set of guidelines produced in the very early stages (BSI 1990) were distributed, presumably with the purpose of detailed examination, to around eight hundred people. Ruston summarises the results of this process thus: 'critical comments were received from about half a dozen sources, all of which centred on two main issues. The first was the definition of the product or output of an educational establishment, and the second was on the use of BS5750: Part 1 or BS5750: Part 2' (1992: 88).

In view of the heated debate that the topic has raised, this all seems remarkably tame – critical comments from less than 1 per cent of those contacted and even then on two fairly minor technical issues! It is perhaps not unlikely that differing terms of reference or a different circulation list might well have inspired a wider range of opinions to be offered. The current chapter will contribute to altering this present state of critical review, and the later empirical chapters will reveal an alternative set of statistics on the extent to which the approach is being welcomed.

In the above discussion reference was made to the involvement of two further education colleges in the process. This is, in fact, indicative of quite a close relationship with this sector in the recent past. Indeed Ruston (1992) notes that the first conference, run on this theme (as recently as the end of 1989) was actually in one such college. While a wider discussion of contemporary QA practice in further education can be found in chapter 3, a few comments about the current situation are of immediate relevance.

To begin with, this marks an instance in which the further education sector might conceivably shape the form of action in the higher education sector. We need to appreciate that the action of individuals within the further education sector has had – and may continue to have – a very real influence on this process of incorporation. The overall spread of BS5750 cannot, of course, be explained without reference to the trends operating at a societal level, but the role of key actors in the further education sector should not be dismissed because of this. Nevertheless, despite the highly visible activity of some within the sector, this should not induce a notion of a 'BS5750 consensus' within further education. Doubts about its applicability are certainly present (see chapter 3) and even amongst those directly concerned with the issue of QA, alternatives are favoured. The Quality Development Network is an example of a loose grouping of people working in and around education whose perspective is certainly one of scepticism on this issue. The experiences within further education are thought-provoking and relevant; they are not, though, all of the same form.

Assumptions and expectations

With that, the shift can be made to deal more directly with those issues which the relevant documentation has thrown up – to a critical review of assumptions and content. A reasonable starting point would seem to be to consider what is actually said about education in the guidance notes, i.e. on what basis the argument is advanced. Although some interpretations of the frequently rather opaque standards find their way into the guidance notes, there is surprisingly little on education itself, as a distinct purposeful entity. The principal exception to this lack of attention comes in the form of reference to the relationship between education and training (raised because the same guidance notes apply to both). There is actually a reasonably promising element in this in the shape of the acknowledgement that 'philosophical and practical differences' (BSI 1991a: 2) do exist between them. What is concluded, however, is that such differences have no bearing on the quality process and no influence on the approach to ensuring quality. There are two related problems here: the general lack of attention to the nature of the context (other than a concentration on the organisational); and, as perhaps illustrative of this tendency, a willingness to lump together education and training.

It is the logic of the overall British Standards approach to quality that is implicated here. Although there is a requirement to interpret the terminology for unfamiliar practices and contexts, because the system is so closely entwined with presentational factors (matters of image) and prevents definitions of quality extending beyond the mechanistic and administrative, not only is there no real need to address underlying questions of purpose and how the procedures relate to these, but BS5750 actually has no way of incorporating such an analysis. Thus, although it can be legitimately argued that the quality of education is a multi-dimensional concern, an approach developed in a context of profit-oriented simplicity is seemingly constrained to deliver a limited approach to an involved issue. As such, the seeds of practical limitations are sown and the inherent mismatch extends beyond the conceptually uncomfortable.

This difficulty in dealing with the specific challenges which discussions of quality in education (and, of course, quality in the diverse parts of education, such as CPE) present is reinforced by the position held by Ruston. For him, 'it becomes clear that virtually every requirement of BS5750 applies in the service sector – and education is no exception' (1992: 87). The problem here is the tendency to imply that education is nothing more than a branch of the service sector, and the service sector is but one half of an all-encompassing dualism of manufacturing/services. Important variations in intent, location and institutional or sectoral dynamics are seemingly discarded by the adoption of such a starting point. It is true enough that branches of the services (e.g. education and social/health/welfare services) have their own guidelines but, as already noted, these translations are only based on a tinkering with the original. The assumed suitability of BS5750 for education seems to emerge from this broad-brush rationale. If education is not a part of manufacturing – the argument apparently runs – then it must be a service. And as BS5750 already has a history of association with the service sector and has 'proved' its worth therein, then its relevance to education is demonstrable. Keeping discourse at the level of generality can serve to hide the inevitable differences hidden by any conception of a service sector. If the definition is limited to public sector services such as health, welfare and education, variation is clear enough; the inclusion of the private sector in the form of, say, banking or insurance shows still more the conceptual and practical insensitivity of a service sector grouping.

The lack of context-specificity is also apparent in the concentration on the source in the quality process – seemingly another hangover from the production process. As Todd (1990) has noted, the standard seems to imply, though not spell out, a transmission model of teaching, i.e. the assumption of the straightforward passing of knowledge from one person to another. Such a model has real limitations, and certainly when dealing with the education/development of highly qualified professionals, it is problematic indeed. It will be from a basis of knowledge and experience that CPE is mediated and interpreted. It will be through a similar process of mediation by a professional that eventual impact of the education will be achieved.

An important aspect of the above discussion, and indeed of the entire character of BS5750, is the apparent 'neutrality of location' it assumes. This brings with it two crucial consequences: that it facilitates application across diverse social and professional territory; and that it induces a homogeneity of orientation frequently incompatible with the very real points of divergence. The suitability of the standard becomes judged less on a considered assessment of circumstances and more on an ideological identity with a system. A claim to hold 'the answer' before (or instead of) formulating detailed questions pertaining to the form of given sectors inevitably places its utility on rather shaky ground. The assumption of universality is difficult to square with the pursuit of a context-relevant approach, it is though an assumption at the heart of the British Standard approach.

There is a further claim made about the way in which the system is constructed which works to promote the notion of its neutral, somewhat time/space/context-free existence. It is that the way in which quality is defined – principally in terms of fitness for purpose and significantly conformance to specification – makes possible the objective assessment of quality (Ruston 1992: 86). Given that most commentaries on the quality issue turn sooner or later to the discussion of the intractable problem of defining the central term, a clear understanding which contains the promise of objectivity is an appealing prospect. It is, though, a difficult perspective to sustain.

Discussion about the possibility for, and desirability of, objectivity (and its accompanying dismissal of value-based approaches) can be put to one side for the moment. There is a more immediate issue to be raised. It is that whatever the claims for the content, effectiveness or objectivity of a system, the initial decision to employ it must inevitably be influenced by subjective criteria. It can be surmised that deciding to pursue a system guaranteed to re-structure a given setting will be based on an implicit (and necessarily subjective) belief in the desired end state. When the approach advanced is a controversial one – one which would have major consequences for the running and orientation of an organisation – the significance of such subjectivity is enhanced still further. Likewise, decisions about targets/standards – those constraints which need to be conformed to – cannot realistically be expected to be 'objectively' derived at (not least because of the commercial pressures involved). At best, a case might be made for the existence of an objective measure of subjectively derived positions and requirements. But that is not quite the same thing.

It will be recalled that this chapter opened with a review of the way the approach is 'sold' at a general level by the BSI and supporters of the British Standards approach. The importance of image, marketing and implied financial gain stood out as the central themes in this. The shift of focus to education has seen no lessening of such emphases.

One line of argument raised in support of employing BS5750 is that as a symbol recognised by the commercial world it can help plug the credibility gap which – it is suggested – exists within industry. This point is frequently coupled with another practical point, namely, that certain organisations holding funds (including the Training and Enterprise Councils (TECs)) may well increasingly come to demand the standard before releasing resources. The large number of representatives from industry on TECs would appear likely to facilitate such a trend. However, there is some suggestion – obtained at no more than an anecdotal level during the research – that a realisation of the practicalities involved might be edging forward a re-think in some of the TECs.

Nevertheless, for the time being at least, the message of 'conform or perish' remains a highly persuasive one. And the point should not be lost that this persuasion is all about being seen, and being able to show, that quality is present. The overtones are negative, the question of looking at quality is relegated to the level of position maintenance and survival.

It is probably not an overstatement to assert that such matters bring to the fore those fundamental issues which relate directly to the nature of CPE as a discipline. Whether or not working to satisfy the perceived industrial/commercial generality is a valid approach can be taken as a particular illustration of a broader questioning of the extent to which instrumentalism should drive action. Responding to pre-set agendas does not aid considered reflection on such matters.

The stage of the discussion is being reached when one of the central limitations to the whole (society-wide) trend of quality assurance is becoming increasingly clear. It is that while across all sectors active in QA attention to the organisation of practice, an assessment of aims and a clarification of procedures hold some potential to improve and re-direct action. Yet, with some degree of regularity discussions are plagued, and not infrequently directed, by conceptions of quality couched in instrumental terms. Rather than the pro-active pursuit of quality, it is the re-active path to survival that often shapes debates. Constructive provider participation must remain pivotal to any approach selected. It is not easy to see how satisfying external demands, and being able to effectively market departments and institutions, might encourage this.

Reference to funding and financial viability is almost guaranteed to secure an audience in 1990s higher education. However, the temptation should be avoided to assume that (for the moment at least!) the BS5750 'badge of quality' is likely to hold greater sway than teaching reputation/effectiveness and scholarship records in the pursuit of resources.

Attempting to shape a system on the basis of objectivity is not only conceptually and practically unlikely to succeed, but also carries with it the implication that there is no place for explicitly identified values. For values – be they educational or social – cannot help but embrace the subjective. In other areas where the objectivity/subjectivity debate has surfaced and re-surfaced over the years, strong arguments frequently exist on both sides (see, for example, Arnot and Whitty 1982 and Hargreaves 1982 on educational research practice). Whether or not an argument for objective procedures can be supported seems to depend on the way it is employed and on the situation it is applied to. The plausibility of Hargreaves's argument (for value-free educational research) rests on the assumption that there is a place for value judgements once objective data have been gathered. It is not in any sense an objective approach to education that is being promoted, merely the objective collection of information about it.

By contrast, in BS5750, quality in education is regarded as being subject to objective assessment in the same way as other products or services. Objectivity is being used as a substitute for reflective consideration at all levels. To consider that such an essentially value-dependent idea as educational quality can be operationalised via objective criteria without close reference to the purposes involved seems somehow to be removing the very driving force from the educative process. It might very well be argued that the offering of a 'value-free skeleton' is appropriate because of the rather restrictive (organisational) emphases of BS5750; and that wider questions might be addressed elsewhere, i.e. that it establishes a sound environment from which to proceed. But this is unsatisfactory in two ways. First (as will be seen a little later), stated objectivity is not the same as actual neutrality. The very process of utilisation helps shape the context and orient it to a very particular way of viewing inter-personal and professional relations. It thereby establishes a situation in which challenging questions are less easily raised. Second, if, following the massive investment of time, money and priority, a 'quality system' cannot extend to incorporate the main issues of education, any sense of its value must surely be undermined.

There is a further necessarily problematic feature of the standard which is at once a function of the principal definitions, the process of accreditation, and of the market rationale within which the approach is located. It relates to the process of third-party checking. For it is important to realise that what is being checked is not a universally agreed-upon structure of quality. Rather, the assessment is merely concerned with verifying that a given unit is doing in practice that which it specified in advance. In other words, there is a policing role designed to ensure 'conformance to specification' – a specification defined and agreed upon in-house. At first sight there appears to be a compatibility here with one of the aspects of an approach to quality which I would favour, namely that such systems should be individually tailored to meet varying requirements. However, the way in which BS5750 dictates that this is done is some way removed from an education-centred and provider-based approach. For instance, the 'individual design' of systems must adhere to the demands of the various universal clauses. Freedom to set certain targets exists; freedom to reject administrative and organisational constraints does not.

If the participation of third-party assessors is not fundamentally concerned with shaping quality then it is safe enough to infer that their role must lie elsewhere. And it does: in confirming quality status. The purpose of this, it will be recalled, is to hold heads high in the market place and enhance commercial viability. Thus, if the goal is the display of this quality identity, and the point at which this can be done is when institutionally defined standards have been reached, what is the message being sent? Quite simply, it is that an institutional examination of quality based on potentially difficult features to quantify, such as the place of provision within a wider context, might delay accreditation. In contrast to this, establishing safe, simple and quick standards which can be assessed on straightforward criteria will ease the path towards the desired goal. If, as is often claimed, the standard is needed to ensure access to funds and secure financial survival, achieving that goal with the minimum of cost and delay might well seem an attractive option.

Such a consequence is a trivialisation of the quality issue. On the one hand, calls are made for a quality consciousness; on the other, structural conditions are established to facilitate the cutting of corners and the setting in place of a facade of quality. Furthermore, if the holding or lack of BS5750 is to be used as a means of making judgements between institutions (a negative but frequently cited possibility), paradoxical situations seem destined to emerge. For instance, take the following hypothetical example and consider which college is to be defined as the quality institution.

College one sets a standard of staff access to a particular form of training once a year. It is easily able to meet this and consequently maintains quality status. A more ambitious second college has a standard of more regular access to training which it just fails to reach. In doing so, it loses its quality label irrespective of its record of offering staff development provision and opportunity at a substantially greater level than the 'quality' institution. It is the kind of problem which would come to plague a BS5750-based quality format. It is a problem of integrating freedom for system development within a structural necessity for compromise. It is a problem of an alien solution to an educational task.

With all the talk of the commercial benefits of BS5750 for the registered party, it is appropriate to draw attention to the fact that the early stages of involvement run counter to that claim. This period is characterised by a quite substantial level of expenditure, some part of which will constitute a shifting of resources away from the educational sector. The required allocation of senior staff time to the task, the probable employment of an external consultant (at perhaps £250–£500 per day) and the inevitability of other fees, combine to reach a total measurable in tens of thousands of pounds. Against a background of the very real restrictions of this approach, such expenditure is hard to justify. As will now be shown, however, the evident unsuitability rests not just on the conditions already described, but extends to the very heart of the type of organisation which the system demands.

What I am referring to is the inter-personal system, the authority system, required by BS5750. It is not an implied or favoured way of going about things, it is a framework for institutional activity demanded by the approach. The sanction of non-registration acts to reinforce the need to comply.

It is a clear and hierarchical structure that is ingrained in the clauses of the standard. It is a no less important element as the matters of content which accompany it. Reference to the text reveals the need for a point of ultimate authority, a clear demarcation of power and, not surprisingly, the persistent use of terminology which confirms such emphases.

Within a section on 'management responsibility' there is a discussion of the nature of the core document – the quality policy. There are two parts of the position adopted which set the scene quite neatly. One of these is that as a part of an overall 'corporate' plan the policy must be 'authorised by top management' (BSI 1991a: 4). In essence, authority relating to the composition of that policy rests squarely with a designated 'top' figure. Doubtless, this would not exclude the possibility of some form of intra-institutional consultation, though that is not laid down in the documentation. It is the ultimate decision-making power of a management figure that is a requirement. The other point relates to the eventual reference made to other staff. This introduction does not address the scope for decision making beyond the management level but, instead, takes the form of an assertion that the policy is to be 'understood, implemented and maintained at all levels' (BSI 1991a: 4). This includes part-time lecturers and trainers, support staff and sub-contract staff. Is this the manifestation of the attention to cultural change? To the (serious) involvement of all staff in quality assurance? To a bottom-up (as well as a top-down) approach? There is no reason to assume that it is. The problem is that while widespread participation is called for, this looks to be little more than a means of ensuring that everyone complies with a policy established some distance from providers: involvement without control.

This is, though, just the beginning. The guidance notes go on to detail how 'responsibility and authority' (1991a: 4) should be formalised. What is stated is that the role(s) and power of each individual whose actions will impinge on quality (assumed to be virtually everyone within an educational establishment) must be formally laid down. Thus, the requirement is for a document to be prepared in which academic, administrative and the range of support staff all have a formal separation of duties; and presumably, a clear indication of limits which must not be broken. It should be remembered that all of this is within a framework of a policy which it is the eventual responsibility of top management to authorise, not the responsibility of colleagues – those in ongoing working relationships – to agree upon.

There are two further clauses which confirm the hierarchical nature of the situation. First, the requirement to appoint a designated deputy to the overall management supremo, presumably on the basis that such institutional threats as may emerge in his/her absence could not otherwise be dealt with! And second, that review of the system should be located at the 'top level' (1991a: 4).

These requirements are especially worth noting when viewed alongside the previously highlighted avoidance of explicit values. For while failing to embrace issues relating to social and educational purpose, and while confidently promoting the notion of an objectivity of approach, what is actually happening is that the system is bringing with it an implicit conservatism embedded in its practical requirements. Claims of objectivity are then weakened further by the realisation that such demands are playing a decisive role in establishing the environment within which quality is addressed. Its existence is then helping to create an environment, and not simply neutrally engaging with one.

The appropriateness of hierarchical working conditions should be examined closely by the university sector. And the mistake of equating involvement with influence should be avoided. For the inclusion of a component emphasising the responsibilities of all staff does not necessarily act to mitigate the effect of a regimented authority structure. It seems, in fact, to be supporting it. For to participate without control or power is to conform to an externally imposed schema. If the ultimate (and indeed practical) authority is concentrated at the top, and is spatially withdrawn, the potential for flexibility and for moulding procedures to provider aims becomes not merely strained but actually incompatible with the whole programme. The institutionalisation of compliance and formalised authority might help to hasten the introduction of a visible system; what positive impact it has on quality is not, however, readily discernible.

The final point of this critique brings into direct focus a recurrent theme in discussions of BS5750. It is that whatever attempts are made; however skills, imagination and diligence are employed; the standard is essentially inappropriate to the educational context. The burden of overcoming the chasm between origin and proposed centres of use is simply too great. This point becomes apparent in several areas of the document. For instance, the notion that books should be purchased to a 'defined specification' (BSI 1991a: 6) inevitably raises questions about whose specification is being discussed and for what purpose. Also the use of the description 'handling, storing, purchasing and delivery' (1991a: 9) as a starting point for procedures to deal with anything from careers counselling (would this equate with 'packaging' of the product?) to lodgings (presumably storage) is highly questionable. This issue of relevance is further driven home by reference to another of the important clauses around which transfer and application rests – the definition and treatment of the 'non-conforming product'.

The interpretation of non-conformance or the 'non-conforming product' is left fairly wide. It is able to encompass inadequacies with the course, with the materials, and, naturally enough, with the actions of the course participant (the student). Thus, what is offered is the very real prospect of an individual having difficulties with one or other aspect of a course, being designated as the non-conforming product. The decision about how to solve these problems is then transferred to that part of the system which details the procedures designed for that situation. The example given (BSI 1991a: 9) describes the actions to deal with a non-conforming product (student failing an examination). These could include a transfer, a re-sit or an expulsion. That these may form a part of a response to exam failure is clear enough; to lay them down as *the* clear options is to inappropriately simplify. There is no mention of a flexible procedure to consider (the frequently complex personal and educational) reasons for failure. Instead concentration is on labelling non-conformance and setting out formal options. By starting with a broad meaningless notion like non-conforming product, a tendency towards de-humanising the situation is largely unavoidable.

The sometimes ludicrous results of cross-sectoral interpretations are brought home by the following statement – intended for the commercial contexts – contained in the BSI executive guide: 'All non-conforming product should be identified to *prevent* unauthorised use, shipment or *mixing with conforming product*' (1987: 13) (my emphasis). If following BSI guidelines the conclusion is inescapable – educational apartheid! It is perhaps all too easy to poke fun at such consequences of the transfer of terminology. But the unavoidable conclusion is that the use of many of these clauses is so contrived and studded with pitfalls that it invites confusion. On the other hand to look at quality in education via language applicable to its own circumstance, and in relation to purposes which relate to that context, actually offers a substantial initial advantage. Rather than a product, conforming or otherwise, the student/attending professional can be viewed as an active participant, both in the course, and in various situations beyond that setting.

A TRIVIAL PURSUIT?

It is difficult to imagine BS5750 falling from favour with quite the speed by which it became a talking point. Unarguably, supporters of its high profile approach are to be found (see chapters 3, 5 and 6). Perceptions of likely benefit seem likely to secure some measure of continued pragmatic allegiance. BS5750 is, though, the centrepiece of an approach which is laden with difficulties. It brings to CPE, or higher education more widely, such a weight of inappropriate focuses that the case for it looks anything but convincing. It has severe difficulties at a number of levels, each of which has been discussed.

It has a vulnerability at the ideological level: in its uncompromising affinity with image and commercialism as the basis of quality; in its lack of attention to the nature, distinctiveness, purpose and influence of education, including its social location; and in relation to its claims of objectivity and its accompanying implicit conservatism. At the practical level, the sheer inappropriateness of content, including its language; the impetus it provides towards easily attained, narrowly defined standards; and its eventually limited emphasis are all serious weaknesses. It has a vulnerability at the financial level (due to the considerable cost involved); and at the organisation level (the required hierarchical structures and patterns of involvement). If and when the enthusiasm for a ready made solution starts to fade, the question of how a system wedded to such problems can actually promote educational quality (rather than administrative compliance and predictability) might well begin to be asked more frequently.

3

QUALITY AND POST-COMPULSORY EDUCATION

In this, the third and final chapter of the opening section, the discussion of quality is developed one stage further – i.e. specifically in relation to education. A central purpose is to locate activity in CPE within the context of developments at other points of post-compulsory education. To this end, research evidence and emerging structural trends are highlighted. A further purpose is to identify and discuss some of the potentially most useful work which has developed within this context. At times these concerns are connected; at different times, one takes precedence over the other. In either case, the chapter will build on (and at some points relate to) earlier discussions in the book with the aim of establishing a wider basis of knowledge from which to proceed.

The opening phase of the chapter – that concerned with the current nature of quality assurance in further education in the UK – is included in order to bring forward some firm data on the sector which has in many ways been in the vanguard of attempts to formalise QA. Evidence on the level at which enthusiasm for BS5750 has been transferred to the generality will be presented. Analysis of higher education begins with a look at broadly based ongoing trends. Details of national emphases in the UK are coupled with a summary of worldwide activity. Two thought-provoking examples are drawn from the latter. The review section of the book is brought to what is perhaps its logical conclusion by direct reference to work dealing exclusively with quality in continuing education. This discussion leads into the empirical analysis of CPE which forms the basis of part II.

QUALITY ASSURANCE IN THE UK FURTHER EDUCATION SECTOR

At various points in the review so far undertaken, the involvement of the further education (FE) sector with quality matters has been acknowledged. In particular, chapter 2 included reference to the support that has been forthcoming for BS5750. My purpose here is to consider whether the quality issue has become central in more than the high profile colleges alone and to discover how far BS5750 is at the forefront of any development. This will be achieved through a consideration of the evidence from two recent reports: one is an official review drawing on selected cases (HMI 1992); the other is a large-scale quantitative assessment of activity (Sallis 1990). Taken together, they will flesh out the nature of quality activity a little.

The Further Education Unit (1991) have identified six major changes to the setting in which further education now operates. Each of these initiatives/trends is noted to have had the explicit purpose of improving quality. The six are: the introduction of National Vocational Qualifications, the Education Reform Act, and the National Curriculum; the higher profile role given to local TECs; the growing links between business and education; and finally, the government initiative for a Further Education Council. It is in the context of such developments, and their interaction with the broadly based impetus to QA, that institutional interest in quality has flourished.

The document produced by Her Majesty's Inspectorate (HMI 1992) was the result of a review of existing quality procedures in FE colleges. It was carried out during the summer term of 1991. The colleges selected for inclusion in the study were identified on the basis of an established and known activity in the area of quality. As a result, this report is a focused consideration of trends within a sub-group of colleges. It is not an assessment of activity in the entire sector.

As the report proceeds, this is made clear. At that point the validity of the approach is confirmed. However, it should be noted that the language of the report sometimes makes accurate and appropriate use of its data difficult. This is because at times the conclusions seem to be embracing generalisations – something to which the approach is clearly not suited. So, for instance, the conclusion that 'colleges of further education are placing the development of quality assurance high on their list of priorities'

(HMI 1992: 1) can neither be regarded as surprising nor informative when seen alongside the following method: 'Twenty-one colleges, *which were understood to have made progress in the development of quality assurance* or were giving the subject serious consideration, were inspected' (1992: 1) (my emphasis). If colleges are selected on the basis of a known interest in quality, then the point that quality is high on their agenda is surely more of an introductory comment than a conclusion! It follows that this report cannot be used for assertions about the sector as a whole. This is essentially a presentational difficulty – a failure to underline the precise nature of the sample (not least in the report summary); to be clear about the consequential scope of the work; and to properly differentiate between discussion of the sample, and discussion about the sector as a whole. Once beyond this initial lack of clarity, though, the report does offer some insights into practice in quality-active colleges.

The following are perhaps the major conclusions of the report.

1 Around one-quarter of the colleges reviewed are some way towards the implementation of a quality assurance system. When recalling that this is a quarter of a pre-identified group and not of the totality, it might be argued that this is a lower proportion than might have been expected. Indeed, changes to the structure of local education authorities and – this is of particular interest – a lack of staff support in some instances are noted as having inhibited development.

2 Approximately one-third of the sample are intending to go for BS5750 approval (see Collins *et al.* n.d., 1991; for details of the application of BS5750 to a college of FE). There is a high level of concern that employers and TECs might come to expect registration.

3 Whilst one-quarter of colleges are embracing principles of TQM, as yet it is rare for this to be transformed into a strategic goal.

4 A lack of systematic attention to non-externally validated work was observed. In contrast, full-time programmes are subject to course review. While such findings can give us an indication of developments, it is to the second study that we must look in order to assess wider trends.

Sallis (1990) approached 466 colleges and achieved a response rate of 56 per cent. Whether or not the survey attracted respondents from those most interested in the field is difficult to judge. It is the kind of difficulty faced by researchers across the board. This study is the best source of data currently available. On the basis of the evidence cited, there is little doubt that colleges are addressing the issue in vast numbers. For instance, 71 per cent stated that they are definitely going to introduce a QA system, with only 6 per cent giving the opposite view. Furthermore 65 per cent acknowledged quality as a high priority, with only 7 per cent describing it as a low priority. Just 2 per cent stated that it is not important at all.

Results which reveal the perceived sources of pressure for the introduction of QA require a closer examination than might initially appear to be the case. The main finding was that 80 per cent regarded college management as the prime movers in this trend. External bodies (whose influence is elsewhere frequently mentioned) achieved much lower citation levels. For instance, the TECs were cited by just 25 per cent of respondents. The author offers a plausible explanation of this. Sallis states '[it] . . . might be that colleges are attempting to introduce quality assurance on their own terms before it is forced on them' (1990: 6). Drawing a clear distinction between management initiative and reaction to pressure is not an uncomplicated matter. In practice, the line is blurred.

With that, we can move to consider the nature of the systems being adopted and the question of whether BS5750 is being embraced at a greater level than that suggested by the HMI Report. In fact, despite the differences in methodology, the results from the two sources are broadly similar. In the wide-ranging research of Sallis, 39 per cent of colleges were developing or considering developing a BS5750-based system; 35 per cent were looking to TQM; and 32 per cent to a college-specific system (figures exceed 100 per cent because some colleges were combining more than one approach). Thus, while the well-known approaches of BS5750 and TQM are doubtless achieving substantial levels of support (see Sallis and Hingley 1991 for a discussion of these in relation to further education), almost as many colleges as accepted either of these were 'devising their own systems . . . in the main, built around course teams, procedures for monitoring and evaluation and client satisfaction sampling' (Sallis 1990: 11). This decision to adopt an independent strategy is likely to be related to the catalogue of problems with BS5750 which were raised by respondents and were cited in the report. Words like: 'bureaucratic', 'gimmicky', 'paper pushing', and 'mechanistic' (1990: 9) give an indication of the kinds of views held.

QUALITY AND QUALITY ASSURANCE

There is little or nothing in these publications which stands contrary to the belief that quality assurance is the big issue in further education at the moment. The extent to which this is occurring under (and as a consequence of) perceived or actual threat (from outside bodies) is less clear. And while the frequently mentioned relationship between BS5750 (and for that matter TQM) and further education is real enough, it is equally evident that there is no single universally accepted approach to the quality issue. Teachers and administrators wary of the demands and emphases of these approaches are seeking alternatives which they consider more relevant to the needs of their own institution.

QUALITY ASSURANCE AND UNIVERSITIES 1: ASPECTS OF THE UK SCENE

Just as the further education sector is undergoing a period of modification, so too, higher education is at a time of significant changes. Increases in student numbers, the end of the binary divide, and the greater institutionalisation of forms of audit and assessment are all important components of this phase. The later terms – those integral to the quality process – are used in quite particular ways. A consultation paper produced by a new institutional player of this period – the Higher Education Funding Council England (HEFCE 1992) – clarifies the situation somewhat. It draws on the government white paper (Department of Education 1991) to differentiate between 'control', 'audit' and 'assessment'. Quality 'control' is deemed to consist of the procedures used by the institutions themselves in pursuit of quality provision. It is, therefore, a responsibility which stays with the universities. Quality 'audit' – of which more a little later – centres on the external review of such procedures: an attempt to consider their potential effectiveness. Quality 'assessment', for which the responsibility lies at the level of funding council, is a more judgemental review of teaching and provision in the universities.

While it is not really appropriate to go into too much detail on these developments, if we accept their likely prominence in institutional planning for the foreseeable future, a flavour of what is involved might be useful. A closer look at one of the discrete categories of action – quality audit – can be used to this end.

Although it is necessary to recognise the long involvement of the Council for National Academic Awards (CNAA) with quality assurance in the now defunct polytechnic sector (see Lewis 1990;

Todd and Tovey 1991), the recent surge towards quality within higher education is perhaps best exemplified by the emergence and subsequent 'transmogrification' – a term favoured by one of the unit's officials – of the Committee of Vice Chancellors and Principals (CVCP) Academic Audit Unit (AAU) (see CVCP 1990, 1991; Perry 1990). Although the AAU has been superseded by an organisation reflecting the post-binary structure, neither its emphases nor its procedures are being lost from the audit process: it therefore deserves our continued attention.

Peter Williams (1992) – writing as director of the Academic Audit Unit – claims that until recently the formalised consideration of quality has been absent from UK universities. Not surprisingly the election victory of the Conservatives in 1979 is identified as a watershed in proceedings. The consequent fostering of managerial and/or industrial values is regarded as having had a direct bearing on developments in education, as it has elsewhere in the public sector.

Williams states that the response of the university sector to both the increasing need to justify its position in the face of this trend, and ever tightening budgetary controls, was a series of CVCP initiatives, studies and reports (e.g. Jarratt 1985; Reynolds 1986) which ran through the 1980s. The AAU was the eventual result of this process. Established in 1990, its instigation was, according to Williams, not peripherally influenced by the threat of the UFC to take matters into their own hands.

In line with the definition of audit outlined above, the role of the AAU was never one of inspection or accreditation of provision or teaching. Instead, its terms of reference were: to review the procedures/mechanisms used to secure academic standards; to assess the extent to which these reflect best practice; to commend good practice to universities at a national level; to review the role of the external examiner and to report to the CVCP. These tasks were to be fulfilled through an examination of: systems for course design and monitoring; mechanisms for quality assurance relating to teaching and communication methods; mechanisms for staff development and assessment; and mechanisms for taking account of relevant interest groups (students, accrediting bodies etc.) (CVCP 1992: 5–8).

The directors' report on the experiences of the first fifteen months of operation of the AAU concluded that the university system as a whole is actively engaged in tackling quality assurance. The AAU

81

itself was observed to be not only reporting on the process, but affecting it: by providing a stimulus to action and by disseminating information which can contribute to change (CVCP 1992: 21).

The body now responsible for audit in UK universities is the Division of Quality Audit of the Higher Education Quality Council. It remains 'University owned'. The short (usually a few days), but concentrated, visits to universities are also retained.

Thus the evolution of 'audit' over the last decade into a clearly defined part of university life seems set to continue despite the current structural changes in higher education. Audit components identified by the AAU are likely to maintain their status, and the process of which the visit is merely the most observable element will continue to require substantial attention at institutional level.

QUALITY ASSURANCE AND UNIVERSITIES 2: ASPECTS OF THE INTERNATIONAL SCENE

By broadening the terms of reference beyond the UK for a moment, a further consistency in the way QA is being encountered across sectors is revealed: that in higher education – as elsewhere – QA is a truly international pre-occupation.

As is apparent from the proceedings of an International Conference which took place in 1991 (see Craft (ed.) 1992), QA is on the agenda in the higher education institutions of countries as diverse as Australia (Kwong Lee Dow 1992); Hong Kong (Sensicle 1992); India (Chandra 1992); the United States (Lenn 1992); and several places in Europe (Staropoli 1992, Frackmann 1992). Despite this, QA practice is neither homogeneous nor interchangeable. Indeed, such variation has itself been the subject of interesting commentary (notably from Bauer 1992). However, before considering Bauer's arguments, brief reference can profitably be made to an example of current developments in policy and practice in one national context – the Netherlands.

There is one unmistakable trend accompanying discussion of quality in Dutch higher education: it is that the government has made the decision to distance itself from the process and invest autonomy in the institutions themselves (Kalkwijk 1992). The consequence is that universities are free to work on their own mechanisms for quality, whilst an external review system based on established procedures, such as expert peer review, serves to monitor practice. Indeed comparison with the emerging system of the UK in the early 1990s is not inappropriate. The intention is, therefore, that by taking responsibility for the mechanisms them-selves, the institutions will be able to establish a more co-ordinated approach than had previously (essentially up to the mid-1980s) existed.

It has been argued that the fairly recent shift in policy has so far failed to match the claims for autonomy with genuine changes in practice (Vroeijenstijn 1992). But for Kalkwijk one part of the change is already proving to be valuable – the location of the ownership of systems with the institutions themselves. What is argued is that this decentralised location of power has encouraged a positive relationship with, and an ongoing acceptance of, quality matters.

There is no reason why the logic of such a position needs to be restricted to any particular (say, national) level. A working principle of allowing those directly involved to have meaningful control over the process could well merit explicit mention within small scale-settings. Despite the existence of particular pressures and emphases, the room for manœuvre allowed within certain national systems permits its retention as a continuing option.

Bauer (1992) in a discussion of contemporary Sweden (and the nature of approaches in Europe more widely) raises several important issues. For instance, it is argued that despite a long history of contact between different countries on issues relating to higher education, this has not been extended to a uniformity of ideas on the way in which QA programmes should be developed. For Bauer, this is a consequence of ingrained cultural and political differences. The argument continues that despite such variation in approach there is a growing pressure towards the internationalisation of ways of assuring and monitoring quality. This should be resisted, Bauer states. Variation should be maintained, local diversity should be encouraged, and any heterogeneity should be interpreted as a welcome contribution to pluralism. It is stated, 'Differences among national evaluation systems, then, are justified if we are not aiming to develop all higher education in the direction of international uniformity. Evaluation systems not only can but should differ' (1992: 135).

It is from this starting point that the discussion of the characteristics of the Swedish experience is undertaken. For our purposes it is the foundations of the likely changes, and not details of the organisational requirements, that are noteworthy. While leaning heavily on institutional responsibility on the one hand, and nationally co-ordinated comparative reviews of approaches on the other, Bauer argues that the Swedish system will evolve into a *quality-promoting* and *development-oriented* one, rather than one in which the guiding forces are *accountability* and *control*. In short, a system primarily motivated by enabling rather than checking. This is a particularly valuable contribution in the light of the themes of this book. It provides a practical – as well as a theoretical – example of an attempt to shape activity towards progressive aims rather than aims of justification and survival. For Bauer, the selection of concepts and the use of one form of terminology over another is crucial. So, for instance, in parallel with a removal from the system of inappropriate terms (such as quality control, because of its industrial connotations) there is a stated need for the formulation of concepts which have an organic unity with the environment concerned. There is evident compatibility in this with the critique of industrially based systems developed earlier. It offers a further impetus to the development of higher education quality in its own terms and for its own purposes, not those borrowed from elsewhere.

As I argued earlier, an objective of seeking to replace existing terminology may turn out to be overly ambitious because of the established nature of existing institutional arrangement. In that sense Bauer's argument may be inappropriate for the UK. The overall line of the perspective is, though, entirely consistent with the task currently faced.

QUALITY ASSURANCE IN UNIVERSITY CONTINUING EDUCATION

Discussions relating to formalised quality assurance have formed an essential element of the recent educational environment of the United States. Despite fundamental differences of setting there is a reasonable amount of literature which can be profitably referred to. However, before concentrating on that there are a couple of features of the UK scene which can and should be raised: the institutional context; and the evolving interest in research and policy development.

UK continuing education: elements of context

The first of these can be discussed by continuing with the 'audit'

84

emphasis. While in practice, the nature of CE may make the relationship with audit more complicated than elsewhere, from its inception the stated position of the AAU has been clear: 'For the purposes of these notes, [for authors], "programmes of study" is taken to mean both award – and non award – bearing programmes as well as their constituent courses or other elements. The phrase includes work in adult and continuing education' (CVCP 1991: 1). Despite the demise of the AAU the expectation (expressed verbally by an official of the unit) is that this is likely to represent one of the many points of continuity with any subsequent body taking over the audit remit. The situation is, however, an ever-changing one.

General trends in higher education are impinging on continuing education. However, like elsewhere (in education and in the non-commercial world more generally) the pursuit of quality is inspired by a mix (in varying proportions) of influences: ranging from a personal and/or departmental desire for quality to the need to 'play the game' of the external bodies.

Probably as a result of the interaction of these influences (though with formal requirements attaining particular importance at given points), the continuing education community has been increasingly engaged in dealing with this issue. This is apparent, for instance, in the consideration being given to the suitability of the type of performance indicators to be used in the HEFCE 'assessment' exercises. It is the original development of these in relation to traditional undergraduate programmes which is problematic for short term and/or qualification-free provision (Brookman 1992).

Matters related to discussions of quality are becoming regular features of research work in the sector. Amongst current and recent topics there have been projects concerned with: student satisfaction; clarification of good practice; monitoring; credit accumulation and transfer (CATS); and performance indicators (see de Wit 1992, for further details). All matters of some significance within the changing climate of university provision.

Work dealing directly with a central theme of quality – educational evaluation – is, of course, well established. This output should not be overlooked. Research has been carried out which deals with aspects of post-compulsory education in the UK (Constable and Long 1989; Hodgson and Whalley 1990); and which considers rather different educational settings (Alkin 1990; Deshler 1984; House (ed.) 1986; Palumbo (ed.) 1987).

Just as in the UK, the interest in quality assurance which pervades continuing education in the US is matched by activity at a much wider level. Indeed, a report resulting from a visit to that country by members of Her Majesty's Inspectorate (1991) emphasised an ever-intensifying pressure towards the development of appropriate quality assurance in the light of apparent public concern about the character of American higher education as a whole.

US continuing education: recent writings on quality

It has been during the last decade that the US has become the site of much discussion around quality and continuing education. Following a brief summary of the kinds of issues this has produced, a little more detail will be provided on arguably the most informative single text of this period – that of Freedman (1987).

Work which is of most direct relevance has not surprisingly appeared within the last decade or so. There is some merit in seeing contributions in terms of their input to one or more of a number of umbrella themes: the definitional; the contextual; and the practical.

The defining and categorising of quality has attained its expected position in discussion (see, for example, Astin 1985). How such matters of definition can become the source of contestation has been examined by Tucker and Mautz (1985). The article serves as a useful reminder of the need to clarify who defines, why, and with what goals in mind.

At the contextual level, the economic rather than organisational determinants of quality have been stressed (Volkwein 1989); as have the demands of the market location of activity (Stern 1982). This latter issue is to be picked up again shortly.

But it is at the level of practice that the depth of contributions is especially evident. There has been reference to the need for continuing educationalists to step back and analyse their own practice, irrespective of pressures of time (Apps 1985). There has been the proposal that collaboration – between various levels and departments within the university, students and the wider community – constitutes the route to quality (Ettinger 1987). And still at the level of the provider, there has been strong advocacy of improving practitioner effectiveness; or to put it in more familiar terms, staff development (Knox 1987). A round table discussion in Shimberg (1983) does add a cautionary note to an over-emphasis on the provider end of the relationship. The gist of the argument is that any reluctance amongst recipients of CE to accept the principle of life-long learning poses significant difficulties not easily overcome by concentration on the teaching professionals alone. With the increasingly 'obligatory' character of CPE attendance in some of the professions of the UK (see chapter 6), this factor might well impinge on provision in the immediate future.

Even without delving too far into the detail of these pieces, their suggestive value is identifiable. Indeed, by-passing (often context-dependent) content allows the essential themes to become more readily identifiable. These reveal a certain symmetry with those which have emerged from the analyses of other sectors. There is: concern about the impact and beneficiaries of different approaches to quality; debate about the role of finance and the role of the market. Also raised are questions about the impact of clients and about the various facets of tutor involvements. These are matters of definition, context and practice which demand attention whatever the national context.

Despite use of the above categorisation, it is obviously the case that writers do not necessarily limit themselves to discussion on just one of these dimensions. For instance, Freedman's (1987) discussion of practice is preceded by reference to the location of contemporary continuing education within an identifiable historical pattern.

For Freedman the growth of interest in quality is occurring during a period in which continuing education is benefiting from (what he chooses to label) the move towards a post-industrial society. This is a term which has been employed in a variety of ways in recent decades in an attempt to explain one or another feature of an apparent move away from the character of early industrial society (Bell 1973; Touraine 1974). Of primary importance in Freedman's use of the concept is that technological developments, and shifts in the basis of knowledge, ensure that education cannot any longer (if it was ever the case) be restricted to a once only, pre-career event.

Despite this apparent historical advantage which CPE now has, there is a separate element of the current situation which is rather less positive in its impact – the market location of activity. Elsewhere, Stern (1982) had earlier signalled the type of clarification needed to deal with the situation. He stated, 'we in continuing education are pragmatic professionals. Up to now, we have been our universities' chief ambassadors to the market place. We are, however, ambassadors, and *the university, not the market place, is our home'* (1982: 64) (my emphasis).

Freedman displays a concordance with such a line in his argument that there is an almost unavoidable temptation to 'include potentially lucrative programs that are inappropriate to the university' (1987: 8). He goes on to state that 'survival is the first law of institutions', and to ask, 'when survival and quality collide, will quality prevail?' (1987: 8). He argues that quality should be adhered to as a means by which survival can be secured. But what is most intriguing is that (in marked contrast to much of the UK debate), far from the market being seen to be the source of quality – through the achievement of client satisfaction or whatever – for Freedman, 'the market-place inevitably forces on all of us some compromises with quality' (8–9).

It is important to reiterate just what is being stated here. From such a perspective the implication seems to be that far from repeat business and institutional survival constituting evidence of quality, they may in fact be providing evidence of the very opposite. As such, quality can be achieved *in spite of the market*, not because of it.

Freedman's perspective on system development is also of some interest. For while he acknowledges that formalised procedures are an essential part of an attempt to ensure quality, he is equally aware of the tendency towards the bureaucratic in such procedures. It is argued that this can work against the achievement of quality by limiting the potential for flexibility and creativity – characteristics which are considered to be the hallmark of continuing education. As a consequence it is argued that: 'The goal for continuing higher educators is to design procedures that provide quality review yet do not destroy initiative, are not unduly expensive, and are based on criteria that take into account the special characteristics of the adult student' (1987: 86). Thus in one step a course is set which is on many dimensions distinctive from the topic of earlier discussion – BS5750.

At least at first sight, the actual headings ascribed by Freedman to potentially valuable procedures appear to have a degree of familiarity and crossover with many systems, including BS5750 itself. Indeed, it is the case that some of these are dealing with similar topics. The difference comes in the extent to which Freedman starts from a clear idea of shaping procedures to context, rather than context to (pre-identified) procedures; and in the extent to which absolute priority is given to the avoidance of unnecessary controls and restrictions.

Practical action is discussed by Freedman in relation to five areas.

1 Review by continuing education staff, as the phrase suggests, is all about the possibilities of collegial interaction. At its simplest this might include the examination of new ideas with fellow members of staff. It might also, though, develop into more formalised feedback systems and patterns of formative evaluation (Deshler 1984). Whatever the process, this theme emphasises the potentially positive influence of internal staff.

2 Input from those elsewhere in the faculty provides the next heading. Flexibility is central to this. Whether comments are received via personal meetings, distributed plans of action or whatever, the aim is to establish a formalised means of drawing in a range of opinions; but in a way which does not exacerbate any existing problems of organisation within a given institution. The idea is to utilise the principle in a way which is of agreed benefit in local settings.

3 This is followed by constituency representation – the inclusion of relevant people from industry, the professions and the community more widely, to help construct course objectives and content which will be valued by those it will affect. Now, this basic idea can be developed for our purposes to note that precisely who these delegates are will be influenced by two factors: the nature of the issue(s) to be covered by the course; and decisions about who has a legitimate voice. While the first of these might move attention towards some 'obvious' external contributors, the second is much more open to interpretation: it is likely to develop from provider (or course team) motivation. For instance, a course deemed to be the domain of a simple provider/client partnership in one quarter could be regarded as requiring more broadly based participation, which moves beyond the professionals to the community in another.

4 Student evaluations must by the 1990s figure in the thinking (if not always the actions) of all those considering the quality of their courses. While in Freedman's opinion the results of the feedback process can be taken seriously, he points out both a continued level of suspicion about them amongst academics, and the partially legitimate basis for such concerns. In particular, the issue of the extent to which this form of evaluation measures performer popularity, rather than scholastic merit and pedagogic proficiency, is raised. For Freedman, though, the tendency for this to influence results is likely to be less pronounced amongst adults, particularly those whose involvement in continuing

education is designed to achieve a clearly defined end. Moreover, it is argued that while the charm element may figure significantly early on in a presentation, a failure to deliver something of value soon overshadows this.

5 All such activity should occur within a framework of written guidelines – the final category. However, it is important to stress that the inclusion of this dimension takes the discussion no closer to rigidity and inflexibility than any of the others mentioned previously. Freedman cites the example of the standards developed for non-credit work in Ohio.

There is a sense of consistency between the emphases in the above discussions and the principles on which the Ohio standards exist (see Anthony and Skinner 1986; Skinner 1987). In particular, the clearly stated intention is that while the standards have a state-wide applicability, fundamental control and responsibility rest with the continuing education specialists and with institutions: a self-study model is the favoured tool. Furthermore, the idea of ensuring that the standards actually have a meaningful unity with continuing education priorities is clearly expressed. The standards themselves are divided into seven categories: mission; organisation; instructional personnel; resources; educational offerings; admissions and evaluations. The main tool is the use of questions relating to each of these aimed at the stimulation of both insight and active appraisal. So, for instance, included within the theme of educational offerings is the question 'what rationale is used to determine what is to be offered?' And in the evaluation section, the cue question 'are evaluation results used to modify and improve continuing education offerings?' is introduced (Anthony and Skinner 1986: 55–6).

As with other work incorporated in this review there is no attempt to hold up the above as the model to follow, as the way in which quality will be achieved. The structural arrangements which exist in the US are not just different from elsewhere, but would in many ways be deemed problematic and unsatisfactory by many in the UK. The cornerstones of the approach outlined are, though, worth repeating, for in many ways they offer an alternative vision – some principles to develop and modify – and a means of sidestepping the flawed basis of industrial and commercial systems. In combination with the themes taken from the wider overview of the US scene, they constitute a considerable resource on which to draw. The centrality of empowering providers rather than asking them to participate in pre-established systems, the need for flexibility rather than rigidity, the avoidance of measures which reduce creativity, and – probably most important of all – the belief in developing approaches to mirror and analyse continuing education as a distinct (though not separate) entity are all stressed. They support the emerging case for the possibilities of context-specificity.

CONCLUSION

Having reached the conclusion of this chapter and, as a consequence, the conclusion of the opening section of the book, two features of the situation facing CPE are clear enough. These are points which can be readily drawn from the review of education and tie in with the review of experience elsewhere. The first is that layer upon layer of nations, occupational sectors, and specialist areas within those sectors are addressing QA as an immediate priority. University CPE in the UK is one of those specialist areas. Left at that, the situation could be seen as fairly daunting: that CPE is merely following a well-trodden (and even pre-determined) path.

But that would be to ignore the second point: that despite pressures towards cross-sectoral and even international uniformity, individuals, institutions and sectors have been prepared to look for locally meaningful solutions. Attempts have been made to develop distinct approaches to QA. Even in areas, like the UK further education sector, which might – at first sight – be assumed to be exemplifying conformity to pre-established approaches, considerable variation is in fact evident. While there is nothing to indicate that these projects are necessarily shifting the terms of reference very far, their existence does demonstrate a desire to adopt self-directed quality strategies. Future work which more readily challenges the assumed nature of quality, and its commercial reference points, can extend the value of alternative approaches considerably.

To respond to the demands of the moment, to those demands made by the central institutions which define the shape of adjudications on quality, will remain a necessary feature of thinking on quality for those involved in CPE. Yet, it seems likely that satisfaction of specified requirements will leave room for flexibility and interpretation about how to develop quality practice, and to what ends this should be directed. Those at the centre of activity in CPE – the providers and facilitators – can retain an influential role in this. And it is to their existing perceptions and practices that I now turn.

Part II

QUALITY ASSURANCE IN CONTINUING PROFESSIONAL EDUCATION

4

EVIDENCE FROM THE FIELD I
Specialist departments of CPE

The empirical analysis begins with the CPE specialists. This group can be defined as the central co-ordinators, facilitators and/or providers of ongoing education for professionals in UK universities. CPE constitutes either a major, or the sole, focus of occupational concern for these members of staff.

Perspectives on quality held by CPE specialists will be revealed in relation to several issues. Each will allude to one or both of the following objectives:

1 A clarification of how quality is presently understood and how it is operationalised in procedural action;
2 A clarification of views held on aspects of the current situation and on possible future developments.

Issues revealed as significant in this context form the basis of the subsequent study of other key institutional players. The full empirical picture will complement the review and conceptual perspectives detailed in part I.

Following a review of methodology – in which the nature of the respondent group is clarified – provider aims (and the definitions of quality which go hand in hand with these) are analysed. The matter of match and mis-match between the two is tackled. The level of knowledge and the type of views held about QA in other sectors are then examined. Evidence on attitudes to BS5750 is featured here. Review of current QA practice in specialist centres, including a discussion of the main procedures actually in use precedes consideration of the barriers which exist – or are seen as likely in the future to exist – to the extension of QA policy and practice. Finally, there is an analysis of subjective judgements and assessments on matters of interest to specialist practitioners.

METHODOLOGY AND SAMPLE

For this phase of the research the means of data collection was a postal survey. Questionnaires were distributed to representatives of central providing and/or facilitating units or departments of CPE in UK universities. As all of our identified population were able to be included, considerations of sampling were not relevant.

The identification of respondents within universities and university colleges was achieved by reference to the members list of the Universities Council of Adult and Continuing Education (UCACE). In the majority of cases the initially addressed people were the ones who dealt with the questionnaire. However, in a relatively small number of institutions the survey was completed by someone other than the originally designated respondent. Whilst this can, no doubt, be partially accounted for by the normal process of delegation, there is a further cause of this which can be identified. It is the varying organisational bases of CPE provision in UK universities. To be more specific, in some universities identifiable units or offices exist with responsibility for CPE somewhat separately from the continuing education mainstream. And in other institutions market-oriented posts exist within established departments (see McIlroy and Spencer 1988: 124–5, for a useful discussion of 'entrepreneurs' in adult education). These variants are the source of a small, but not insignificant, number of the sample.

Fifty-five questionnaires were distributed. Thirty-seven of these were completed and returned. A completion level of 67.45 per cent was therefore recorded. It can be noted, however, that two institutions were sent two questionnaires. This was because of a particular structure which indicated two parallel sources of CPE provision. In each case one was returned. As such, 37 of 53 institutions (70 per cent) surveyed are represented in the data.

There are two points of particular interest in the above.

1 Due to the fairly tight (and therefore inevitably limited) nature of the research population, all of the units able to be so classified were given the opportunity to contribute to the research.
2 A large proportion (over two-thirds) chose to be involved. This not only increases confidence in the likely validity of the data, but perhaps gives an indication of the priority being ascribed to matters of quality assurance at the present time.

CPE has traditionally been perceived as existing on the periphery of university education. The figures from the present study illustrate that (in terms of scale) such an interpretation needs to be questioned. The extent of provision is now such that its component parts (including quality assurance) merit independent consideration. From the 28 institutions which provided data on this topic an estimated total of 7,788 courses were reported to be conducted each year, undeniably a considerable level of provision. This is not, though, to imply an even distribution of activity. Different universities and university colleges detailed substantially differing patterns of activity. Indeed, the range of course numbers was from 25 at one institution to 1,250 at another.

Differences between the central units of institutions can also be identified in terms of the extent to which they provide or facilitate activity, i.e., whether the role is one of co-ordination of university-wide provision or the actual laying on of short (or other) courses. The total estimated number of courses provided by the responding central departments was 2,137. Although this is clearly a substantial output for a relatively small number of departments, it does represent little more than a quarter of total provision.

Thus, from these initial data alone we can see that: CPE has a significant place in the educational provision of the modern university; that there is a substantial level of decentralisation; and that there is variation in the extent to which central units perform a providing and/or facilitating role. There is not just one *raison d'être* amongst the responding units.

PROVIDERS AND FACILITATORS: AIMS AND DEFINITIONS OF QUALITY

Whilst it is undoubtedly the case that quality assurance has been able to secure a central position in debates concerning the organisation of educational provision, we should not lose sight of the fact that QA itself is but a support mechanism, or set of mechanisms, designed to increase the likelihood of attaining a high level of success (as defined) in the specific area to which it is applied. Thus, the procedures and practices are to a significant degree neutral tools which must be activated on the basis of particular objectives. A perspective on purpose is required for the complete picture to be constituted.

This is entirely consistent with the theme of context-specificity which ran through part I. It is an issue which influenced the research design of this study. Whilst necessarily concentrating on details of policy and practice, an early section of the survey to specialist providers was reserved for questions which would elicit information on identified aims of provision and the definitions of quality around which that provision revolved. Although separate issues in their own right, there is an element of overlap between them which will be highlighted.

As can be seen by reference to table 4.1, two approaches were used to gain data on the aims of respondent involvement with CPE. Column (a) provides details of the level of identification with any or all of a presented list. The notable feature of respondent evidence here is the consistently high rate of affinity with the majority of the aims listed. While this gives an indication of the multi-faceted nature of the aims of these professionals, this measure was unable to provide details of priority.

A supplementary question, constructed in an open-ended form (for which answers are listed in column (b)) was designed for just that purpose. In this, respondents were asked to identify their 'primary aim'. Although a singular response was expected, 56 responses were recorded from the 32 participants. The percentage

Table 4.1 CPE specialists: aims of provision

Aims	Column a List offered (%)	Column b Primary aims (%)	Column c Single primary aim (%)
Income generation	95	31	12
Satisfaction of individual participant	95	28	6
Satisfaction of commissioning body	95	22	0
Improved professional practice (for the benefit of society as a whole)	84	44	35
Research and development	68	6	0
Links with industry	84	22	12
	N = 35	N = 32	N = 17

Note: A small number of other non-listed aims were offered; a maximum of one respondent per aim.

figures indicate the number who include a given aim within their 'primary aims'. This measure produced a greater degree of differentiation between various aims than had been previously highlighted. An improvement in professional practice for the benefit of society (44 per cent) stands a little way clear of remaining aims in citation rates. Income generation (31 per cent) and satisfaction of individual participants (28 per cent) also gained support.

As stated above, these figures in column (b) were calculated on the basis of all identified 'primary aims' – including those which formed a part of a multiple response. The data were the subject of a further stage of analysis, one which dealt solely with those respondents who detailed a single primary aim. The rationale behind this was that if one such aim was able to be identified it was likely to be of some import to the individual subject and may, potentially at least (though this is, of course, a matter of conjecture) influence practice. The biggest difficulty faced by an analysis of such respondents is that their numbers drop considerably from those available for other calculations. However, having noted such a proviso, the figures are both valuable and largely supportive of the tentative conclusions resulting from a review of column (b) data. Even more marked here is the extent to which improved professional practice takes centre stage (35 per cent). The figures for the remaining aims do become small indeed, but again it is income generation (this time accompanied by links with industry) that stands out.

There are features of this evidence which deserve particular attention because of their direct relevance to the development of quality CPE. Foremost amongst these is the consistent level of identification with the notion of CPE as an activity which has, or should have, a positive impact on the nature of the society of which it forms a part. Despite its location in the market, it is apparent that for a number of those involved the provision of courses has a basis in educational principle like any other. Thus, the argument against conceptual relegation of CPE, advanced earlier in abstract terms, is given support by the expressed aims of currently practising CPE specialists.

However, although there is clearly this identity with the ideal of improving professional practice, the more practical and pragmatic responses based on income generation and developing links with industry are far from ignored. This is likely in part to be influenced by the somewhat contradictory position in which CPE currently exists. This was described earlier (see introduction) in terms of pedagogic impetus on the one hand, and financial restrictions and underpinnings on the other. Demands from a range of sources apparently compete for priority. As well as the dual or multiple influences operating on individuals and within single units, the range of responses may have been influenced by the diversity in the style of departments which co-ordinate CPE across different institutions. For instance, it is certainly theoretically feasible that the aims of a department (and respondent) working within an overall (liberal) continuing education remit may well differ from a more focused one concerned solely with, say, industrial liaison. And, as will be raised again later, differentiation is not solely confined to variation between styles of units or departments. The hypothesis that varying aims and purposes will relate to organisational structure and individual background is certainly one worth pursuing, though it has to remain a hypothetical assertion at this stage. The ambiguous nature of job titles held by some specialist respondents, and the option for anonymity taken up by others in the sample, act against the possibility of such an analysis of the data.

The approach adopted to the collection of data on 'elements in the definition of quality' was quite straightforward. It was to provide the respondent with the opportunity to describe these as s/he deemed appropriate. The item itself was included for two reasons. First, in looking to devise a system to assure quality, some conception of what an 'ideal type' of quality is actually being taken to mean is of paramount importance. It seems logical to assume that without an identified point of reference, claims for quality are rather less satisfactorily substantiated. The second reason is rather more theoretical in orientation. The concern is to help develop an understanding of the *kind* of references that are made when the term quality is introduced – an attempt to judge how far the terms of reference used to define much of the current debate are influencing ideas about a notion which could in actuality be the subject of significantly varying interpretations.

Despite the fact that no 'cues' were given there was a significant degree of consistency in the answers provided. Almost half (48 per cent) of the respondents made specific reference to the standard of the pedagogic experience as a whole, and the same amount stressed the need to provide a satisfying experience for the learner. In the light of the point raised earlier concerning the competing influences on the provider, it is interesting to note that nearly twice as many respondents stressed the importance they attached to meeting the needs of the *participating* 'student' (48 per cent) rather than the *paying* client (27 per cent). But with over a quarter mentioning the latter, this influence should not be overlooked.

These figures give an indication of the aspects of provision which those involved are rating as central to the assurance of quality. Hence, they offer the first pointers towards the required shape of future policies.

What then of the *type* of responses that are inspired by the introduction of the term quality? Reflection on the listed criteria will reveal that in the main what are included are those components of practice which can be regarded as the building blocks of practical provision; those aspects to which procedures can be applied in the hope of securing a better performance on that dimension. For instance the delivery of classes, administrative arrangements, matching the needs of students and clients etc. are the kinds of references consistently made. This is, of course, fully appropriate. However, the question can be raised as to why only 6 per cent referred to meeting the needs of society (or any parallel concern) as integral to a definition of quality. Why is it that definitions of quality remained tied to one (albeit important) level? I suggest that this is bound up with the way in which quality as a concept has been utilised in the recent past and the practices with which it has become associated. I suggest that this is an empirical manifestation of the link between quality, industry and consumer society previously identified. Quality as a concept of increasing acceptability is essentially being seen to correlate with a particular facet of provision (i.e., its organisational arrangements), rather than being open to qualitatively differing interpretations which could include the articulation of concerns and debates of purpose, meanings and implications beyond the immediate.

Support for this view can be drawn from the earlier part of this sub-section, that dealing with aims. It would seem reasonable to assume that there should be some consistency between people's aims for the provision of CPE and the same group of people's understanding of what the quality of that provision should be. In essence, if provision is not ensuring the achievement of, or at least the consideration of, one's aims, does it make sense to see it as quality provision? It can be recalled that the dominant aim was improved professional practice for societal benefit, yet as an element in the definition of quality, it was peripheral.

Quite clearly, therefore, there seems to be an intervening mechanism having an impact on the absence of any consistency between the answers offered to these particular questions. It seems a justifiable contention that that influence is the understanding held about the meaning of the principal terms and concepts in question. In this instance, it is a consensus of interpretation encouraged by the commercial and market orientation of many publications in this field that is identified as crucial.

The discussion of QA is certainly not able to remain as a uni-dimensional one once the issues of aims and definitions of quality have been brought on to the agenda. It has been the intention to both detail the priorities and central concerns of providers and facilitators and draw attention to some of the complexities involved. It is from this basis that further elements of attitudes and practices can now be considered.

AWARENESS AND CONSIDERED APPLICABILITY OF QA PRACTICE IN OTHER SECTORS

This section deals with the extent to which knowledge of QA activity beyond CPE is characteristic of the specialists. Of some importance is whether or not external developments are seen to be of significance for CPE. An overview of knowledge of, and decisions about, a range of sectors is to be followed by a separate consideration of BS5750.

The data for the level of awareness of QA practice in the NHS, the construction industry and the social services were obtained by direct reference to each of these on the questionnaire. These were selected as the most likely sources of knowledge about QA given the relatively high levels of attention it has received in these areas. The remaining results were collated by means of an open-ended question.

The assumption that awareness levels would be highest in the three identified areas was partially borne out by the data. But in none of the examples can knowledge be described as widespread or extensive. Manufacturing (22 per cent) and other branches of education (19 per cent) were noted with approximately the same frequency as the social services (21 per cent) and the construction industry (26 per cent). Only the NHS provided a figure notably in excess of these (43 per cent).

Even here, however, it would perhaps be premature to assume a widespread knowledge of practices internal to the NHS rather than a basic knowledge of their existence. Notes to this effect were frequent additions to the responses provided. It may well be accurate to infer that the widely publicised organisational re-structuring – of which QA has been an integral part – is implicated in the achievement of the 43 per cent level to at least some degree.

In turning to the position held by respondents concerning the potential applicability of experiences and practices adopted in other sectors for the development of QA in CPE, a particularly clear picture emerged. It should be pointed out, of course, that the relatively low levels of knowledge across the board acted against the receipt of comments from the full sample, but still twenty-one considered themselves to be in a position to comment.

By far the most consistently recorded observation (45 per cent) was that the experiences observed elsewhere were only ever likely to be of use as a basic guide. And this only in so far as it is always valuable to have a background knowledge of a given area. A further 14 per cent stated that the practices had no relevance at all. Amongst the remainder there was no universal advocacy of the need to draw on these established practices, although certain tentative suggestions, that one sector may hold more relevance than others, did appear.

If a patchy awareness is characteristic of respondent knowledge to the QA policy and practice of individual sectors of British society, the same assertion certainly cannot be made of the component of QA discussions which seems to be an ever present, irrespective of sector – BS5750. In the sample, 95 per cent had heard of BS5750, a figure which stands in marked contrast to even the most widely known about of the areas detailed above. This high level of awareness can be traced to identifiable factors. For instance, it is cross-sectoral; therefore coming across it is not dependent on having any particular subject specialism. Also, it has been the subject of concerted promotion. And on a related theme, education is currently perhaps *the* area on which attention has been focused for its utilisation.

In itself this provides an interesting but essentially incomplete picture. The fact that virtually the entire population of CPE providers and facilitators have come across the standard in one form or another does not reveal the impact it has made and the consequent likelihood that it may develop into a major component of practice. An open question was used to raise the issue of perceived applicability with the CPE specialists.

The data reveal a definite lack of unanimity on this issue. Despite this, it is accurate to say that a trend towards the negative is discernible. Comments such as 'The application of BS5750 is limited because it can only be used for administrative procedures. This is an important aspect of quality but not the only one' (head of a university CE department); and 'since it is not designed for this [CPE] purpose it is unlikely to be effective' (director of a department of CE) were not unrepresentative of one set of opinions. However, on the other hand, some (at least qualified) support for the standard existed amongst the specialists: 'I believe it could be useful in improving the customer/provider relationship' (head of a CE department). A further group remain undecided or uninformed. In fact, if those who have yet to formulate an opinion (27 per cent) are coupled with those veering towards one side but accepting at least something of the converse position (43 per cent), we are left with just 30 per cent who hold a clear unequivocal position. Of these, 22 per cent rejected the possibility of any relevance, and a mere 8 per cent gave support without reservations. It may well be that further consideration may re-affirm a position somewhere between the two ends of the continuum for some people. Yet it is also quite possible that an accurate interpretation of the evidence is that for a large proportion of the sample the debate is far from complete and the argument remains to be won. This view is supported by the recognition that in the vast majority of cases initial inclinations (and the recent involvement of the standard with education suggests that these are early positions) had yet to be acted upon. Awareness of the experience of BS5750 in further education and the perceived attractiveness of alternative strategies are sure to influence the course of these developments.

These findings, from the two related, though distinct, parts of the above sub-section, are at once revealing consistency and possible elements of divergence. Concerning the former, it is undoubtedly the case that there is no widespread interest in following the example of other sectors in any direct or comprehensive sense. Similarly, there is no wholesale tendency towards the adoption of BS5750. Having made that point, however, it must be recognised that the lack of affinity to BS5750 is less complete than that expressed towards the overall practices of particular sectors. There is clearly some interest in following the British Standards approach to QA in CPE.

Overall, there seems little in the above evidence to suggest that the importation and modification of standards or approaches devised in non-educational contexts are regarded at the present time with any regularity or conviction to be the means by which QA can be put on a firmer footing in CPE. Thus, the way seems open for alternative and more context-specific approaches to be considered.

THE NATURE OF POLICY AND PRACTICE AND PERCEIVED BARRIERS TO IMPLEMENTATION

In moving on to the analysis of actual QA activity, a number of elements will be considered. The initial task is to establish the current condition of QA in CPE. This is achieved by looking at the extent to which written policies exist and the level of utilisation of various techniques, whether part of a formalised system or not. This is followed by the views expressed concerning the varying require-ments of open and closed courses and the issues of tutor selection and involvement. The identification of barriers to the imple-mentation of QA rounds off this section.

Whatever form QA may take, if it is to be established as a coherent organising tool then some form of written document can reasonably be expected to be a legitimate element of it. This provides a constant point of reference from which particular programmes and courses can be planned and implemented. As argued in part I, rigidity, complexity and inflexibility are not endemic to this, they are simply the companions of a particular expression of the written format.

On the basis of the evidence collected in this study there can be little doubt that written policies are in the main absent from central providing and facilitating units. Only 14 per cent noted their existence. This is perhaps a slightly misleading figure given the currently dynamic nature of the whole area of QA. In several cases comments were added to the effect that such policies were either being considered or were actually in the process of development. This, however, is an indication of future trends. For now the data informs us that written QA policies are available for consultation in only a minority of departments. And so it is on that basis that discussion should develop.

Despite the limited number of policies which were available for examination in the early 1990s, one that was can be turned to at this stage. This policy has three features which mark it out as particularly worthy of note. The first is that it incorporates an acceptance of, and makes specific reference to, the political context in which it was developed: that the influential bodies of higher education are stressing the need for such policies. From the start, then, there is a sense of context. But what is important is that this willingness to recognise the influences at work has not led to superficiality – to looking to purely and simply satisfy outsiders. Instead, whilst the implicit agenda is one of meeting external requirements, actual practice is developed in line with context. Therefore, the second point is that explicit mention is made of the character of CPE and that QA policies and practices relate to that. So, for instance, it is stated in the document that the policy has been devised solely in relation to the work of that department; it is not meant to be applicable beyond it. Moreover, it is made clear that the policy develops from a recognition that the nature and practice of CPE is rather different from other areas of higher education. That attenders will be qualified and will be experts in their field is very much part of this. The third feature of the policy is not surprisingly its mechanisms. While many of these are standard enough, an attempt to develop these in relation to context is discernible on some levels. For example, particular attention is paid to composition of planning groups.

Of course, this is just one early policy. But its value is as an illustration of how policies can be broadened to reach beyond the mechanistic. Political context is seen to influence quality; it therefore attains a place in policy. Likewise, the nature of CPE is regarded as having a bearing on practice, so it too merits explicit mention. Although neither are extended to their fullest potential, it is the fact that they are included at all that is of immediate importance.

Returning to the data as a whole, the low level of written policies stands in marked contrast to the response received when respondents were directly asked whether or not QA procedures were used within their department. Ninety-seven per cent stated that they were. The remaining 3 per cent noted an inability to comment, rather than giving a negative response.

Thus, these two figures (illustrating the very low level of written policies on the one hand and the near total use of some form of QA on the other) provide a stark contrast. Clearly, providers are virtually without exception concerned to include in practice mechanisms which facilitate quality in one sense or another, yet this has not been translated into clear policy statements. This should not be read as necessarily indicating that QA procedures are not being effectively utilised, although it is apparent that a single document can certainly provide a co-ordinating function. Such an unequivocal 'Yes' to the present employment of procedures is also inevitably but a starting point. The logical next step is to establish a breakdown on the component parts of QA and gain evidence on the level at which they are represented. Table 4.2 details the results gained on this theme. It is immediately noticeable that a number of the procedures produced very high rates of use, especially when compared with the lack of written policies. As such, the initial comment must be a confirmation of the near unanimous assertion of a general involvement with QA procedures. The priority given to three such procedures stands out: evaluation sheets (exit surveys) 89 per cent; informal feedback 83 per cent; and feedback from tutors 86 per cent. The potential for each of these to provide insight into aspects of course provision is recognised; however, in the absence of generally adhered-to formalised systems, difficulties may well exist. For instance, the consistency and regularity with which each of these is employed is unclear. The case of evaluation sheets can be used to elaborate some of the problems faced.

Table 4.2 CPE specialists: procedures included in current QA practice

Procedure	Procedure forming part of practice (%)
Joint planning groups with clients	72
Use of planning guides and checklists for providing departments and tutors	37
Participant evaluation questionnaire (exit survey)	89
Participant evaluation questionnaire (post-course, i.e. several months later)	11
Other follow-up evaluation	22
Informal participant feedback	83
Feedback from tutors	86
Other	30

In theory, these forms provide an excellent source of immediate feedback, not least because participants are able to comment whilst the details of the events are still fresh. In this context, an 89 per cent use rate would seem to provide a highly satisfactory state of affairs. However, this is a figure which reflects all use at any level and, therefore, not the extent of application within each institution. There is, as such, inevitable doubt over the level and consistency with which these are applied within universities. The large level of decentralisation of provision adds an extra variable. The lack of a formal policy often leaves individual providing departments to define their own QA needs with the consequence that definite variations occur. To be fair, 56 per cent of CPE specialist respondents stated that all departments in their institution used some QA procedures. This, though, leaves another half where QA is rather less widely employed. Indeed, in these institutions the reported levels of departments using any or all of the techniques ranged from 95 per cent down to a mere 10 per cent.

Once beyond this question of involvement with particular mechanisms, the design and utility of the tools themselves have to be looked at. During the course of the project, evaluation sheets from a range of sources have been collected and analysed. Some of these have clearly been designed with definite objectives in mind; others, though, incorporate ambiguous questions and related problems of structure. Furthermore, although the issue of whether procedures are adopted to secure high completion rates was not part of the survey, the limited discussions undertaken suggested that this is not always the case. Despite the ostensibly high rates of use, the practices surrounding evaluation sheets are, therefore, not invariably satisfactory.

The above discussion of evaluation sheets should not be taken to indicate a negative attitude towards them. Instead, what is stressed is that their degree of success, and their value as an aid to QA, rests on their form and mode of operationalisation. Specifically, when clearly designed, their objectives identified and the subject of proper distribution and consistent analysis, they are valuable. When offered as a token without consideration of a full rationale (or not offered at all!) the situation is somewhat different. The establishing of departmental principles and guidelines may well be beneficial on this matter.

Not all procedures received the high level of citation experienced by the above. Perhaps the most interesting example of this is the low level of follow-up evaluations (some months after the event). At a mere 11 per cent, when compared with that other expression of post-course evaluation (the exit survey) the difference is considerable. Concluding anything about the perceived relative merits of these would, though, be perhaps unjustified. The fact is that follow-up evaluations are notoriously more time consuming and troublesome to conduct than on-the-day evaluation. The issue of time and resources seems likely to be the fundamental one, an assertion supported by evidence later in this section. Although currently underused, the follow-up evaluation does offer an angle on proceedings largely unobtainable in the immediate term. For that reason, it could well constitute a suitable topic for discussion and inclusion within departmental guidelines. The practicalities would ensure that the frequency of its use would not be the same as for the exit survey. But a considered approach towards the sampling of participants, in a manner consistent with the varying need of particular providing units and institutions could secure a place for such follow-ups in QA procedures. The issue of long-term evaluation is tackled in more detail in chapter 5.

Open and closed courses

Although discussion has in the main been in terms of CPE as a homogeneous entity, variation is ever present not least in access to courses. One key variable is whether a course is fully open or is in some way closed, i.e. commissioned for a specific group of people.

Respondents were asked whether they felt different approaches were needed to deal with the particular requirements of the two types of courses. Just over half (54 per cent) believed that this was indeed the case. When asked to elaborate, the answers provided were largely those predicted; they were, though, no less relevant for that. Essentially, respondents discussed the relative levels of control which exist in the provision of the two course types – open courses being less directly controllable and closed ones more so. In practice this has a number of implications. For example, the kinds of points raised in relation to open courses included the need for more attention to be given to the background of participants and requirement for more detailed pre-course information including a wide awareness of objectives. They were regarded as less easy to evaluate. Conversely, the ability to take account of particular client needs on closed courses was seen as making objective fixing and evaluation altogether easier.

As stated above, such findings are unlikely to provide much in the way of surprises, especially for those directly involved with course planning. Incorporation of an awareness of such conclusions into future policy, however, is worthy of consideration.

Tutors: selection and development

It is perhaps something of a statement of the obvious that the quality of CPE is in no small degree related to the nature of the tutors. Evidence relating to aspects of the place of the tutor will now be examined.

The selection criteria used in employing tutors again holds little in the way of surprises although it is important to underline the attention displayed to selecting those with key skills. The priority ascribed to academic knowledge (44 per cent), general (33 per cent) and adult-specific (25 per cent) teaching ability, and an enthusiastic and professional approach (19 per cent) stand far in excess of the practicalities of availability (despite the latter's obvious and continuing significance).

It is one of the characteristic features of CPE that tutors are not necessarily staff with established or full-time involvement with the university in question. Indeed, it is a recognised part of the CPE that external expertise will be drawn upon. The figures provided by the survey on the level of tutors drawn from inside the providing university demonstrates both the widespread, at least partial, use of external tutors and the variation across institutions on this issue. Figures ranging from 0–98 per cent for reliance on internal tutors reveals that in no case is the external tutor unused.

The identification of this adds an extra dimension to the quality issue. Inevitably, individual tutors whose association with institutional life may constitute as little as one day a year, provides a situation somewhat different to the norm.

As a result of this acknowledged involvement, respondents were questioned on the way in which they felt quality was affected by the employment of external tutors. Some interesting results emerged.

In the majority of cases, respondents detailed a situation with a two-fold character, i.e. one composed of the perceived co-existence of pluses and minuses. However, despite this tendency one response was still given in many more instances than any other: 47 per cent stated that external tutors offered a positive input by bringing in otherwise unobtainable expertise, up-to-date information and experience from the field. It should be re-stated that even those expressing such a view were not averse to the identification of problems in certain circumstances. Difficulties of detachment, less potential to be influenced by feedback, the need for more support and a lack of theoretical knowledge were all noted (by just one respondent in each case). They demonstrate the range of problems which may exist. The need for careful selection to ensure a positive outcome was mentioned by 20 per cent. This once again draws attention to the notion that it is the way in which an element of practice is conducted as much as that component itself which affects results.

The physical and at times intellectual distance between the tutor and the department is an umbrella idea to which much of the above relates. One possible way of integrating external tutors into the expectations of the providing institution is 'staff development' programmes. Twenty-nine per cent of respondents reported that their external tutors were given some kind of training under this heading. This could be an area where impact on quality may be considerable, although the temporary nature of involvements presents a not inconsiderable hindrance.

Overall, the evidence on tutors can be interpreted as being rather encouraging. There is an absolute reliance of criteria of appropriate pedagogy, for selection and external tutors continue to be regarded as valuable despite the difficulties endemic to their use. Staff development programmes are, though, at present an under-utilised resource; their existence as a bridging mechanism should not be overlooked in future planning.

Barriers to implementation

Table 4.3 contains the views expressed by the sample on those factors which have already acted as a barrier to the implementation of clear QA procedures or are likely to so act in the future.

A number of the pre-identified factors can be seen to have struck a cord with a large number of the sample. The clash with academic independence (42 per cent), fear of institutional imposition of measures with which they disagree (44 per cent), the fear of negative personal consequences (36 per cent) and disregard for the significance of quality assurance in itself (29 per cent) were all seen as relevant. The levels of identification can be seen to be remarkably similar across these themes – a variation of only 13 per cent between

Table 4.3: CPE specialists: perceived barriers to the implementation of QA

Barriers	Level of identification as actual or future hindrance to the development of quality assurance (%)
Inherent clash with academic independence	42
Staff fear of institutional imposition of measure with which they disagree	44
Staff fear of negative personal consequences	36
Quality assurance being regarded as a peripheral issue	29
The time-consuming nature of quality assurance procedures	83
A lack of interest from clients	6
A lack of participant motivation	14
Other	22

the four. One further factor stood out far beyond this group, though, in the frequency with which it was cited by respondents. It was the time-consuming nature of QA. This was described as a barrier by 83 per cent of those filling in the questionnaire.

So while there is evident disquiet about the relationship between QA and the established practices of a university, the concern uppermost in the thoughts of those surveyed was the rather more mundane, yet invariably crucial, dimension of time. Such a finding should be neither ignored nor trivialised for it carries with it a clear implication for the way in which QA policies are developed. What is important is that such policies must not be an unnecessary burden if they are to gain the support of those who will be needed to operationalise them. Furthermore, if we now take together the results on time (83 per cent), on imposition (44 per cent), and dependence and independence (42 per cent), the nature of what is and what is not likely to constitute a successful mode of QA on the basis of provider evidence is beginning to take shape. This seems to have little in common with the kinds of emphases which, say, BS5750 would bring with it. This is not to overlook the fact that

BS5750 had a reasonable level of support, but rather to affirm that the same sample are expressing concerns on just the kinds of issues with which the British Standards approach has been identified. Not only is a flexible, non-time-consuming, department-centred approach more likely to satisfy social and educational principles, but it is also possible that it represents the sort of approach which stands the best chance of incorporation into institutional practice.

PROVIDERS AND FACILITATORS: JUDGEMENTS AND ASSESSMENTS

This final section draws together the views of respondents on a small number of further issues – each of which contributes towards a clarification of the nature of attitudes and priorities.

When asked to identify the reasons for (actually completed) courses being either a success or a failure there was a high priority ascribed to pre-course activity. Although within-course activity was not excluded, matters were frequently seen to hinge on planning, on design, and on the setting of clear objectives to meet the needs of the audience concerned. For instance, the single most cited determinant of a successful course was good planning (43 per cent), with poor planning (including a failure to define audience needs) being the most frequently noted influence on an unsuccessful course at 39 per cent.

Such priorities fit in well with the whole idea of assuring quality rather than simply controlling, checking or evaluating it. To put it another way, the emphasis on the planning stage is striking at the heart of what is required – i.e., establishing and fostering *preventive* action. Thus, whilst recognising that other elements were included, the assertion that good planning facilitates successful courses and poor planning acts against it is identifiable as holding a pivotal position in thinking. Covert acceptance of this is likely to be widespread but a more explicit incorporation of it is appropriate.

There is an implication for policy to be drawn from these findings. For another way of describing the data is to note that where courses fail they often do so for both identifiable and potentially avoidable reasons. Furthermore, these reasons are frequently concentrated in the pre-course period. Unforeseen circumstances will always effect provision, but consistent and detailed attention before the course begins seems from the evidence to be accepted as paying dividends. Although elements of evaluation may perhaps offer a more observable image of quality consciousness, an approach seriously concerned with assuring quality cannot simply or even mainly rely on post-course procedures.

The appropriateness of accepting the value of procedures at various points in provision is confirmed by reference to the next data set. It details those procedures with which providers are currently most happy. Concentration on a different phase emerges. It would perhaps be expected on the basis of priority given to planning in the above section that this 'pre-course' emphasis would continue here. This is not the case. Instead, the highest level of mentions was secured by immediate formalised feedback – i.e., exit surveys (50 per cent) – for those practices with which people were most content. (Interestingly, exit surveys also figured relatively highly in the 'unhappy' section. Although this confirms the difficulties which can arise in the use of exit surveys in some quarters, the results can also be interpreted as showing a possible spur towards their improved utilisation).

Possible reasons for the high level of satisfaction with exit surveys can be identified. One is that although planning was identified as being crucial when conducted correctly, it was seen to exert a powerful negative effect when inadequately performed. Therefore, it may not yet be carried out in a consistently helpful manner. On the other hand, evaluation sheets may not hold as much potential in terms of likely influence on the effect of the whole programme, but within their terms of reference they may be performing a role considered effective by providers.

Another explanation rests rather more on the interpretative elements of questions. It could be argued that as QA practices were asked for, the distribution of the evaluation sheet may be more readily perceived to fit this criteria for a discrete policy or practice than general patterns of pre-course action. Doubt is cast on this possibility, however, when comparison is made with those other procedures which were ascribed high use rates. For instance, 83 per cent stated that they used informal feedback, but only 12 per cent considered it the essential practice; and 86 per cent employed feedback from tutors, with 17 per cent giving it priority. Thus other visible and recognisable procedures did not secure anything like the same support; in itself awareness of a practice was not enough to induce support. Consequently, it seems reasonable to assert that evaluation sheets are seen to be fulfilling an important role at present for a large proportion of respondents, despite both their inherent difficulties and citation by some respondents in the 'unhappy' list.

Thus, it can be deduced that while immediate formalised student feedback is, for around half the respondents, the most *effective* of their established procedures, it is not necessarily the most influential and *determining* in its impact – that distinction goes to various dimensions of planning. The implication is that evaluation sheets are seen to provide a valuable contribution. The careful design and distribution of these amongst the range of providers would seem likely to be worthwhile. However, their impact will remain a limited one if their construction is framed within an approach which treats evaluation as the linchpin of the process rather than regarding it as a final support mechanism.

Attention can now be turned to consideration of what are regarded as ideal and irrelevant procedures. Of those procedures which respondents were keen to see, both evaluation (33 per cent) and planning (34 per cent) again figured, as did the development of formalised systems (30 per cent). However, staff development (30 per cent) was mentioned in a similar amount of cases, and there does seem to be some potential for its incorporation.

The opinions expressed about those procedures unlikely to contribute to QA make very interesting reading, although the smaller than average number of respondents in this case should be recognised. What is important here is that BS5750 was included in the answer by 29 per cent of respondents and inflexible, narrow, defined, time-consuming procedures were stressed by a further 47 per cent. Now, while there was some doubling of answers by single respondents, a further analysis reveals that 59 per cent of those answering the question included one or both of these two in their answer. Considering the open nature of the question this has to be noted as reflecting quite a strong base of opinion. Taken together, the concern to avoid rigid, cumbersome approaches is quite marked. And when viewed alongside the evidence on barriers to QA (detailed earlier), the direction of thinking amongst a significant strand of respondents is seen to have a certain level of consistency. It seems that within this section the need for flexibility and appropriateness are as integral to requirements for practice as they are to the critique of the overall approach to BS5750.

115

CONCLUDING NOTES ON SPECIALIST
PROVIDERS

In the first half of the book much was made of the need to move towards a context-specific understanding of quality. Indeed, I began by drawing attention to the particular characteristics of CPE which distinguish it from much other higher education. In this chapter, empirical backup has been given to this emphasis. The aims of provision identified by providers relate closely to the nature of CPE. This is particularly evident in the expressed concern with the professional practice in real-life situations and with finance: two distinctly CPE-centred concerns.

A sense of how influential a knowledge of aims might be in the formulation of strategy is brought into sharper focus by the failure to endorse external approaches. If the desire is for a profession-specific approach – one linking aims to quality and both of these to procedures – this needs to be a constant reference point.

But the value of the data is not restricted to conceptual concerns. On the practical level, we now have a better idea of procedural preference, as well as the use and under-use of individual mechanisms. Of equal importance, what might act to prevent the introduction of a workable strategy also emerged. There is, though, one question which this coverage has not been able to answer: whether or not these are views specific to CPE specialists or whether they are shared by the diffuse collection of non-specialist providers located throughout the universities. Only once this is known can policy-related decisions be made. Chapter 5 fills this gap.

5

EVIDENCE FROM THE FIELD II
Non-CPE specialist departments

University provision of CPE is not isolated in, or restricted to, one central department. To stop the analysis of providers with the CE community – the specialists – would be to bias the data collection to an unacceptable level. Decentralised CPE is a significant part of the current university norm. A proportion of this provision is inter-disciplinary. However, the profession-specific nature of much work (e.g. that for teachers or civil engineers) encourages the co-ordination of courses by those departments with the highest concentration of relevant expertise. It is on those individual providing departments that this chapter concentrates.

A brief return to the evidence of chapter 4 can be used to quantify the extent to which responsibility for CPE is spread throughout the universities. Of the total of 7,788 courses put on in the responding institutions per year, only 2,137 were run through the central units. To put it another way, approximately 70 per cent of CPE activity is to a large extent the responsibility of individual providing departments. Thus, although it would be neater to restrict the analysis to one specialist group, the diversity of providing sources calls for more opinions to be sought. The evaluation of quality will depend, in no small measure, upon this heterogeneous band of providers.

As a short-hand, the term non-CPE specialists (as opposed to the CPE specialists of chapter 4) is used. This is merely a way of differentiating on the basis of primary activity. For this group, continuing education is not (as a rule) the specialism of the department, or of the respondent from that department (though it could be argued that certain centres and individuals interrupt this picture). They are specialists, but in another discrete subject area.

In the vast majority of cases CPE must fit into a portfolio of activity grounded in the traditional activities of undergraduate and postgraduate teaching and academic research. Thus the respondent group is in a very real and practical sense approaching CPE from a differing starting point – one which raises the theoretical possibility of a differing approach to provision. The non-specialists, therefore, offer an invaluable perspective for a number of reasons. For instance, while – as a consequence of the sampling technique used – they practise CPE in the same institutions as the specialists, they do so in a way which supplements their main activity. Also, a part of the unusual character of the group is that despite this peripheral or partial involvement, collectively non-specialists form the majority of providers. So, irrespective of the limited involvement of particular individuals or departments, the long-term quality of CPE can be directly affected by this diverse group.

The character of non-specialists as providers in their own right, and as providers whose work is juxtaposed with the practice of CPE specialists, is reflected in the organisation of this chapter. For each of the major themes, the discussion of non-specialist attitudes and experience is accompanied by a comparative analysis. This is an examination of the extent to which the differing (specialist and non-specialist) forms of involvement with CPE are empirically discernible in relation to quality issues. Where appropriate, the data is subjected to statistical analysis. In order to accommodate the comparative emphasis, issues are tackled in an order broadly consistent with that used to review specialist providing units.

NON-CPE SPECIALIST PROVIDERS: PARTICIPATION LEVELS

Non-CPE specialist departments involved in CPE provision were identified by the central units of their university. While some omissions from the lists will be inevitable, only one specialist respondent described the list produced as incomplete. All providing departments identified as being currently active in the post-qualification education of professionals were included in the sample.

Twenty-six universities and university colleges forwarded details for inclusion. A total of 150 were reported as CPE active in these institutions. Inevitably – and purely as a function of the lists provided – the number and range of academic departments contacted at each university were variable. Suffice to say that in cases where only one or two departments were sent questionnaires, that was the total of identified non-specialist CPE activity in that university.

Responses were gathered from a good range of sources. Of the 26 institutions included, questionnaires were completed by at least 1 department in 22 of them. Thus 85 per cent of institutions included in the sample contributed data. Taken as a whole a 50 per cent completion level was obtained: 75 departments participated. The mean number of departments which responded per institution was around 3.5. But this is not a particularly informative figure given the variation involved. Perhaps more useful is to note that the single largest level of returns from one institution was 9, with 14 of the 22 universities (64 per cent) providing between 1 and 3 returns.

The 50 per cent response rate – although around the normally expected level – did not match that achieved with the CPE specialists. It is perhaps worth briefly suggesting the reasons for this. It seems probable that there are four contributory factors. These are reasons suggested by correspondence and feedback of the research period.

1   That identified departments are no longer 'CPE active'. It is certainly the case that (especially amongst those whose participation in this form of education was never substantial) phases of inactivity, or indeed a termination of all provision, have occurred.
2   That the level of provision is so small in a particular department as to produce in the potential respondent a feeling that s/he is not 'qualified' to discuss the quality of the subject.
3   That an internally announced intention to establish courses has yet to move beyond the developmental stage.
4   That because of the limited role of CPE within the output of some departments, QA may not yet be receiving the level of attention that it is amongst CE specialists.

It should be remembered that I am not attempting to explain a low response rate here, but rather the failure to match up to a very good one. As will become clear, however, there is no attempt to draw unnecessary distinctions between the two samples. The intention is simply to establish that differing influences do – to some extent – inevitably affect the conditions of activity for specialists, and for non-specialists. Whether views about, and the practice of, quality assurance varies amongst those who did respond is, as will be seen, a separate matter.

The number of courses provided by individual departments each year was, as a general rule, fairly small. This is entirely consistent with the contributory rather than dominant role of CPE in the *raison d'être* of most units. Eighty per cent of departments questioned provided 25 courses or less per year. Provision at the upper end of this category is certainly not insignificant when bearing in mind other forms of output; however, it does show the generally limited extent and scale of most involvement. Increases in course numbers per annum brought a corresponding reduction in department representation. The relevant figures were: 26–49 courses per year (11 per cent); 50–99 courses per year (8 per cent); and between 100–149 courses per year (1.35 per cent, i.e. one department).

NON-CPE SPECIALIST PROVIDERS: SUBJECT REPRESENTATION

As the technical and the pragmatic are major influences over the present form of CPE, certain subject specialisms and areas of expertise could have been expected to predominate in the make-up of provision; this proved to be the case. The single largest discipline represented was engineering. This is a composite category incorporating all the various sub-areas such as civil, mechanical, electrical etc. Sixteen departments (21 per cent) of the sample could be so categorised. The second subject area to be well represented was business/management studies – 10 (13 per cent). Beyond these two main disciplines, education 6 (8 per cent); law 5 (7 per cent); computer studies 4 (5 per cent); biology, geology, pharmacy and languages, all 3 (4 per cent); and politics 2 (3 per cent) accounted for most of the remainder. Specialisms as diverse as history, chemistry, Arabic and dance each provided one case.

Thus, while it is certainly legitimate to acknowledge that the sample incorporated a genuinely diverse range of subjects, it is also crucial to recognise that over a third of it is made up of academics working in engineering and business studies. This is relevant to the theoretical clarification of the orientation of CPE. But it is also of direct and practical relevance to research on quality. For it means that a substantial number of the sample are active in, or associated with, areas in which the concept and practice of QA are fairly well established. Within the sample there is likely to be a significant number of individuals with a degree of familiarity with those interpretations of QA (notably BS5750) which evolved beyond education and are being pushed forward within it. While the impact of a sub-group of just one-third of the total should not be overstated, a failure to endorse such approaches (as BS5750) in a sample constituted in this way would certainly raise questions about the likely acceptability of these systems to others in higher education.

Clearly, participants in contemporary university CPE, and any sample derived from them, are not a microcosm of university academics as a whole. There is a diversity of representation, but also a concentration of emphasis. This is the nature of CPE at the moment.

CONTINUING PROFESSIONAL EDUCATION AS INCOME GENERATION: THE WHOLE STORY OF PROVIDER AIMS?

The earlier discussion of CPE specialists demonstrated that for many providers, aims were broadly based: they frequently (though not always) referred to the social as well as the financial. With CPE as a/the primary responsibility of their professional activity this avoidance of minimalism makes a good deal of sense. But will such an extension beyond instrumentalism be evident amongst the non-specialist providers? Is not their partial involvement likely to work towards a rather more concise interpretation of the purposes of activity?

A revised procedure based on that used to elicit information from specialist respondents was used to collate the new information on aims. Drawing on the tendency exhibited by specialists to acknowledge the relevance of virtually all listed aims, it was decided to focus purely on the identification of 'primary aims'. This was again interpreted in different ways by different respondents. Fifty per cent gave multi-response answers, while the other 50 per cent identified a single aim. An analysis of those expressing a single aim will follow a review of the full data set.

Although a reasonable degree of affinity was expressed with a range of aims – satisfaction of the participant, satisfaction of the client, increasing the likelihood of consultancy and developing links with industry were all cited by between 20 and 34 per cent of respondents – it was the remaining two aims which stood out. Income generation (50 per cent) and improving professional practice for the benefit of society (54 per cent) were clearly the most frequently cited. Thus, an expectation that short-term involvement with CPE would be equated with a greater restrictiveness of purpose than found amongst specialist providers is seen to be groundless. In fact, the findings provide a further piece in the empirical and theoretical jigsaw which has led to the characterisation of CPE as existing at the centre of conflicting pressures.

It would be difficult to give too much attention to such findings, for they seem to impinge directly on the very core of the discussions. The evidence can be used to build on the commentary establishing the understanding of aims as a vital pre-requisite for the pursuit of quality. The impotence which may result from a failure to do this is clearly illustrated by these findings.

For instance, it is entirely feasible that the market orientation of some provision could lead certain providers to establish the 'satisfaction of paying clients' as the key indicator of quality. Derived from the now popular notion of the centrality of the customer, a reasonable assumption from such a perspective could well be: satisfied customer = likely future courses = income generation = departmental security and/or expansion = quality. Such a rationalisation is certainly understandable when the two pivotal conditions (a CPE provision dependent on its place in the market and a logic inspired by commercial notions of QA) are recognised. But once attention is shifted back to the identified aims of providers, the evident limitations of the above are uncovered. This is because that aim included by 54 per cent of the sample (improved professional practice for the benefit of society) simply has no possible place in the equation. That this positive consequence may (and certainly may not) evolve from course provision anyway is not really the point. If the task is to address quality in CPE, and quality is to relate to aims (of educationalists), then such thinking must be in an approach from the start in order to establish a shaping rather than dependent role for it. Indeed, the apparent difference in orientation between an approach established on this basis and one of commercial origin can only add fuel to a discussion of whether a significant shift in terminology might not be appropriate. A consideration of issues couched in their own terms would doubtless provide a more substantial challenge, but the rewards achieved may be rather more fundamental.

The results gained from those offering a single primary aim are perhaps even more suggestive than those achieved from the complete data set. Forty-two per cent of this smaller group cited improved professional practice as their single aim. The next highest citation was income generation at 18 per cent. The remainder achieved only very small levels.

Two statements are immediately necessary on the basis of these data. To begin with although appearing in a rather differently weighted form, evidence for the perceived as well as theoretical dual character of CPE is available. Again when judgements are made about aims, the elements of the pragmatic and the educational are both clearly represented. And second, although the same two aims figure most consistently, the degree of equilibrium is removed. Quite simply, far more respondents were wanting to identify their sole aim as improved professional practice rather than income generation. Therefore to re-cap: when respondents were offering multi-answer primary aims income generation virtually kept pace with improved professional practice; where a single aim was decided upon around two and a half times more chose the latter. What this seems to be implying is that for a large number of respondents income generation is an active element in their decision to participate in CPE. But when prioritising further, for many respondents it achieves only a supportive significance. It has a place in thinking, but one frequently subordinated to those kinds of social and educational concerns which can be assumed to figure largely in their motivation for involvement with pre-practice (largely undergraduate) education.

A direct comparison of the data on identified aims between specialist and non-specialist providers can be used to develop the analysis further. Table 5.1 provides evidence of a real symmetry in expressed attitudes. In each of the four 'pairs' of data, improved professional practice achieved a higher score than income generation.

Table 5.1 Aims of provision: a comparative analysis

	CPE specialists (%)	Non-CPE specialists (%)
Primary aim(s)	(a) 31	(a) 50
	(b) 44	(b) 54
Single primary aims	(a) 12	(a) 18
	(b) 35	(b) 42

Note: a = income generation; b = improved professional practice for the benefit of society as a whole.

Also in each of the samples the size of the difference between the two aims increases with the shift of the analysis towards the single most important aim. At no point does one aim dominate to the exclusion of the other, although a narrowing-down of options does seem to reduce the allegiance to the financial dimension.

This consistency has important implications. For evidence of the dual character of CPE is seen to be provided from two empirical sources. That an understanding of CPE in these terms can be theoretically argued for is one thing, to see this reflected in the composition of the aims of those active in the field is another. This dual character may manifest itself in the co-existence of individuals with identifiably distinct aims, or it may be evident in the complex composition of the orientations of single providers. In either case to see CPE as solely dominated by instrumental motives or as something which is perceived as a peripheral activity of somehow lesser worth (even by those who do not regard CPE as their primary specialism) is far from the whole story. This is despite the fact that it is in the nature of its complex situation that CPE may be so undertaken in some instances.

The consistency is also significant in terms of what it says about the distance between CE specialists and non-specialists. The evidence on aims provides the first measure of whether the seemingly different starting points have an impact in practice. As is now clear only slight variation between specialists and non-specialists was observed. Amongst specialists, 23 per cent more identified with improved professional practice than with income generation; for non-CPE specialists the gap was 24 per cent. Corresponding differences of 12 per cent and 4 per cent were recorded for multi responses. Clearly, there is a stronger parallel in the range of motivations between the two sectors than might have been first imagined. For similar numbers of both groups an ideal approach to quality would be one which extends some way beyond the mere achievement of repeat business.

DEFINING QUALITY

The importance attached to the understanding of quality expressed by respondents was discussed at length earlier and details need not be repeated here. However, the major concern can be re-introduced: the extent to which quality is being used either in a restricted or in a wide-ranging sense.

From the 65 members of the sample responding to the question, 189 elements of definition were recorded. These embraced a wide array of themes. But as was the case with the CPE specialists, those concerned with the practical provision of courses dominated. Meeting the objectives of clients (44 per cent), using appropriate styles of presentation (41 per cent) and ensuring an up-to-date and relevant course content figured highly. Certainly this constitutes the road to the ensuring of success within an allotted 'course space' and period of time.

What, though, of that intention, so widely expressed, to attempt to make the first point of reference in their work improved professional practice? Just as with the specialist providers such wider considerations are conspicuous by their near total absence. Only 8 per cent made any reference to considering 'the effect on professional practice', and even then this did not necessarily include an unequivocal need for 'social benefit'. Once again, in that short step from the identification of aims to the definition of quality, the attentions of providers have been drawn away from the social implications of an educational experience to the means of satisfying short-term objectives. That the practices listed are required, indeed demanded, by any serious provision of CPE is accepted without question – but the results demand discussion at a level beyond that. The data are forcing on to the agenda the need to accept that in talking about 'quality assurance' people are not necessarily talking about a quality CPE in any fundamental sense. The danger is of a failure to recognise that QA, as currently understood, is by its nature by-passing those issues (e.g. of wider aims) which a discipline at a crucial stage of development (of which CPE is certainly a prime example) needs to address in order to achieve effective maturity. This can only reinforce a stilted conception of CPE in an age when professional status and professional qualifications continue to be a pre-occupation of both established and aspiring groups.

At this point it is perhaps worth pausing briefly to take stock of where such discussions fit into an overall analysis of CPE and its quality. To my mind, the significance lies on two levels. The first of these is in relation to developing the case for a soundly based understanding of the process at hand; one which accepts, and incorporates, the difference between quality assurance and (absolute) quality. This requires reference back to the origins and points of introduction of QA into CPE. The equation of quality (assurance) with narrowly defined organisational activity is the aspect of particular importance. For – as argued earlier – the concept of quality assurance results in a taken-for-granted definition of quality which is derived from the dominant original. This explains the orientation of the responses of non-specialist as well as specialist providers. What may be reasonably viewed to constitute absolute quality in CPE (in view of the evidence of aims), namely a provision which addresses its social value, and its impact on those who are affected by the education (ultimate recipients, clients etc.) as well as on those in receipt of it, becomes marginalised. This is because if the quality of provision is measured and perceived one way on a day to day basis, there is little room for a second, potentially contradictory, interpretation. As such, a theoretical distinction between 'assuring the quality of sections of CPE provision', and 'pursuing/assuring a CPE of absolute quality and value', needs to be accepted. It is, though, recognised that in practice a fusion based on such a clarification would be appropriate.

On the first measure QA is indeed all about the smooth running of an aspect of provision; the second measure of quality operates at an altogether more fundamental level. It is the unrelenting spread of QA to the point where it is assumed (perhaps unwittingly) to be one and the same thing as absolute quality that is problematic. It acts as a diversion from theoretical clarification. When the concept of QA is applied in industry, manufacturing and commerce there is no such difficulty; it is unlikely that a wider conception of quality could be legitimately argued for and sustained. That education must be socially responsible as well as responsive, where industry and commerce (essentially) does not, is a real disjuncture which the transfer of both policy *and* terminology from one to the other can only exacerbate.

The other point of significance relates directly to the contributions which an awareness of the theoretical base can make to the utilisation of appropriate procedures to assure the quality of individual courses. This would not, of course, necessitate constant reference to detail during the process of course development. Acceptance and integration of the principles would instead contribute towards the selection and operationalisation of procedures with a purpose not necessarily limited to the immediate. These are points for individual providers and departments to consider. Decisions about procedure utilisation and the relationship between particular procedures and particular aims cannot be generally prescribed. The shape will vary with adopted perspectives. But whatever the eventual content, an awareness of aims and intentions should be a conscious and initial element of a formalised process of course production in CPE.

It may well be that providers who rate income generation (and as a function of this 'paying client satisfaction') as all important will adopt very different approaches to those for whom improved professional practice rates as the primary motivation. So be it. An approach based on flexibility and context-specificity can and must accept that. By the same token, however, those who do see provision as potentially achieving something wider can profitably acknowledge a difference between the micro and macro expressions of quality and select procedures on that basis. This issue is developed and given a practical dimension in the discussion of procedures later in this chapter.

FURTHER PERSPECTIVES ON BS5750

Attention can now be returned to that feature of the quality assurance debate which has (if nothing else) attained a position near the pinnacle of 'points to be considered'. What follows is the final major part of a three-phase research process aimed at clarifying what it is that BS5750 has to offer those providing (and experiencing) post-qualification professional education in UK universities. Whilst the opening part of this examination was a critique of the organisation, language and orientation of the approach; and the second went on to offer an empirical analysis of those continuing education specialists on whom the system would initially concentrate; this last element shifts the focus one stage further: to the views from individual providing departments. It is on this topic that the composition of the non-specialist sample is potentially at its most influential. For, as suggested earlier, if BS5750 is to find favour anywhere in higher education then – it might be hypothesised – it will be amongst those whose primary area of expertise has provided an introduction to it. Such specialisms as business studies and engineering are – it can be recalled – well represented in this group.

As with the analysis of this theme with the evidence of specialist providers, discussion needs to be undertaken in relation to two aspects of the data: the level of awareness of the standard (and, therefore, the attending controversy); and attitudes to its perceived applicability.

It can be recalled that there was an extremely high rate of familiarity with at least the name and basic meaning of BS5750 within central providing units (95 per cent). Interestingly, this is not matched around the universities: 79 per cent of the sample confirmed that they were aware of the standard, leaving around one-fifth (in comparison to one-twentieth of the first sample) for whom it meant nothing. This difference proved to be statistically significant (χ^2 = 4.660, df = 1, significance reached at χ^2 = 3.8415 at 0.95 level. However, with just two respondents falling into one category, chi square is not at its most powerful).

Thus, both groups exhibit high levels of awareness, although this is particularly pronounced amongst the specialist providers. It is in the nature of CPE that external meetings will be extensive; regular contacts with industry and the professions are certain to have played a part in knowledge formation. Moreover, the organisation which figured largely in the lives of CE specialists until the early 1990s – PICKUP (Professional Industrial and Commercial Updating) – had several representatives more than keen to discuss, or promote, the benefits of the standard.

For individual departments modes of knowledge formation about this issue can perhaps best be understood (with key exceptions) as rather more general and indirect. For instance, while the educational press and informal contacts are certainly successful in disseminating awareness, they rarely target one subject specialism over another.

One supplementary point of clarification can be made at this stage. It was stated earlier that within the most recent sample individual departments' association with industry and commerce (and therefore potentially the British Standards approach) is at a high level. In apparent contradiction it was also noted that a general and undirected process of information receipt can be assumed for the sample. This is to be explained by the fact that while in the context of university life as a whole (individuals involved with CPE or not) those most likely to have industrial links will be found in the sample, they still far from constitute the entire group. Small-scale and/or non-industrially orientated providers of CPE maintain a significant level of representations. For the first sample such contacts are endemic to their situation.

What then were the expressed opinions concerning the perceived applicability of BS5750 to CPE? The results can be accurately summarised by the following three conclusions.

1 A full range of opinions, taking in all options, were present; no single viewpoint dominated responses.
2 Although this is the case, there is a tendency towards the negative in the results. This is particularly pronounced amongst those subjects holding unequivocal – as opposed to less definite – views.
3 A remarkable degree of consistency is displayed between these figures and those gained from specialist departments.

Evidence relating to these findings can be explored in a little more detail.

One way of examining the results is to re-define the original six response categories into three larger ones. They are: (a) in favour (i. fully and ii. with reservations); (b) no comment (iii. undecided, iv. no knowledge) (c) Against (v. with reservations and vi. fully). The spread of opinion is apparent when the percentage response rates within each of the three groupings are noted (a = 25 per cent, b = 37 per cent, c = 37 per cent). On this first broad measure, therefore, consistent representation is found in each of the groups – not least in the 'undecided' category. This is a section clearly bolstered by the relatively higher number of people who had not heard of the standard, but also includes 16 per cent who had yet to reach a positive conclusion, despite some degree of familiarity. Some indication of the tendency towards a negative perception of the standard is given in the above figures. But it is only when these are broken down into their component parts that the situation becomes clearer.

For out of the 25 per cent who are located at the positive end of the spectrum, a mere 9 per cent were expressing unequivocal support or calling for the full-blown integration of BS5750 into CPE. So expressions of the view that it is 'very applicable' (a professor of mathematics) were few and far between. 'It is applicable but may not be worth the effort' (short courses manager, computer studies) is the type of statement which emerged from the more well-supported 'ambiguous positive' group.

In comparison, of the 37 per cent lodged at the other end of the continuum 25 per cent (a full quarter of the complete sample) were totally against any role for the standard. One respondent entirely familiar with the standard from his main teaching and research area expressed 'amazement' that it should be taken so seriously and continued, 'I do not believe that BS5750 is applicable to QA in CPE (or elsewhere in HEIs). It is based on manufacturing practice and is not appropriate to higher education teaching activity' (a head of civil engineering). And another respondent went further – to doubt the motivation behind its use. 'I have some concern that quality and BS5750 are ideological and that the standard will only serve to limit improvement and divert energy and resources away from primary activities' (a CE officer, computing).

Thus, there is strength of feeling on both sides. However, in terms of the quantity of support the situation is clear enough: nearly three times as many non-CPE specialist providers unreservedly reject the standard than unequivocally argue for it. Once away from the extremes, though, slightly more subjects were recorded as 'accepting with reservations' than were 'rejecting with reservations'.

A comparative analysis of *attitudes* between specialist and non-specialist providers provides no evidence for a continuation of the difference which characterised levels of *exposure* to BS5750. On the contrary, a striking similarity is revealed, not least in the key zones of unequivocal support or rejection (see table 5.2). At these extreme points of the response continuum the results are virtually interchangeable. It can be recalled that amongst respondents from central providing units 30 per cent had established a clear viewpoint: 8 per cent expressing the positive view, and 22 per cent the negative. In this sample (of around double the size) 34 per cent fell at either end: 9 per cent revealing a favourable position and 25 per cent a negative one. With hardly any discernible differences, the statistical significance of such differences is not an issue.

Table 5.2 Attitudes to BS5750: a comparison

	CPE specialists (%)	Non-CPE specialists (%)
Fully in favour of applying BS5750	8	9
In favour with reservations	24	16
Undecided/heard of it but no comments	22	16
Never heard of it	5	21
Against, but can see same minor advantages	19	12
Against unequivocally	22	25

A position has been reached in which an amalgamation of the two empirical research strategies will yield interesting conclusions. For instance, despite all the hype, there is certainly no consensus on the merits of employing BS5750. And while opinions do not all fall in one direction, it seems reasonable to deduce that should a consensus of any sort emerge, it would be an anti – rather than a pro – British Standard one. This expectation is consistent with the opinions expressed in both surveys.

The opportunity to draw on the opinions of these two distinct groups of respondents must be of some value to policy makers, and those involved in CPE more generally. For here is detailed the kind of reaction which the introduction of such an approach might well induce. When discussed alongside the theoretical critique and other elements of the data germane to BS5750 the complete situation will be clarified further. Such an overall perspective will be developed in the concluding chapter.

QUALITY ASSURANCE: THE NATURE OF PRACTICE

Parallel findings on the nature of practice can now be highlighted. Following a brief description of the overall level of activity and the degree of use of written policies, each of the principal procedures identified will be reviewed in turn.

Quality policies: established and emerging

The extent to which concern with QA has been translated into a specific written policy for the undertaking of CPE is limited: 16 per cent of the sample had such a document. It is certainly possible that for some respondents there was no perceived need to separate CPE from undergraduate and postgraduate provision, either conceptually or in terms of documentation. Limited references to such integration were made, though there was nothing to suggest that this was a widespread position. To enter a note of realism, the impetus to produce such a document will not necessarily be strong for the whole of the sample. While a number of respondents will have provided a significant number of courses annually, it should be remembered that 80 per cent of the sample were responsible for 25 or less per year, with a significant number at the bottom end of that range. This is not to offer a judgement on such a position but rather

131

to offer an explanation of trend. This lack of a written statement, though, as was demonstrated earlier, is not a tendency peculiar to this group. Those policies of non-CPE specialist departments which were available for consultation were very much of the practical variety: they conformed to the image of quality as beginning and ending with the administrative. Indeed, in a couple of cases differentiating between a quality policy and a checklist was non too easy. For example, in one 'policy' of an engineering department, supplies of chocolate biscuits were given equal prominence with booking lecturers; issues of intent or purpose were not included.

Any idea that the lack of an extensive array of formally identifiable policy documents can be equated with a failure to consider and adopt individual (or multiple) practices aimed at securing effective provision can though be immediately dispelled. Ninety-six per cent of respondents regarded one or more of the main procedures as recognisable in their own work. As with the central units, we are not faced with an empty space to be built upon in a wholly fresh way. Educationalists have evolved approaches from their own experience. These are sometimes formalised, sometimes not; sometimes extensive, sometimes not. That these can be re-assessed and re-constructed from a fresh perspective is apparent; that this requires a wholesale replacement of current practice is less so.

The activity surrounding an ongoing CPE venture established in the early 1990s shows how the lack of a written policy is not necessarily indicative of a lack of attention to quality, nor to the imaginative implementation of procedures. The course – which can be called the Diploma in Professional Practice – was based on four separate one-week units over two academic years. It therefore varied considerably from the structure of a 'short course'. While considerable attention was given to the planning stage, putting the course through the relevant university committees etc., it is the evaluation phase that is unusually wide ranging. At least five separate elements of the process can be differentiated: within-course evaluation sheets; informal contacts; graffiti sheets; post-course meetings; and long-term work. For now I will restrict myself to comments on a couple of the mechanisms.

The use of within-course evaluation sheets was initially a failure. Distributed at the end of the first week, attending professionals found it difficult to recall the intricacies of various classes. By adopting the simple measure of distributing forms at the start of each unit, and requesting daily completion, their value was enhanced considerably. Thus a straightforward procedural modification, borne of a willingness to modify an agreed strategy, produced a mechanism of use to all concerned.

The graffiti sheets were prominently positioned flip charts available to course attenders to comment anonymously (or not!) on any aspects of the course. The course director had developed this idea from one suggested by Rowntree (1981). As well as coming together with the other forms of evaluation in post-course discussions, they offered a genuinely immediate source of expression for attenders. They offer a similarly immediate source of information for providers to gauge the responses to a new mode of provision. The course team noted a decreasing use of the graffiti sheets as the course became more established. This was possibly the result of having ironed out initial difficulties; possibly the result of having formalised other ongoing forums for comment.

These are but selected examples of practice in a course which has, as yet, no written quality policy – no written framework for action. The course is still at a relatively early stage in its development. It is expected that forms of evaluation – and all quality mechanisms – will continue to evolve in the light of experience.

Quality practice: procedures in use

At 79 per cent the level of participation in, or use of, joint planning groups with clients is substantial. And once it is acknowledged that the predominantly 'open' character of provision in some departments would not always be consistent with such a practice anyway, the extent to which providers are aware of the benefit to be derived from preventative rather than corrective action is seemingly confirmed.

There is evidently a greater reluctance to employ planning guides and checklists for tutors – only 46 per cent reported such practices. Perhaps earlier discussions about general concerns surrounding the controlling nature of some approaches can be re-introduced to help understand what may be going on here. It may well be that there is something distasteful about modes of organisation like these for many people. Here, as elsewhere in the issue of QA, perhaps what needs to be addressed is the way in which some procedures are applied and incorporated within a wider whole. It seems reasonable to argue that there is nothing inherently problematic about the use of aids to facilitate successful preparation. Indeed, they are rightly seen to fall within the remit of a planning/prevention-orientated approach. The issue quite probably rests on the source of such guides, and how far they are grounded in an approach which draws providers into the organisational process. There is some difference between guides perceived to be written in tablets of stone – instructions to be followed – and those regarded as controllable tools, able to be directed towards the satisfaction of particular aims. Nevertheless, this simple support mechanism does have a fair level of use. It might well achieve a dramatically increased level given a shifting locus of control.

The use of participation evaluation questionnaires (exit surveys) was discussed at length in the previous chapter and doubtless the kinds of concerns raised there are similarly relevant in this context. The popularity of this procedure is borne out by a use rate of 93 per cent, although that figure does not necessarily describe their inevitable and consistent application to each and every course.

Just as evaluation is but one component of a successful approach to QA, so too the exit survey is only one mode of formalised feedback. Indeed, it is my contention that one alternative mode, the post-course evaluation, whilst in no way a panacea, does constitute an under-utilised resource.

Questioned about the extent to which post-course evaluation of participants is carried out, only 21 per cent confirmed current activity. A similar figure of 25 per cent was recorded for other miscellaneous forms of follow-up evaluation. There is clearly a range of forms and focuses of such evaluation, but the link between all of them is the desire to establish a different perspective – probably with the help of course participants and certainly with the aid of spatial and temporal distance – to consider whatever features of the provision seem most pertinent to those involved. This is, in fact, offering a further point of continuity with the discussions of aims and purposes of CPE and definitions of quality which have been frequent points of reference. For here is a mechanism (or set of mechanisms) by which an extension is offered beyond the practical and the immediate, towards a consideration of the eventual value of the work undertaken. The potential is significant; the potential difficulties (not least the time required to operationalise such procedures) no less so. But in opening up the possibilities those respondents whose aims were identified as existing beyond the financial are offered a means of assessing the value of provision and feeding that back into future work. For in establishing this as the final link in a chain which necessarily begins with the clarification of purpose, a contribution is being made to extending the perceived limits of 'quality assurance procedures'.

To find an example of this we can return to the case of the Diploma in Professional Practice first cited at the start of this chapter. For the course director (a non-CPE specialist), the purpose of the course could only be expressed in terms of the impact that might emerge in the practice of the professionals concerned. The quality of the course was not demonstrable without reference to that outcome. The selection of forms of evaluation related to this aim. Evaluation questionnaires were distributed to attenders between each residential phase to assess impact on practice. At the time of writing, the first two-year course was just being completed. To date, the course team have data on how the attending professionals felt their practice had changed at each of four points over two years, and what aspects of the course – if any – had induced or encouraged that change. Around nine months after completion of the final residential component, a further evaluation form will be distributed. Again impact on professional action will be a major concern. Matters relating to participant satisfaction retain a place in the questionnaires; the practical and administrative details are not overlooked. But the long-term development of the course is seen to be dependent upon the extent to which provision is matching socially located aims. Ongoing evaluation acts as a quality mechanism directed towards this intention.

Thus, with this extra dimension a sequence can now be established which runs something like: recognised overall aims → specific course requirements → QA procedures up to and including delivery based on the first two stages → modes of long-term evaluation based on the first two again. Therefore, a process which frequently becomes squeezed into: course aims identification → QA procedures to meet these immediate evaluations, is given extra dimensions. And the first part of this process – explicit recognition of aims – need not seriously impinge on time.

The value and relevance of continuing/post-course evaluation will vary both in efficacy and in applicability depending upon both the subject matter and, crucially, the value base of providers. What I am suggesting is that for that substantial proportion of providers for whom CPE is primarily about improving professional practice for the benefit of society as a whole, there is a component of the provision process which can contribute to just that end. There are, of course, established means of doing this. For instance, there is the participant evaluation questionnaire at a given point which produces data on a re-appraisal of the course or a view on its value following a period of practice. But the options are more extensive than that. Whilst some of these will only be possible infrequently, the point is to encourage a creative approach and confirm that the option of extending rather than limiting the concerns of CPE is not simply a theoretical matter. A process which begins by offering a challenging and broad conception of the role of CPE; a wide notion of quality within that context; and aims which reach beyond the didactic transmission of technical knowledge can be supported by an approach to course design and appraisal which is equally wide ranging: one which incorporates a look into the world of professional practice.

The above will certainly be noted to be inappropriate to some. Just as the distinction amongst specialists between the entre-preneurs and the 'liberal' educators (McIlroy and Spencer 1988: 124-5) is seemingly getting at something quite concrete, so too there is likely to be a persistent entrepreneurial element to non-specialist provision. Nevertheless, because the discussion builds on the actual evidence from providers – that in large numbers their aims extend beyond the instrumental – a formalised adoption of an intention to include such longer-term evaluation becomes a high profile option.

To summarise, it is not consistent with the approach proposed to dictate procedures to follow or aims to achieve. Nor is there any suggestion that the general orientation of the procedure discussed above is new (although applications, such as contact with clients of professionals, could certainly be so in certain circumstances). What is stressed is that the research evidence has revealed on the one hand, the co-existence of a high regard with a low use rate for this procedure; and on the other, a widespread concern with the societal impact of provision. The argument is that the re-appraisal of quality and quality assurance in many departments and universities can incorporate a range of elements. Varying forms of evaluation would be but one of these. In so doing, both a sound practical base for course provision and the intention (depending upon resources and individual circumstance) to work towards a constructive societal role for CPE could be established.

The results relating to two further procedures used during the pre-course (and to some extent within-course) phase are worthy of mention. Both informal participation feedback (86 per cent) and feedback from tutors (85 per cent) seem to be fairly well institutionalised as means of gaining information. Both have the considerable advantage of being easy and flexible to manage. And they are able to be carried out within the normal run of events. They are nonetheless effective. They are relatively painless to deploy, and their continued use offers testimony to their perceived value.

The comparative treatment of the earlier themes has produced findings of some import for the project. The rate at which the main procedures are used is no exception.

Similarity rather than difference again characterises the relationship (see table 5.3). This impression is confirmed by a chi square analysis of the two samples as a whole (χ^2 = 1.714, df = 6, 12.59 or above needed for significance at 0.95 level). Not surprisingly, none of the comparisons between specialists and non-specialists on individual procedures revealed a different trend. Even the largest chi square value, for post-course evaluation (χ^2 = 1.574, df = 1, 3.8415 needed for significance at 0.95 level) did not seriously threaten statistical significance.

The emerging proposition emphasising the compatibility between specialist and non-specialist providers, therefore, requires little modification on the basis of the latest data set. It should be borne in mind that on this behaviourial rather than attitudinal measure the likelihood of differentiation is inevitably reduced.

Table 5.3 Procedures forming a part of practice: a comparison

Procedure	CPE specialists (%)	Non-CPE specialists (%)
Joint planning groups with clients	72	79
Planning guides and checklists for tutors	37	46
Participant evaluation questionnaires (exit survey)	89	93
Participant evaluation questionnaire (post-course)	11	21
Other follow-up evaluation	22	25
Informal participant feedback	83	86
Feedback from tutors	86	85

Interaction between specialists and non-specialists, as well as shared knowledge of what constitutes institutionally specific assumptions on good practice for course provision, might draw together results in a way which would not be so relevant to matters of perspective and purpose. Even so, rarely, if ever, is practice entirely directed from the centre. Autonomy remains, and individual choices are made.

UNNECESSARY BURDENS AND UNWELCOME EFFECTS

Five actual or potential barriers were identified by CPE specialists in such numbers as to call upon policy makers to take them seriously. Each of these again (the first five listed in table 5.4) stood out with the second research group.

One-third of the non-specialist respondents noted that the identification of QA as a peripheral issue was likely to prevent appropriate policy development. It is possible that one cause of this is the distance that can exist between individual providers and decision making about practical requirements. If providers are making judgements about the peripheral nature of a process from a

Table 5.4 Perceived barriers to quality: a comparison

Barrier	CPE specialists (%)	Non-CPE specialists (%)
Inherent clash with academic independence	42	24
Staff fear of institutional imposition of measures with which they disagree	44	27
Staff fear of negative personal consequences	36	23
Quality assurance being regarded as a peripheral issue	29	33
Time-consuming nature of quality assurance	83	80
Lack of client interest	5	14
Lack of participant motivation	14	14

starting point of resignation and expected compliance to establish systems, then there is clearly a legitimate basis to the perception. It is certainly pertinent to ask: if one-third of academic staff genuinely do consider that QA is a peripheral issue, then what kind of interpretation of quality (providing the catalyst for change) have they been exposed to and internalised? And as a supplementary question, it could also be asked: whether such an interpretation can be explained away by arguing that the provider view of QA is a distorted one? Is it not the case that such a sense of isolation from, or ambivalence towards, the process will only be tackled by an amalgamation of QA with actual activity; and in view of earlier evidence, by an integration with actual aims? This seems to be a pre-condition for overcoming the disinterestedness amongst this substantial minority of academics.

There is a certain degree of overlap between the ideas raised above and those which relate to the next set of barriers. Although the extent to which each of the following have been identified is relatively small (that is, around one-quarter each), it is perhaps indicative of the process having gone a little awry that such fears should be surfacing at all in a situation which should reasonably be expected to be all about committed staff developing their work to its fullest potential. The three themes of concern are: the identification of an inherent clash with academic independence (24 per cent), staff fear of institutional imposition of measures of which they disagree (27 per cent), and staff fear of negative personal consequences (23 per cent).

What each of these individual aspects has in common is a loss of power over the process of QA. Each suggests a feeling that developments are operating at an organisational level which is to some extent beyond them, yet is still demanding certain things from them. The discovery that such views are presently held throughout UK universities must lead to a querying of the kind of approaches to, and images of, quality existing in the mainstream. Certainly, issues relating to the active or passive ways which people believe they may be undertaken should form a part of this: a consideration of form as well as content.

The question of the location of power on the various dimensions discussed has produced a consistent, though in no case over-whelming, level of identification. One important methodological point should be clarified here, however. For the question on which the results are based asked respondents to assess which issues have acted or may in the future act as barriers to QA. As such they are voicing opinions based on their understanding of general trends as well as personal feelings. Thus an indication is given of the levels of those who consider one factor or another to be affecting institutional life. To gain data on the actual level of concern with these factors amongst academics at large is a slightly separate issue.

The final barrier to be discussed is one bound up with institutional arrangements of university life as a whole. And it is also one which, given current expansionist trends, centres on a commodity which is likely to be in increasingly short supply. It is time that is the issue, and in particular the feeling that the greatest difficulty in the application of a process of QA lies in its inevitable consumption of this resource. Eighty per cent of the sample felt that there was a very real problem here. In doing so they find affinity with the comments of John Westergaard who suggests that working in universities is currently characterised by an 'accelerating scarcity of space, books, facilities – and of time, time, time' (1992: 585).

If such an interpretation is accepted, the conclusion might well be reached that the problem is an intractable one. However, working on the assumption that QA mechanisms will be adopted in one form or another and, therefore, that some re-scheduling will inevitably result, a positive utilisation of the evidence is called for. In the present circumstances, the choice is not between no approach and an elaborate time-consuming one; it is between one which exists with very real purposes in mind, devised (not least in relation to time commitments) and operated by practitioners; and externally imposed systems which do not equate with the requirements of individuals. Coupled with a similar concern emanating from central providing units, the implication is clear and simple; yet it is potentially far reaching in its consequences for an adopted approach: the rejection of all unnecessary/cosmetic (with providers having a direct role in defining the necessary) time-consuming measures, and the use of that time in ways perceived to be enhancing the character of actual provision.

It could be argued that this point on time does not fit easily with my earlier promotion of long-term evaluation. However, a closer look at the issue shows the contradiction to be confined to the surface.

There are several guiding principles – of which limited demands on time is one – which can be drawn from the research to suggest what is likely to produce a workable and valuable system.

Simplicity, flexibility and relevance to defined aims are amongst the most important of these. Whilst these are essentially sympathetic to each other, decisions of prioritisation will have to be made. For instance, dealing with elements in the pursuit of agreed-upon aims will demand a time commitment. But what is of real importance is that this will be positive time consumption supported by the retention of flexibility and control. In other words, the *nature* of time consumption as well as the *total* expenditure of time is of significance. In circumstances that allow for a directive role to be played by providers, choices can be made about how to operationalise procedures in line with particular aims. So, time consumption is an inevitability. But as long as the basic construction of an approach is one which is context-relevant in form there should be no reticence in making the case for the utilisation of those features which can offer a formative contribution. What is not defensible is the expenditure of time and resources geared more to image maintenance than towards genuinely established aims.

The comparative analysis of 'barriers' (see table 5.4) has a degree of complexity not found elsewhere in the data. By this I do not mean that a great divergence of opinion is found. Indeed, the overall analysis of specialist responses against those of non-specialists yielded a χ^2 value of 6.201, df = 6. (Significance at 0.95 required a χ^2 value of >12.5). Nor do I suggest anything but consistency on arguably the major discussion point: time ($\chi^2 = 0.233$, df = 1, χ^2 value of 3.8414 needed for significance at 0.95 level). There is even a similar grouping of the 'control' dimensions around the same levels *within* each sample. What table 5.4 does show, however, is that there are sizeable differences between specialist and non-specialist responses on several of those dimensions related to control of the quality process.

None of these (clash with academic independence, $\chi^2 = 3.262$; fear of external imposition, $\chi^2 = 3.121$; fear of negative personal consequences, $\chi^2 = 1.964$; all df = 1, all required 3.8415 for 0.95 significance) reached statistical significance. Irrespective of that, the tendency towards differentiation is observable in a comparison of the relevant percentage levels.

Having failed to achieve the point of 'significant difference', the variation may be little more than a quirk. But assuming that this is not entirely the case, some comments are appropriate. For instance, on the basis of the evidence, it could be asked whether CE specialists are more concerned with the independence/control implications of QA than academics across the board. And if this is accepted as so, then the pursuit of explanation can begin. One possibility is that we are seeing a manifestation of a 'liberal' concern with academic independence etc. But not only does this tend to imply the rather doubtful idea of a lesser concern elsewhere in the university, it also runs into difficulty because of the presence of the non-traditional providers – the 'entrepreneurs' – in the sample.

Perhaps then the explanation can be found at a more practical level. Could it be that the greater level of awareness of BS5750 amongst specialists is being transferred into concern about the likely development of QA? It might also be that the specialists have simply over-estimated the degree of reticence amongst colleagues towards QA. But that only returns us to the why? questions.

Whatever the explanation it should be remembered that this is dealing with just one deviation from a pattern of consistency. And the range of that consistency is such that it suggests what will not work, or at least what will only work under duress. Matters of control and independence, and to an even greater extent time consumption, are ignored at the risk of institutionalised dissatisfaction.

SOME FINAL COMMENTS ON QUALITY

Much of that which is of concern to providers is department- or institution-specific. As a consequence, the identification of satisfactory and unsatisfactory procedures; contributors to good and bad courses; and ideal and irrelevant components of QA systems, in part provides a forum for the expression of one-off non-generalisable concerns. Having said that, themes of broader applicability are not entirely eclipsed.

In looking to the evidence on elements of practice which induce satisfaction, we are drawn back to a consideration of evaluation in its various forms. The only exception to this pattern is the inclusion of appropriate planning (38 per cent) in the list of positively regarded procedures. That category was dominated by the exit survey, 58 per cent of respondents including them within their list of valued approaches. Informal feedback from participants also received support, though at a rather lower level (28 per cent).

The double-edged nature of opinions on evaluation sheets is characteristic of the non-specialists as it was with the specialists. A little over one-fifth (21 per cent) expressed dissatisfaction with them.

It was, though, a further feature of the evaluation process which was most frequently cited as a source of dissatisfaction. Moreover, it was not so much a difficulty with actual practice as something absent from it, post-course evaluation (23 per cent). Its presence here adds weight to the claims already advanced in support of its usage. Quite clearly, immediate means of evaluation are seen to be only able to offer so much in the quest for quality provision, and follow-up work is identified as one way in which such gaps as are inherent in the capabilities of on-the-day questionnaires can be plugged. The need for more post-course evaluation (equal highest response with improved planning – 24 per cent) also topped the list of 'ideal' procedures. This demonstrates a consistency of thinking within the non-CPE specialists on related issues. It is true that the figures are not high in absolute terms. This is explained in part by the vast spread of 'one-off' citations. However, a consistent figure of 1 in 4 raising this issue (especially as these are the people who would be in line to activate it) means that at the very least there is a strong case for consideration of its potential at the department level.

The elements of practice regarded as holding a determining role in the production of a successful or unsuccessful course will perhaps, on the basis of what has been learnt to date, be the ones that would have been predicted. The reliance on good course design and planning, meeting recognised needs and drawing together the knowledgeable and committed course team (all 33 per cent) are the elements which head the list. These were also represented in the listed causes of a poor course. A significant feature of this list was though the claim by 29 per cent of the sample that they had never had an unsuccessful course. The interpretation of such a result is one which would doubtless be affected by one's position in the debate. It is perhaps diplomatic to state that neither pedagogic perfection nor gross complacency constitutes the whole story.

Having consistently adopted a position which embraces the importance of the professional being able to establish control over the procedures used in an aims-orientated manner, the work has necessarily dealt with what is inappropriate as well as what is appropriate to this task. Analyses of favoured procedures, of aims of provision and even the explicit consideration of the value of BS5750 have all contributed to this. A further step towards this is to examine those procedures which were deemed irrelevant by the sample – a finding which can then be seen alongside those emerging from the above issues.

In a similar way to the treatment of the data of CPE specialists (more of that relationship in a moment), points raised could often be grouped under one of two headings. One was a rejection of any approach which relied on British Standards and a centralised determination of system content. Twenty-six per cent recorded such comments. At 27 per cent, the other major response set can be identified as incorporating time-consuming procedures and those which squeezed human and financial resources unnecessarily. As with data from the specialist providers, the evidence was the subject of a second level of analysis, one which assessed whether or not such concerns were concentrated in a small number of respondents. There was, in fact, very little doubling of comments. Approaching half of those replying (44 per cent) provided a statement which fell neatly within the boundaries of one or the other of the categories.

There are many features of the above sub-section which might provide the basis of comparative analysis: the issues surrounding planning, immediate evaluation and post-course follow-up have all been noted as consistently relevant. The data on those procedures identified as irrelevant to the needs of CPE are particularly informative. It is summarised in table 5.5.

It seems that several things are being indicated by the data. First, that across the board around a quarter of respondents felt impelled to express a rejection of BS5750 (and/or the kinds of national approach it represents) in a question not explicitly related to discussion of it. Second, that while existing or potential procedures could have been expected to dominate responses, the theme of the burden of time was again raised. And while the high citation rate amongst central units is especially noteworthy, when this data is read alongside the earlier evidence (see table 5.4), it is clear that it

Table 5.5 Identified irrelevancies for the quality task: a comparison

Irrelevant 'Procedures'	CPE specialists (%)	Non-CPE specialists (%)
Centralised British Standard approach (BS5750)	29	26
Time/resource-consuming approaches	47	27
Inclusion of at least one of the above	59	44

would be unwise to under-estimate the feeling in individual departments on this issue. It would be equally inappropriate to focus on differences rather than similarities between the groups. Third, that around half of each sample would react negatively to any system which was established in a manner which incorporated either of these two elements.

On this, as on other measures, the (obviously not unbroken) continuity between the results from CPE specialists and from non-specialist providers is substantial. The consistency on the latter themes should be especially noted given the open nature of the question.

CONCLUSIONS AND COMPARISONS

Prior to the research, little was known about how the internally diverse group of non-specialist providers might influence the quality process. We were able to work solely from deduction, from assumptions about action in relation to circumstances. What then do the results say about the way in which CPE is perceived and quality envisaged? And what can be made of the relationship between the data from the specialist and non-specialist populations.

A measure of the expectations which a provider has about CPE are the aims that that same provider adheres to. Had income generation – a reasonable enough indicator of instrumentalism – predominated, claims that CPE for this group was a side-line, a less important adjunct to primary provision, might have been able to be supported. The substantial allegiance to broader aims illustrated that this was far from the case for many providers. Many academics are engaging in CPE with a seriousness which has often been lacking in the conceptualisation of the subject itself! Definitions of quality, though, operated on a different level: the worrying absence of a tie-up between aims and quality is seen to be widespread.

While the sample was very broadly based, it will be recalled that business and engineering representatives together accounted for over one-third of it. The failure of a group so constituted to identify with the British Standards model of quality was a major result of the study. Moreover, the concern with time-consuming approaches as a whole, and with systems which impose, threaten, or appear to threaten, limits to personal freedom has to be taken seriously. But the results also revealed what was valued as well as what was rejected. From the preventative to the evaluation, individual procedures are being examined and utilised.

145

Whether analysis was of these trends outlined above, or of isolated components of study, it was similarity rather than difference which characterised the relationship between the evidence from specialists and non-specialists. The seemingly different starting points, and the apparently opposing modes of affinity with the subject area rarely, if ever, became exhibited in quantifiable form. By briefly returning to some of the main areas of discussion, some reasons for the complementarity can be suggested, and some aspects of the significance of this finding can be identified.

Whether aim(s) were described in the singular or plural, in relation to the financial or the social, variation did not occur on the basis of being assigned to one or other of the two groups. In general, respondents from the CE community were no more likely to have wide ranging, socially located aims for CPE than the non-specialists. One way of looking at this is that non-specialists proved less instrumentally oriented than might have been expected. But this is perhaps more of an observation than an explanation. It is, though, a warning against over-simplification: there is no single orientation amongst subject specialists, just as there is not just one amongst the CPE specialists.

Instead of trying to explain the high levels of interest in the effects of provision amongst non-specialists, perhaps a more profitable route might be to look at the primacy ascribed to income generation by a substantial (though not overwhelming) number of specialists. Now, this might be a manifestation of the emerging role of the entrepreneur in specialist departments (McIlroy and Spencer 1988). On the other hand it might be indicative of an attitude to CPE – as essentially vocational, practical, or near-industry – amongst some established academics. For if CPE is perceived as different from the 'main' traditional activities of university adult education, it could be that the normally wide ranging purposes of provision are scaled down for CPE. Conjecture certainly, but the shifting form of university CE might well, in one way or another, be influencing outcomes.

Whatever the cause of consistency, consistency there certainly is. And if this says one thing above all else, it is that to see CPE as a straightforward satisfier of technical needs, or as a means of making money, is both theoretically insufficient and stands against the orientation of the full range of those actually delivering the education. Single level notions of quality look ever more ineffectual against such a background.

The fact that the two samples were drawn from the same institutions goes some way towards explaining the similarity of existing practice. These results on procedures can directly assist the clarification of future strategy. This is self-evidently the case in relation to the full range of those mechanisms already employed. Correctly used, certain procedures work and should be retained. However, comments on procedures valued in theory (e.g. continuing evaluation) but to date under-used, can also assist policy development. The aim is to enhance effective use of the former, and work towards integration of the latter.

Alongside the identification of aims, attitudes to BS5750 could well have been regarded as a possible source of divergence. The fact that this did not occur, and in particular that the non-specialists failed to identify with the standard, has an important implication. For if a structural shift of the type demanded by BS5750 is to be achieved, a consensus, or at least a lack of antagonism, would seem to be a necessary, or at least a sensible, pre-condition. As neither environment exists; neither, it would appear, do adequate grounds for pursuing with the standards-based solution.

Of course, although I have differentiated between the two groups, the individuals within them are subject to many of the same constraints and concerns. After all, each respondent works within the same university system. When viewed from this perspective, the identification of similar opinions on likely barriers to QA is understandable. The same institutional trends are affecting perceptions. These will also influence attitudes to policies and practices of varying forms.

At the theoretical level, the failure to find an empirical basis to the separation of CPE specialists and non-specialists raises important questions for the subject area of CPE. Is it necessary to differentiate between types of providers? Would specialists and non-specialists express differences on other variables? Should any differentiation between providers be on the basis of expressed aims? Are the entrepreneur and the liberal the categories by which this can be achieved? Attitudes to quality are but one way of examining the nature of CPE providers and provision. However, the evidence does suggest that the notion of the dual pressures on – and character of – CPE (the market and socially located provisions) remains an effective conceptual tool for understanding CPE. Interpretation on that basis seemingly cuts across the more obvious distinction between specialists and non-specialists.

147

When looking towards the practical level, this complementarity has an immediate positive benefit. When taken together, the results from the two groups of providers suggest directions for practice which – as will be seen later – can support the development of a strategy for assuring quality.

6

INTEREST GROUPS, QUALITY AND CONTINUING PROFESSIONAL EDUCATION

Some case examples from employers and professional institutions

For this final substantive chapter, a somewhat different approach is to be followed. So far this section has been all about discussing the nature and implications of large-scale (given the size of the relevant populations) surveys. It has, therefore, been based on the quantitative and generalisable. My focus here differs from that in relation to subject matter, and in relation to methodological style.

Concerning subject matter, the analysis moves beyond the confines of academic institutions to draw on evidence from other groups with a strong interest in the nature of CPE in universities. As for method, the main point of departure is that there is no attempt to establish a sample as such or to identify generalisable conclusions. The individual cases were selected solely on the basis of their known activity in the area of post-qualification education. The expectation was that if the study of these respective sectors was to yield anything of interest it would come through an awareness of policy and practice in high profile exemplars. Given the current enthusiasm for a customer-driven basis for action, the intention is to illustrate some of the practical features of involvement with professional development courses amongst employers and professional institutions; whilst also considering – at a more general level – the value of incorporating perspectives on quality which emanate from vested interests. Before bringing in the new empirical evidence, both the nature of the groups considered and matters of method can be addressed in a little more detail.

INTEREST GROUPS AND QUALITATIVE ANALYSIS

Varying forms of relationships with external groupings and their representatives are clearly an essential feature of the nature of CPE.

Quite simply, the subject area fails to have meaning once divorced from professional practice. Because of this existence at the interface of the academy and the outside world, a number of groups could have been introduced into the discussion at this stage; one or more of those not included here could well be picked up for analysis in future work. Individual practising professionals might have been selected; so too might ultimate recipients of professional wisdom (the eventual clients of professions). My focus is, though, on employers and professional institutions. These represent institutional interest in the process of course development.

Employers frequently – though not exclusively – constitute the paying client. A recognition of the primacy of profit and the need to fend off competitors, suggest that conceptions of CPE are likely to be closely allied to business needs. The analysis of the selected cases will offer empirical evidence by which to examine such a proposition. Moreover, the research will be used to look at how quality is operationalised and what compatibility there is between the objectives of the commercial setting and those of the university.

Professional institutions and professional 'good practice' can be expected to go hand in hand. The very purpose of these representative bodies is after all to promote and enhance the position of their members within a particular occupational (and social) structure. Moreover, a secure place for members ensures a secure place for the institution! Therefore, the perpetual improvement of skills and knowledge of members is a central issue; as is, at least by inference, an interest in good quality CPE. Pronouncements on CPE make interesting reading against such a background, as do the varying responses to matters of QA.

There are numerous sources of information which can be drawn on in the course of a case study (Yin 1989: 85–104). Selection between these must relate to the needs of the task at hand. In each of the case studies undertaken here, the following three-part approach was followed: (1) to gain background information on the development of the institution or company; (2) to identify key personnel (concerned with CPE/CPD and its quality) and to carry out semi-structured interviews with them; and (3) to collate and analyse any available internal documents or publications which illuminate policy and practice on CPE/CPD.

Thus, those studied are companies and institutions which may well be forwarded as exemplars of best practice in each of the two sectors. Because of the focused nature of the work, the guiding questions were not those which might be used to quantify activity (e.g., is CPE on the agenda?). Instead, questions began from an assumption of some form of involvement and a search for more information (e.g., amongst those who are known to be CPE active, what is their rationale for participation? What is their attitude to quality, and their relationship with the universities?). Building up a statistical picture of the extent of CPE/CPD activity beyond universities is a potentially useful study in its own right; it is not, though, an issue with which this research has been concerned.

A total of six case studies were conducted: three employers and three professional institutions. They were carried out in 1992. Each of the commercial examples were drawn from the same geographical region in the north of England. The professional institutions represented members on a national level. The bodies selected were connected by membership of the same umbrella organisation, yet they retained a strong sense of autonomy. Brief details of the six are given below. The actual names have been replaced in order to preserve anonymity. All employee numbers are based on 1993 levels; all membership figures for professional institutions are drawn from 1992 data.

Regional services is a recently privatised company. It has around 6,500 employees. The number of those who might be classified as professional would – as is the case in any organisation – be dependent on definition. The company's interest in CPE has led to the development of detailed, formalised policies, and to participation in regional and national award schemes for provision.

Monopolex is also a company which was privatised during the 1980s. It has 4,300 employees. The emphasis on CPE can be directly traced back to the enthusiasm of a few key personnel. Each of these individuals is well known for this activity throughout the local business community.

John Jeffreys Ltd is a long established private company. They produce several nationally known household products. The figure for employees is 866. The opening of a lavishly equipped development centre is a notable recent feature of the company's CPD programme.

While the pseudonyms (and acronyms) chosen for the professional institutions do allude to something in the character of the bodies, the titles are first and foremost a means of labelling, a means of differentiation. They are not meant to define or characterise the institution in any strict sense.

151

The Professional Institution of Theoretical and Practising Specialists (PITPS) has 15,400 members. It is an institution which is the site of any ongoing debate about the relative value of theory on the one hand, and practice on the other. While some members stick rigidly to activity on just one of these levels, many straddle both.

The National Institution of Established Professionals (NIEP) is probably the most well known of the three to people beyond its immediate specialism. It has 22,333 members. It has a traditional image and might be described as representing high-status professionals. The profession of its members has a high profile.

The Institute of Recognised Professionals (IRP) is by far the largest of the three bodies. It has 77,909 members. It is probably also the most troubled. There is a sensitivity among members about a poor(ish) public image. The institution is aware of prevailing criticism.

In order to contextualise the following discussion, several features of the perspective which inform it can be signalled in advance. This serves to confirm the sense of continuity between analyses conducted on these case studies and the other forms of analysis presented elsewhere in the book. Each element will be returned to at the end of the chapter and clarified in relation to the evidence of the cases.

1 The opening point is simply a statement of the legitimacy of reaching beyond the university for input. It is to do no more than to acknowledge the presence of CPE activity, opinions and practice elsewhere, and to value an analysis of them. The theoretical possibility of utilising mechanisms is noted.
2 This represents an extension of point 1. It stresses the potential impact of varying conceptions of quality (courses). This is not unrelated to the evidence of chapter 1. The relationship between aims and sectional interests is an issue here.
3 This suggests that a critical awareness of the concept of the customer may well impinge on discussions.
4 The final point draws attention to the need to be aware of the consequences of market dominance. Difficulties of establishing a clearly defined, theoretically grounded subject area (of CPE) are implicated.

Having established the context, evidence from the case studies can be introduced. Discussion is split into three sections: conceptions of continuing professional education and its relationship to institutional dynamics; the approaches to qualify for in-house provision (including descriptions of innovative, or otherwise relevant, examples); and relationships with, and attitudes towards, universities.

WHY CONTINUING PROFESSIONAL EDUCATION?

The essential requirement for inclusion as a case example, namely, the known commitment to CPE, has brought together a range of institutions for whom ongoing post-qualification development has become, or is becoming, increasingly ingrained in day to day activity and institutional ethos. This is an intriguing trend, the parallel identification with an apparently similar educational process occurring in two seemingly very different sectors. Why is this? Do motivations take on the same form across institutions and sectors? These are the kinds of questions which the qualitative case evidence will help to answer.

These are important questions for a consideration of quality. If CPE is entered into on the basis of varying motivations, the identification of either a successful course, or a quality provision as a whole, will be correspondingly variable. Moreover, issues concerning the degree of correspondence between these emphases and those of university providers will inevitably be highlighted. Similarly, the potential tension for university departments of achieving a precise fit with the expectations of just one group, as opposed to meeting the perceived needs of the generality, will be underlined. This reintroduces the potential problematic of a disjuncture between aims and the pursuit of quality. For complications may emerge should the aim of these institutional players conflict with those of university providers. Clearly, an indication of institutional motivation is a necessary precursor to establishing the details of modes of quality assurance.

We can turn first to the commercial organisations for evidence on that motivation, and for details of the main thrusts of activity. The training manager at Regional Services, a recently privatised company, expressed an unequivocal position. For this individual, and for the company at large, the primary motive for involvement with a co-ordinated programme of CPE is the achievement of business ends (as defined at that time). It was stated, '[we] are seeking to develop people in a way consistent with business needs' (interview 1992). Such a strategy, *designed* to maximise the effectiveness of one or more elements of the company development plan, *may* have benefits for the individual professionals, and indeed, *may* be providing a function of latent benefit to recipients of professional practice, but the starting point – the base from which involvement stems – is commercial profitability. Taking on board the nature of such companies and the social structure into which they fit, it is readily understood that this is entirely consistent with the dynamics of the situation in which they find themselves.

These are the priorities. For us, it is the identification of motivation that is necessary. And that motivation, for a major CPE-active organisation is clear: it is institutional self-interest.

It should be confirmed that individual professionals are far from excluded from the decision-making process surrounding course development (as will be seen later). However, it is undoubtedly the case that the context within which this is occurring is fairly restricted. For instance, the respondent elaborated, 'we will prioritise [about what is included in CPE] according to the circumstances of the time'. And continuing in the same vein, it was stated 'Institutional [Professional Bodies] and individual needs are *not* as important as business needs' (my emphasis) (Training Manager, Regional Services, interview, 1992).

It is particularly informative to realise that the respondent was both making an active decision to adopt this policy and in doing so was fully conversant with the kinds of institutional conflicts which may result. The example cited by the interviewee was that of the potential incompatibility of decrees from professional bodies and the commercial needs of the company. Although we should be careful not to draw these out into polar opposites – as the institutional positions are clearly not mutually exclusive – it does highlight the very real practical consequence of an approach to CPE which is wedded to narrow institutional objectives. Furthermore, it also indicates the limits imposed on the nature of CPE which such a policy dictates.

Alongside decisions about type of CPE come judgements on amount. At Regional Services there is no enthusiasm for set targets; individual professionals are not expected to complete a given number of hours in a specific period. This can be seen to relate to the practical and pragmatic approach which was noted above. In it, the point of involvement is to *meet* a demonstrable *need* rather than participate in development for its own ends. This is a matter of institutional emphasis: the set target approach is regarded as appropriate elsewhere in the commercial sector.

An examination of the second case – Monopolex – reveals a variation in institutional practice, while at the same time showing a similarity of underlying ethos. Essentially, CPE in this company is all about establishing a climate of training which enhances the opportunities for professionals to participate in education. This is clearly a genuine phenomenon. However, again such priorities are dictated not in the first place by a belief in education in its own right, but rather by the need for company profitability. It was stressed by the company co-ordinator of CPE that, 'In order for the company to prosper, important professionals are being developed to meet the demands of the market place' (Regional Training Manager, Monopolex, interview, 1992). The respondent went on to reveal a further impetus to their support for ongoing professional education – the need to attract 'good' individuals to join the company in the first place. Offering the 'carrot' of educational opportunities was seen to be an essential feature of this process. Once in position both the nature and amount of that CPE the employee is involved in is to some extent flexible. Matching individual requirements to company needs is seen as much more commercially viable than any policy of specifying these in advance. There is again no place for a minimum annual involvement.

The third company – John Jeffreys Ltd – provides an example of a commercial organisation which offers the reverse view: its policy is one of formalised minimum involvement. Currently standing at three days a year, it is intended that this will be raised to ten days per annum by 1996. The rationale behind this lies in the perceived nature of the business. During the course of discussions the relevant staff member stressed how the industry required little in the way of capital expenditure on machinery etc. producing a situation in which the main focus of investment is on their human resources, 'people are the greatest assets and it is they who make business' (Employee Development Manager, John Jeffreys Ltd, interview, 1992). Although some concern was expressed that such a regulation may lead to an emphasis on quantity rather than quality they remain firmly committed to it. Thus, while a continuity is being revealed by the primary importance of business priority, a different industrial and commercial context is inspiring a different basis of operationalisation for CPE.

In each of the cases institutional variation was evident. Crucially, both that variation and its underlying rationale were seen to be inextricably linked to the need to sustain or develop a position in the commercial market place. For these companies at least, therefore, both what can be legitimately included in educational provision of this sort and what can accurately be described as quality CPE have to be judgements grounded within such a framework. One important implication of the discussions in chapters 4 and 5 is that such a restrictive interpretation of aims will not always rest easily with those held by a significant number of university providers. While this does not negate the possibilities for particular partnerships, it does throw up a potential contradiction. Just how professional institutions fit into this pattern can now be considered.

Earlier in this chapter, it was noted that the very nature of professional bodies is consistent with the ideas inherent in CPE. That it does indeed form a significant part of institutional priority in a number of practice areas is supported by the emphases of the bodies themselves. One such institution clearly intends to use the general trend to encourage participation from their own members. Whilst the following quotation does not attempt to quantify such trends it does recognise that one exists. A recent internal document states, '[You] . . . are not the only professionals who are being encouraged by their institute to make a more conscious effort on continuing professional development. This note explains the continuing professional development policy and schemes of [our body] and other institutes and helps set [our] scheme in a wider context' (IRP, members' guide).

A discussion of the institution which I am calling the PITPS introduces a number of issues pertinent to the place of professional bodies in this discussion. The opening point may at first sight be seen to be a rather peripheral one, yet it brings with it a quite significant emphasis – it is the matter of terminology. Although I have employed the term continuing professional education in this text (a usage in keeping with that frequently accepted in the university sector), there was a considered and explicit rejection of the term in the professional association, or to be more accurate a rejection of a part of the term – education. The position expressed was based on the belief that the use of this word hindered the possibility of widespread take-up amongst members. It has, as a consequence, been substituted by development – producing the term of continuing professional development (CPD). The use of education was seen to be likely to induce negative reactions amongst practising professionals, due to the perception that as qualified practitioners education as such is complete. Leaving aside any conceptual considerations, this awareness of, and sensitivity to, the fears of members can certainly be seen to be indicative both of the actual purpose of such bodies, and the perspective from which they enter into the situation – namely, as the supporters and promoters of member (and institutional) interests. This is a point which will be developed.

At the moment CPE is not compulsory for the 'ordinary' members of PITPS. However, this is not to say that a clear indication is not given that it is advisable. The term chosen to demonstrate this approach is 'obligatory'. This is clearly not the same thing as 'voluntary'; yet in its avoidance of compulsion the institution aims to perpetuate the notion of the preservation of professional independence. But, this position on CPD, which stops short of any potential challenge to professional integrity, is not seen as fixed – a situation is envisaged in which compulsion could be introduced.

As and when such a change comes about, the expectation is that it will not be bound up with decisions about the perceived benefits of CPE. Instead, falling out of step with comparable professional institutions is regarded as being the most likely impetus to the re-orientation of policy. In such a circumstance the credibility and professional status of the body may be put in jeopardy and thus the potentially difficult decision may be taken. This is, of course, the crux of the matter. Just as business needs dominated CPE action of the employers, both institutional viability and prosperity and the professional status of members serve as directors of policy in this instance. The fact that we are dealing with groups with a vested interest concerned with but a small part of the social, occupational and educational totality is becoming clear.

For now, though, the approach is one of encouragement and of highlighting enlightened self-interest. It points out to members that their interests are best served by taking up CPD without undue pressure. In a document to be distributed to all newly qualified professionals in the field from now on, the reason for taking this on board is explained thus: '[Our] profession, like all professions, is constantly changing, [we] need to keep abreast of these changes and expand [our] knowledge to *maintain [our] professional status, both in the eyes of the public and [our] colleagues'* (my emphasis) (PITPS internal document).

This stress on reinforcing the position of members was confirmed during an interview with the co-ordinator of CPD in this body. It was stated, 'First and foremost we are a service to members and so policy will be influenced by that' (Head of CPD, PITPS, interview, 1992). Clearly, CPD like anything else fits into an institutional dynamic and is directed by the rationale behind it.

In moving on to the second professional institution – the NIEP – a number of the issues detailed above are confirmed as significant. Both the preference for the term CPD over CPE, and a belief in a policy based on trust rather than on the policing of members are noted. On the latter point, there was a particular desire to avoid boxing themselves into a corner: to be forced into a situation in which following a policy of compulsion introduced the possibility of having to discipline members, and having to eventually expel them from the profession for non-compliance. Such a result is clearly one which the body would wish to avoid if at all possible. Rejection of the rule and consequential exclusions may well both weaken the image of the professional and the professional body – precisely the opposite outcome anticipated by the promotion of CPD in the first place.

Although it was noted that CPD has been on the institutional agenda since the 1960s, it has been the period since 1987, or thereabouts, which has seen the big boom in interest. Again, the importance of activity around them had the determining influence in pushing the issue forward. In particular, it was 'an expectation of professionalism from clients, keeping in step with other professional bodies and [that] the institution always wants to be seen to be leading rather than lagging' (CPD Officer, NIEP, interview, 1992), that were influential factors.

Evidence from the IRP (the third and final institution selected) re-affirms the rejection of the terminology of education and both confirms and extends the previously mentioned reasons for involvement in this area. A wide range of influences were cited which together made the pressure for change irresistible. These were: first, a government requirement to 'keep their house in order' (CPD officer, NIEP, interview, 1992). This is a particularly profession-specific reason. As mentioned earlier this was influenced by a degree of public disquiet about their work and the possible threats which the single European market poses to them. The fact that in Europe no comparable profession exists means that a need to legitimise their existence and establish their credentials is of some immediate significance. Second, there is the need to assert that members are skilled professionals in comparison to other UK professions. Again, the question of legitimacy and survival are uppermost in the minds of those involved. Third, pressure from their own younger members, not least because of the need to secure long-term viability. Fourth, to reduce the potential for complaints against members by raising standards.

Thus, while the specific character and emphases of the reasons cited may have a degree of peculiarity to this profession, the underlying strands of thought are familiar enough – to maintain the position of individual members and the profession and to correspondingly secure the future of the institution which represents them.

The examples drawn from the ranks of commercial employers and professional institutions illustrated points of divergence within and between groups, as well as consistencies in their reasons for involvement with CPE/CPD. Whilst an explanation for variation can perhaps be most profitably undertaken by means of an analysis of individual institutional dynamics, the similarities can be seen to be influenced by concerns at a rather more fundamental level, at the level of location and structure.

In each case what was evident was that regardless of the specifics of content, CPE/CPD was a part of a strategy aimed at securing the position of the key players and/or the institution itself. Thus, it can be deduced that input from such groups (certainly for those encountered here) on matters relating to the aims and objectives and range and content of the education will be made from that point of reference. It therefore seems appropriate to note that while contributions from such groups are valid, they must be gauged against this background. Judgements will have to be made about how consistent these are with objectives which reach beyond immediate sectional interests.

QUALITY AND IN-HOUSE PROVISION

The discussion of the reasons – or underlying philosophy – for institutional involvement in CPE raised important issues which will continue to feed the ensuing analyses. The next immediate focus is in-house provision. This is a broad term used to draw together any or all professional and educational development (usually short course) activity conducted within and/or by the company or professional body concerned. Bearing in mind the concerns of the work as a whole, the focus will be on the process by which courses come into being, and on the way in which quality is addressed – if this occurs in any formalised way.

Two features of the review are of particular relevance to the ongoing discussion. One is essentially practical. It is the issue of whether there are any features of practice – any individual mechanisms used in these contexts – which may (in suitably modified form) offer anything for university CPE provision. Again, it needs to be borne in mind that what follows is not intended as an exhaustive survey of such possibilities. But, having said that, these are organisations operating at the forefront of their respective sectors on this issue, and so if such features do exist, at least some indication could be expected to be revealed by these cases.

The other issue is of rather broader interest and, at least in part, looks to develop the themes addressed earlier. It is the assessment of the varying ways in which this matter of provision is addressed and whether the nature of institutional priorities impinge upon this. Examples from industry and professional institutions will again be cited.

At Regional Services, the work conducted in-house did not constitute the whole of the short course provision that employees were involved with. The concentration was on those aspects which could be identified as management skills. Courses based on the extension of technical expertise were dealt with, virtually without exception, by outside bodies.

The mechanics of the organisation of provision were fairly well formalised. At the first stage – planning – we can see both a careful integration of the various interests and influences; and significantly, a continuity into practice of the commercial rationale around which CPD has been seen to be constructed. The period of planning is developed around attention to each of the following elements or factors.

The opening stage relates to yearly performance review meetings held with individual members of staff. These are somewhat akin to the individual performance review (IPR) of the National Health Service, or the system of performance review now operating in UK universities. The relevance to CPE is that a part of the meeting involves the setting of training objectives, identifying needs and the like.

The next phase is just as important, arguably even more so, yet cannot be pinned down to something as explicit as the outcome of a single yearly meeting. It is the integration of the above *personal* needs with the established *business* needs. Such training as is identified by the opening procedure must not contradict, or even fail to contribute to, the underlying commercial emphases. Here, then, is confirmation of the importance of establishing a context, a meaning for CPE, within which individual actions can be understood. Thus, a continuity between expressed purposes at a general level, and restricted practice in terms of educational provision, is recognised.

The following stage is to take the result of the fusion of the first two and consider to what extent the courses which exist in the established portfolio are suited to the achievement of the newly defined objectives.

This initial phase of activity is clearly all important. For in it, the nature, limits and purposes of practice are being defined and those definitions are being made on the basis of underlying aims (which in turn are influenced by the needs of institutional survival and market-based self-interest). Although the nature of these resultant emphases may not be satisfactory for university provision, the central implication – the need to tie in practice with aims – certainly is.

At this point the relevant internal staff are introduced into the process to undertake course design, based on a clear appreciation of aims and objectives. This design period will involve consultation with those considered to hold a valid input.

Up to the point of delivery these are the means by which quality, as defined in relation to identified goals, is considered. Attention to the actual nature of the delivery is perhaps a little less formalised, with a heavy reliance on the value of selecting experienced people. Modifications on the basis of evaluations are expected.

On that very matter of evaluation, the approach adopted had two distinct strands, each dealing with a separate facet of the operation. That ever present of the evaluation process – the exit survey – has been designed solely to elicit information on the actual efficacy of the course. Questions used are intended to discover whether the course actually met its stated objectives. So, for instance, it might be used to confirm the delivery of planned content. There is no interest in individual consequences and subjective experience. Whether such a limited agenda is the best use of evaluation sheets, or indeed whether this form of monitoring requires an evaluation technique as such is debatable. However, the clear identification of a purpose for the questionnaires and their use in tandem with a second approach on a regular basis demonstrates a definite rationale behind action. It was expected that the data collected from exit surveys would be fed back into the (re-)design of future courses.

The complementary element centres on the impact of provision for individuals. Each attender is encouraged to have both a pre-course meeting with a supervisor to determine exactly what personal expectations of the course are, and a post-course discussion to see how far these have been matched. In so far as this concentrates attention on the provision, its value is recognised. There are, though, problems with this. One is that in practice such meetings do not always occur. This is largely a matter of organisation and, of course, is not insurmountable if they are considered to be genuinely beneficial.

There is a further concern which is rather more fundamental. Again this relates to the breadth of purpose to which CPE may or may not be put. In a commercial setting where the purposes are simple, and therefore relatively narrow and identifiable at an early stage, noting 'what one wants and needs from a course' is, in theory, possible. If the content – say in a university setting – of a course extends rather beyond the narrow and/or technical to address complex social issues which cannot easily be learned or pre-identified, the approach becomes problematic. For instance, courses on AIDS awareness for teachers or racial awareness for magistrates may well (hopefully) throw up issues which had possibly been beyond the experience or terms of reference of attenders prior to involvement. In such cases, pre-course meetings are only likely to be able to identify increased awareness as a broad, largely unproductive and unfocused aim; or else they would encourage the pre-selection of principal issues which could actually act against an openness required to experience and embrace a challenging issue fully. Thus, although in certain circumstances a strong case could perhaps be made for this approach, for the purposes of university CPE, it is not quite so clear cut.

Even though the procedures were well established, the evaluation process in this company was not considered to be beyond debate. Other forms of follow-up evaluation were being actively considered. Certainly, the range of approaches that this may incorporate, adopting a less pre-defined structure could – as discussed earlier – introduce kinds of procedures of more widespread value.

One additional finding which is perhaps a little surprising is the absence of a written policy to co-ordinate this fairly detailed activity. The reason given for this was simply that one was not necessary and, indeed, that such a document may lead to an increase in bureaucracy which – by rhetoric at least – company policy was firmly against.

In many ways the process of putting on in-house courses has a significant level of similarity across all of the industrial examples. Thus, to avoid unnecessary repetition these will not be discussed in detail. It is the case, though, that the variation of approach which does exist throws up points which merit consideration in their own right.

Despite this broad compatibility of practice, there is one feature which is intended – over the course of the next three years – to affect the way in which quality as an issue is addressed for in-house work within Monopolex. It is the intention to go for BS5750 accreditation. The motivation behind this policy is revealing, especially when seen in relation to the critique of the standard presented in chapter 2 and, indeed, the misgivings about (as well as the support for) the standard expressed in chapters 4 and 5. If BS5750 is to be considered as the centre piece of an approach to quality, the first question to be asked has to be whether or not those who are adopting it believe that it will achieve the ultimate end – i.e., to secure a significant leap in quality. When this issue was directly raised, the surprising yet highly informative response was an unequivocal no. In line with one element of my earlier critique of the nature of the standard, the justification for the time and expense involved with its implementation was that in the end they would *be seen* to be quality providers, thereby enhancing and developing their position against competitors. The rationale was purely commercial. It was image based. Whether or not quality as such was to benefit was not really the issue. If it contributed to the commercial viability of the organisation then that was the aim satisfied.

At present the policy at Monopolex relies on the integration of results of an annual review with commercially grounded aims as the basis of action. The emphasis on the latter element is institutionalised into practice through the requirement that an individual's immediate line manager must sponsor a training request; its direct value to the com- pany must form the basis of the decision-making process.

At John Jeffreys Ltd a co-ordinating role, in a process similar in structure to that outlined above, is performed by a development sub-group. In this instance, the responsibility to ensure a business payoff is removed from the immediate manager and placed in the hands of this group. It was stated that 'Any request for provision has to be approved by the training group, who must be convinced there is a business need for the training' (Employee Development Manager, John Jeffreys Ltd, interview, 1992).

One contentious (at least it would seem to be from the perspective of an outside observer) feature of practice relating to in-house (and other) CPE opportunities at John Jeffreys Ltd is the policy of giving graded access. What this means is that certain high-flyers (usually the most highly qualified graduates) are given priority access to funds, and to time, to develop professionally. This pre- sents a clear point of departure from any attempt at establishing quality either within professional bodies or universities. Although CPE is, by its very nature, restrictive (i.e., to post-qualification professionals), this form of limiting access to continuing education within professions is something distinct from that. There are suggestions that this policy may be reviewed in the future. But it has been an established part of practice for several years, presumably on the basis that it suits the ongoing requirements of the company.

Across the professional institutions, the approaches taken to quality and in-house work were rather diverse. One of the systems presented was written, formalised and considered in some detail. Approaches elsewhere were significantly less so. A brief review of the latter style will follow details of the well-established and ingrained mode of operation.

At PITPS quality assurance had until recently been addressed in a rather half-hearted way. In the period since 1988, however, there has been a fundamental revision of the process.

Although they do not operate as a profit-making concern – breaking even is considered the guide – there is an awareness that alternatives to their own provision do exist and that offering something members will want to part with their money for is obviously needed.

The institution uses two systems for the provision of short courses which can fall under the banner of in-house. In one of these, they are responsible for the whole thing, including the technical details and speakers. In the other, they contract in a commercial company. From the point of view of QA, however, this is claimed to hold little practical consequence as both forms need to go through the same system. Thus, whatever the source, the institution now has a major influence over the composition and quality of the range of courses. Interaction with outside agencies is based on the assumption of participation and modification. They do not simply buy in the finished article.

Figure 6.1 is an approximate reproduction of a diagram currently distributed within the institution. It forms a schematic representation of the policy process as a whole.

When a course is planned explicit attention is given to two important elements: (1) the skills and experience of speakers; and (2) the quality of the technical information being presented.

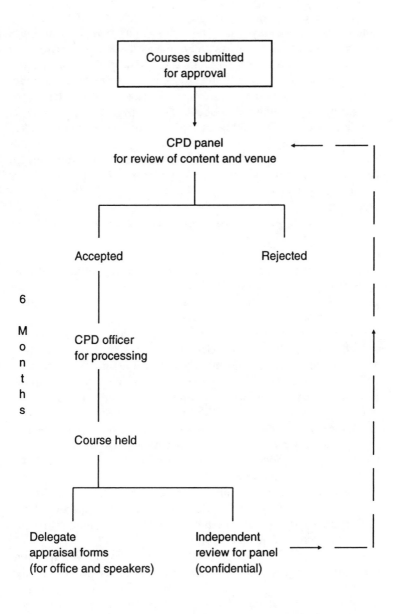

Figure 6.1 QA systems for CPD courses (PITPS)

Initially, a course going through the system will be termed 'authorised'. It is only when the course has been run and has evaluated successfully that it can be re-classified as 'authorised and approved'. When a course is in the 'pre-approval' phase, the preference is to present it to the largest audience possible (in practice in London rather than in the regions). This is in order to provide the strongest potential for feedback. The ultimate fate of a course is decided by the CPD panel (a specialist grouping within the institution). This is not simply a matter of acceptance or rejection but could, for example, involve approval for course content but only on the condition of the removal or replacement of certain speakers. The evaluation process (described below) forms the basis of such adjudication.

The planning process is regarded as flexible and variable. In theory, however, the elements of it should contribute to the acquisition of skilled tutors presenting up-to-date relevant information. While the early stages of planning are open to shaping the most appropriate form by those involved, this phase always involves a presentation to the CPD panel who consider both the individual course components and overall viability. From that point the process of putting on the course continues into subsequent stages.

The delivery phase is acknowledged as not yet having received as much attention as it requires. There was a feeling that this could well be the point at which developments are likely to occur in the near future. The immediate problem is the current lack of guidance or training given to speakers. Although, some effort is made to detail the nature of the audience, as assessed by age and experience, that is as far as any assistance or development goes. As a result, the institution is dependent upon selections made in the planning phase (meaning that this assumes greater importance still) with no potential to iron out emerging difficulties between selection and completion. The result is that shortcomings are only apparent at the evaluation stage, a situation which to some extent undermines the underlying ethos of quality assurance.

In practice, the biggest difficulties have been found with speakers brought in from contexts where professionals are rarely the audience (notably universities). There was an acknowledgement by the interviewee that staff development on this issue could play a valuable role.

Evaluation receives at least as much attention as any other phase in the system under consideration. It provides another example of a two-tier approach. The first utilises the evaluation sheets used widely in most centres of CPE provision. Distributed and discussed early on in the event, they are collected at the end of the session. These are always analysed both by central office and by the speakers. Significantly, despite their prominence in the whole QA cycle, the CPD panel infrequently receives the data from this mode of evaluation. In fact, they only see this evidence when they make a direct request for it. This is quite important, for it signals a degree of apathy towards the value of this form of appraisal and reinforces the significance of the second element of evaluation which is routinely a part of the panel-based decision-making process.

This feature that is afforded greater respect than the on-the-day evaluation sheet is a written report by one of the delegates (a senior member of the institution) on all aspects of the course. The report is produced under conditions of anonymity – i.e., the identity of the reviewer is known neither by the tutors nor by the CPD panel. For each course a report is passed to the panel and this report assumes a high level of importance in the formulation of decisions about the success and future viability of the event. Such a procedure brings with it – in glaring form – the problem of individual bias. Quite simply, these reports are the views of just one professional, a person who will inevitably bring a fairly restrictive focus to the evaluation. The institution and its representatives were fully aware of this. It was not, though, regarded as a serious enough drawback to bring into doubt its continued use.

This element of the system was claimed to be unique to the institution. It had evolved over the period in which the institution has provided courses for its members. There is no doubt that it offers a means of obtaining an unequivocal judgement on events. However, the emphasis it places on a single person's involvement, especially when this occurs in isolation from other modes of evaluation (long-term evaluation was acknowledged as useful but not possible under the existing institutional arrangements), makes its value somewhat debatable.

The situation at the NIEP was virtually the full reverse of the above. Quality assurance was not considered to be a part of the remit of centrally located CPD staff. In part this can be explained by the rather more decentralised approach to provision which exists in comparison with PITPS. But the suggestion from the interviewed CPD officer was that systematic treatment of QA did not exist in the regions either. This is not to say that courses are not developed in a manner which permitted the consideration of quality by individuals, but rather to stress that no co-ordinated approach is involved.

Perhaps a clue to the kind of rationale shaping such a pattern is given in the evidence from the IRP. As the central role is seen to be one solely of facilitation and an attitude exists which stresses the individual responsibility of professionals to select courses for themselves, a laissez-faire attitude to QA evolves. Market forces are seen as the true arbiters of quality – an attitude not restricted either to these institutions, or in fact to this sector. The implication is that professional autonomy and responsibility may be jeopardised by an overly controlled approach to course provision – something which does not seem to concern the (no less independent) professionals and representatives of PITPS.

Across the two sectors a variety of approaches and practices are evident. Indeed, individual procedures adopted – such as varying forms of evaluation – are worthy of consideration. But once beyond the practical level, it is the nature of differences in relation to institutional priority that particularly warrants attention. What this is re-affirming is that procedures, approaches or systems do not exist in isolation from the dynamics and priorities of the institutions into which they fit. Moreover, such factors are not determined – and cannot be predicted – by the identification of structural location alone. Variations between one company and another, as well as between one professional institution and another, were apparent. The structural factor should not though be dismissed, as again business needs for the commercial enterprises and members needs and institutional survival for professional bodies were often the touchstones. All in all, the position is that whatever the variation, systems of (or approaches to) QA must be grounded in an understanding of overall intent. This is clear to those who are shaping policy in the above examples. It is something which those in the university sector could profitably address to avoid obtaining a quality which conforms to the (market-orientated) preferences of interest groups rather than to their own expressed aims.

UNIVERSITIES: LINKS AND COMMENTS

For the final part of this chapter, I will move the focus towards universities and university provision. The aim here is not so much to detail the range of links between these bodies and individual universities – that is the task of a more quantitative approach. Instead it is to use the experience (or indeed lack of experience) of these institutions with the higher education sector in general, and universities in particular, as a means by which points of interest can be raised. Thus, the range of elements which I will cover includes both written guides to quality and verbal expressions of the way in which quality needs to evolve. In a manner consistent with the earlier discussion, such positions are regarded as inseparable from varying institutional priority with no guarantee that the bases of action will be consistent across sectors.

For Regional Services, involvement with universities existed only on an ad hoc basis; no regular pattern was established. Moreover, the attitude expressed by the company training manager displayed a pragmatism about future links. The feeling was that CPE providers exist in various sectors and that universities had to compete against these. This is not to suggest there was a call for universities to enter the mass market, indeed the opposite can be seen to be true. The intention was to stress the market position of universities whilst suggesting that their strength lies in its knowledge-at-the-cutting-edge. This was perceived as the most appropriate focus for universities.

Having noted this, however, a quite clear plan of action was advanced by which, according to the respondent, the quality of university provision could be enhanced. The features of such an approach, detailed below reflect the fact that the understanding of quality underlying it, is derived from a commercial ethos. While it was not the case that the lessons-to-be-learnt were regarded as being all one way – from industry to universities – there was a clear feeling that quality would be more likely to be achieved if attention were paid to the following.

1 A modified approach to customers. In particular, the incorporation of commercial language to address the business sector was identified as necessary.
2 An awareness of business culture, i.e. learning what businesses expect.
3 Use of appropriate marketing. This point returns to the belief that university work is frequently of the very highest calibre and yet even award winning departments fail to capitalise on such accolades.
4 A generally increased responsiveness.

Coupled with the view that university offerings are often too theoretical, these are the main features of a quest for CPE as advanced by Regional Services' training manager. Whether or not this is acceptable, totally or partially, is another matter. It is a decision which like many others demands a return to an examination of purpose. I will return to this crucial issue again shortly during a look at the third industrial case example.

The long established private company (John Jeffreys Ltd) whilst putting a lot of attention into their own training centre, also paid for their professionals to attend university courses – so long as the important 'meeting a business need' criteria had been satisfied. An occasional reluctance among members of staff to use universities was reported by the company development manager. This was grounded in what was described as customer perceptions. While the reputation of universities for expertise was rarely questioned, certain features of the practicalities of university provision are seemingly a problem for many employees. Examples which have recently been raised by company professionals with this manager include: poor university facilities, unhelpful caretakers, and even the presence of students on campus! There is a serious issue which was raised alongside, and was in parallel to, the latter point. It is a perceived unease about involvements with universities per se. The 'unfamiliar culture, and a concern that tutors would be talking over their heads' (Employee Development Manager, John Jeffreys Ltd, interview, 1992) were raised as problems inherent in the situation. However, perhaps this says a little more about business culture than university quality.

Beyond such details one message for university providers was again clear: the guiding force should be a customer-driven approach. The business of the continuing education of professionals in universities was regarded as no different – in basic terms – as the production of any given product. From this perspective while the operation may be complex, the foundation of it is certainly simple – satisfy the paying client and quality is assured.

Although Monopolex undertakes a small amount of regular work with universities and a certain level of satisfaction is achieved, there is an underlying problem which prevents more interaction. It comes in the form of the company's requirements that what is learned should be at all times directly and immediately applicable to tasks within the commercial environment. Thus, we are in the territory of technical information transfer rather than education in any general sense. So this provides another practical illustration of the already theoretically established difficulty of an over-reliance on customer-based criteria. A restriction is being placed around what CPE can be and how its quality might be assessed. This inevitably leads back to questions about the nature of CPE, not the least of which is whether the case for CPE as a primarily educational entity can be maintained without a re-consideration of its funding base.

The demands made by a company such as this are illustrative of the conflicting and potentially contradictory location in which CPE currently exists. It is further testament to this existence at a point of tension that the only easy answers are those which blatantly over-look one or another of the key facets of its existence. Perhaps the main point is that if the income generation/customer-driven path is chosen then limitations and restrictive consequences will become ingrained. Whilst under the current structure, dismissing such requirements will induce financial pressures, it will only be when the whole debate about purposes (individual, institutional and societal) and funding of the continuing education of professionals is widened, that questions of quality will be able to be addressed unhampered by the unique and difficult position currently experi-enced by university CPE.

The debate about whether or not universities should be used to any significant degree by the PITPS actually revealed a deeper ongoing dispute within the ranks of the profession (or at least the professional body) as a whole. At the present time, there is in fact very little use made of higher education. The extensive network of courses provided by the institution can be seen as instrumental in this. However, further influences can be found in both the perceived nature of university work and in the composition of members themselves.

The problem was traced by the interviewee to that characteristic of this institution identified earlier – that there is a real and perceived split amongst members between those regarded as practising and those regarded as theoretical. This conflict of interest hits at many features of the organisation. For instance, there is currently con-siderable debate about how far their journal should reflect an ethos of the discussion medium for a learned society or be the point of dissemination for practically based skills. As the academics will frequently be university based (and, therefore, potentially providing courses), the perception among practising professionals is that what is offered will generally be of little direct relevance. If they are to pay for CPE, they want that provision to be distanced from the theore-tical. Such courses are seen to be more appropriately served up by the institution itself. Of course, certain individuals will at times cross over these boundaries. They will act as providers in universities as well as in the institution; they may also at times be both theoretical and practising professions. But these are in broad terms the divisions which are shaping the overall context at the moment.

Thus institutional involvement with universities is limited and, as a consequence, so is the influence over, or the interest in, the means of assuring quality. In fact, there was an assumption of quality about university provision in general. So long as those attending were not demanding something immediate and applicable in every case there was a general sense of satisfaction. It was only when the emphases of the two distinct sections of the profession were inadvertently integrated that the difficulty emerged.

The situation at NIEP regarding involvement with universities was in some ways similar to the above. Although, as a whole, this profession is well represented throughout higher education, and at a regional level many connections have been established, the institute does not, and indeed consciously will not, validate or even recommend courses falling under the banner of CPE to its members. The nearest they come to this is the current move towards building up a *non*-evaluative database of events. This is not seen as a precursor to a more direct involvement.

Having observed the impact of this kind of rationale in action earlier, it should be appreciated that this is no oversight, but is actually something which is related to the very idea of professionalism which is held. The knowledge and experience of university provision of undergraduate courses has introduced an assumption of quality. Any suggestion of the need to shape the organisation of CPD courses is resisted. Personal judgements and informal contacts are regarded as far more suited to the situation.

In the final example – the IRP – a considerable number of members are involved in university courses after initial qualification, yet once more a direct role for the institution is not seen as appropriate. So, for instance, they have not to date commissioned any courses, and this is not seen as a potentially significant route to exercising influence over the quality of provision. While a central information-providing role is accepted, that is the limit. An essentially practical reason was expressed for this approach. It was stated that the institution puts a considerable effort into undergraduate provision and that this must remain their priority. As a consequence, the relative new-comer of CPD – although wholeheartedly supported – is left to other means of securing quality. As such, the 'healthy' competition between providers, the informal approach to quality assurance (personal recommendations), and the need for academics to be seen to be exhibiting a professionalism remain the preferred routes.

These are the approaches of individual institutions. It can be recalled, however, that each of the above is a member of an umbrella organisation concerned with the promotion of CPD in their respective fields. On the one hand information emanating from this source seems to reveal an allegiance to a distanced approach. However, a rather more interventionist stance is also discernible in its literature.

As a member of this grouping each of the above institutions utilise the document which has been produced (sector umbrella group, guidance paper). It is, though, a paper which is essentially limited in scope. While it can be viewed as a contribution to the quality debate, it in no way undermines the individual strategies outlined.

Although the document is designed to provide guidance to providers, it clearly establishes the context of this by the following statement. 'It is generally felt that the quality and relevance of events must be a matter for the user firms and individuals to judge.' However, in response to what it describes as 'requests from continuing professional development providers', it has established certain criteria to be followed. It has to be made clear, though, that what is detailed is not an input to the quality of the course as such; it is merely a statement of the most suitable way of giving the prospective user an advance indication of the aims, content and emphases of the course. Therefore, the actual quality of provision remains the responsibility of providers and the judgements on that quality remain firmly rooted with the experiencing client.

The document states that the following should accompany details of administrative arrangements in pre-course material.

It is recommended that the following information be included in addition to that relating to administrative arrangements:
- The objectives of the conference, short course, seminar etc.
- A clear description of those for whom the event is primarily intended and separately those that may find it useful.
- A clear indication of the subjects to be covered, their content and level.
- The qualifications and experience of the chairman, course leader, speakers etc.
- A timetable which indicates the amount of time to be spent in formal learning sessions.

- Details of the material (reports, speakers' contributions etc.) to be supplied to supplement the event and to enable participants to undertake further studies.
- The extent, if any, to which a particular professional institution is willing to recognise the event for continuing professional development.
- Arrangements for the provision of certificates of attendance if required by participants.
- Arrangements for feedback, including participants' views, to employers and others.
- The definition of continuing professional development.

(Sector umbrella group, guidance paper)

Thus, the document is by inference suggesting areas which may well be worth concentrating on in the pursuit of quality; it is not, though, actually devised for that purpose. It might well be difficult to follow the guidance principles for information dissemination without having first addressed associated issues in a concrete, course-specific way, but that is not considered a matter which should be pursued any further.

Overall, the discussion of the cases in these two sectors and their forms of association with universities have shown the importance of the notions of institutional priority and sectional interests in influencing positions. Be it the push to define quality in terms of satisfying commercial needs or the overriding belief in informal judgement and professional selection, the themes are continually relevant. These are among the main themes discussed in the concluding section.

CONCLUSION

This chapter has drawn illustrations from what is a considerable range of potential sources. Those with a vested interest in CPE constitute a significant number, both within and beyond the ranks of professionals themselves. The decision to select cases where the institutional ethos already included a commitment to CPE/CPD meant that a focusing of attention was possible. An understanding of the situation was not feasible by reliance on the assumption of either pure similarity or complete differentiation, both were involved. Of some importance, though, is the frequently found internal consistency – i.e. the relationship between stated priorities and actual practices. The roles of institutional dynamics and

sectional interests in influencing the conceptualisation and operationalisation of CPE were confirmed as pivotal.

These kinds of points relate to the four elements of the perspective outlined in the introduction to this chapter. It is now
appropriate to return to these and develop them somewhat on the
basis of the evidence.

The opening point acknowledged the validity of at least considering the transfer of mechanisms. In fact a comparison of the
experiences of these groups with the accounts of university providers described earlier would tend to suggest that there is little in
these examples which has not been considered and/or incorporated
in higher education. However, a couple of interesting examples did
emerge, notably in the area of evaluation. For instance, the use of a
'delegate' report as practised by the PITPS merits discussion, though
as detailed earlier, this approach is not without its problems.

Although an openness to consider elements of approaches from
elsewhere is potentially of use, the second point is really the one
that puts this into a proper, and rather more complete, context. It is
that the classification of a course as constituting 'quality' involves
not just setting procedures in place, but also that these are directed
towards the achievement of aims. These aims will be determined by
sectional interests. This was fundamental to the discussions within
each of the sub-sections. The absolute determining role of commercial success or institutional survival in the decision to participate in
CPE in the first instance was substantiated. Crucially, this starting
point was integrated with CPE practice in activities within and
beyond the institution concerned. As such judgements on quality
were above all concerned with satisfying localised aims.

In effect, this is supporting the assertion that quality in CPE, and
the procedural means of securing it, is less dependent on any
abstract agreed meaning than on what is considered to be either the
immediate or long-term interest of a given party. We have seen how
perspective influences procedures in each of the business
examples. Within the management structure of each case a procedural level or directive was established to prevent the undertaking
of CPE by staff unless a clear commercial benefit could be
envisaged. This is clearly an aid to quality continuing professional
education (as defined in this business context) for those heading the
hierarchy of the commercial concerns, because it limits the allocation of resources to situations which can be positively identified as
being of direct value to the company. But, if the resultant narrow

conception of a quality CPE of this sort may be a little contentious – at least for the individual professional – in relation to the business world, it would certainly raise serious questions about purpose in the university sector.

This seems to hold a couple of important lessons. First, when drawing on opinions about quality in CPE from external sources it should be recognised that, what is offered is a sectional interest. Also that practice in the context from which observations are drawn may not be consistent with what is required for, and applicable to, university provision. This is despite an apparent overlap in some of the procedures employed. Second, that quality depends on link- ing appropriate procedures to acknowledged aims. Moreover, there should be no reluctance to assert that aims within higher education can and do encompass rather more complex phenomena than those found in other sectors.

The third point – that the following of a wholly customer-driven approach may lead to problematic consequences for university CPE – is certainly confirmed. If these customers are the same as those whose interests lie squarely with commercial viability, there would be an inevitable squeezing of educational aims.

This leads on to the fourth element. In many ways it is the one which underpins the whole of the work. It is the component which directs attention towards the relationships between market domin- ance and subject (CPE) identity. The central point is clear on the basis of the examples cited. Interest groups have a definite under- standing of what CPE is for and without exception that reason relates to personal, institutional or commercial needs. These are, by definition, limited in the extent of their concerns. If university-based CPE is to become established in its own right then the ability to move beyond a reactive (to commercial and/or sectional interests) position is essential. The ability to shape pedagogic terms of reference would permit the incorporation of views from varying groups without being overly influenced by them. It could be stated that it is a task which the inherently contradictory nature of the area is acting against. But it is arguably one on which the long-term viability of a quality CPE depends.

CONCLUDING COMMENTS
Towards a framework for quality

At an early stage of this book, I made the point that it is possible to look at QA as both a feature of modern higher education deserving academic attention in its own right, and as an essentially practice-related matter. In working within the themes set out in the introduction, issues relating to one or both of these have been covered. But because of the breadth of the analysis – its examination of other sectors, its analytical elements, and its empirical strands – possible implications have tended to emerge at irregular intervals. In this, the concluding chapter, I will draw together those themes and issues which I regard as being potentially the most useful. In fact, this also serves to highlight many of the most illuminating features of the analysis regardless of possibility for application. However, the main purpose is practical: it is to establish a framework for quality.

THEMES, ISSUES AND QUESTIONS

The first task is, then, to ask whether there are features of the analysis which are suggestive for future action. As a means of making such an assessment, the main themes of the book (expressed in their entirety in the opening chapter) can be re-introduced and examined. At the risk of over-simplification, it is possible to distinguish four principal themes. They are neither entirely distinct, nor do they cover every nuance of the work; they do, though, collectively encapsulate the primary practice-related concerns. They are:

1 Quality assurance has been shown to constitute both a cross-sectoral and an international feature of contemporary societies. Of what relevance are existing practices and experiences to university CPE in the UK?

2 On the basis of analytical review and empirical analyses, what judgements can be made about the value of BS5750? What implications for practice do these judgements bring forward?
3 University CPE depends upon both specialist and non-specialist providers. What can be drawn from the evidence collected from these two groups (about aims, concerns and practices) which might inform a quality strategy?
4 CPE can be at least partly understood in relation to the dual pressures (socially located education, and the market) working on it. Are the objectives of interest groups and these of CPE as a discipline compatible? Are quality in CPE and customer satisfaction synonymous? Is the customer always right?

Discussion relating to each of these four will go some way towards, highlighting their practical relevance as well as their academic interest. Each will be taken in turn.

Lessons across boundaries?

All those areas within education – the UK based, the international, the CE specific etc. – and beyond education – construction, health, and welfare – are relevant to this opening theme. In order to most effectively use the mass of available evidence, our purpose will be best served by turning this into two distinct issues. One of these queries the extent to which the direct transfer of approaches is possible or desirable. The other is rather looser, and introduces a whole range of possibilities: it asks what can be learned in the broadest sense from the experience of these sectors.

On the first of these, there seems to be little or no basis on which an argument for the direct transfer of systems can be sustained. Systems have in general been developed to address the needs of particular situations. By this I am not simply referring to the obvious differences of work content, or professional activity, but rather to the purposes of provision and to the touchstones of quality which these engender. Across sectors priorities differ; across sectors notions of what it is that constitutes a satisfactory situation – or indicators of quality – also differ. Furthermore, work patterns and interpersonal structures are established in varying ways. Management structures accepted as normal in one context may well be alien in another.

The example of the construction industry can be re-introduced here. Although there is little doubt that some of the principles on which activity is established will have relevance beyond the immediate context, it is equally clear that this is a partial crossover of interests, and in no sense a complete match. For this is an example in which technical effectiveness and commercial viability are the points of reference – the basis on which the achievement of quality is assessed. It is certainly true that (in revised form) both of these elements are relevant to CPE, but to see them as providing the sum total of what is required is replete with difficulties. Engineering and CPE have different objectives; quality is dependent upon meeting objectives. The development of approaches must begin from a recognition of purpose.

While this may at first seem to frustrate the search for practical applications, in fact the opposite is the case. This is because difficulties of transfer can be traced back to the incompatibility of work structures and of objectives. We can extrapolate an important lesson from this. For it is but a short step from here to the affirmation of the principle of context-specificity. And it is that which provides the first illustration of the lessons of genuine promise which can be derived from these sources.

The value of starting an assessment of quality from sector-related, value-embracing, concerns emerges strongly from Maxwell's (1984) discussion of the health field. For example, it can be recalled that in Maxwell's context-specific schema, effectiveness was included alongside efficiency, and equity alongside economy. In other words, health quality, according to this model, needed to relate to more than the technical and commercial criteria dominant elsewhere – it needed to be built around elements which were context-specific.

What is implicit in this, and indeed was explicitly stated by Maxwell, is that tackling quality issues in health is far more complicated than in, say, business. There is no reason to distance education from health in this regard. The dimension of profit and loss as a measure of quality does not transfer easily. In fact a reliance on it excludes the central impetus to both health and education – its human and social character. The review in chapter 1 showed just how problematic the transfer of business-based systems can be if pursued. Systems purporting to deliver quality by following a commercial model will – almost by definition – be restricting the range of its concerns. Systems purporting to deliver quality by actively engaging with the needs of the situation and by incorporating a willingness to embrace, rather than shun, values can broaden discussions considerably.

179

Thus, the viability of quality starting from a basis of commitment to values emerges from the review. In the field of welfare, Pfeffer and Coote's (1991) insistence on building quality around principles – of, for instance, democratic participation – offered insight into the structure of such a system. And in bringing forward the need for an up-front consideration of the relationship between ethnic minorities and quality developments, Johnson (1991) can be seen to be operating within similar terms of reference. The issue of how health (or educational) quality is to be established, is never going to be an easy task when bearing in mind the circumstances of varying groups in a culturally pluralist society. It is, though, only through the incorporation of such issues into strategies that policies can be formulated.

How continuing educationalists in the US have dealt with quality also contributes to a sense of the importance of context-specificity. They have been exposed to the same kinds of business-oriented models as their UK colleagues. The response of the CE community to that context is therefore of some relevance. The preference for sector-specific policies was clear enough. And the allegiance of writers such as Freedman to flexible and non-imposed systems revealed a welcome concern with the form of the policy as well as its procedural detail.

There is one further 'indirect' lesson which can be drawn from the review. At several stages I included reference to the way commentators within particular fields have described the influences on how quality became a big issue. Invariably these lists extended beyond an agreed need to tackle a local problem. In each case there were institutional, political and social factors at work. Quality and quality assurance could not be understood as somehow neutral phenomena. Quality arrived on each agenda by virtue of a mixture of factors. Thus, at any one time, what is sought from that place on the agenda will vary from individual to individual; institution to institution; political location to political location.

This seems to be a matter of some importance when deciding upon how to approach the question of pursuing quality in a given setting. It is only when individuals, trends and ideologies shaping the quality process have been identified, that decisions can be made about how consistent or inconsistent these are with desired outcomes. And it is only then that a strategy can be agreed upon to achieve acceptable results.

The implication is that a procedural stage might be preceded by one addressing these issues of context. In no sense is the isolation of political (or other) influence a precursor to a withdrawal from the process. Instead, what it suggests for policy development is that before going along a pre-set path, it is worth considering the direction of that progression, and why any given process is being followed. If quality is acknowledged as a social and political construct, rather than a pre-determined entity, the option of re-interpretation is opened up. And the satisfaction of external requirements need not exclude the parallel pursuit of localised understandings of quality.

Consideration of the question of cross-sectoral relevance does not, then, provide the ready made solution which may have been sought. These experiences can, though, act as a formative influence for CPE. These are events and commentaries to be *used*. They can help inform policy development, but only once decisions have been made about where CPE is heading. But that takes us on to a later issue.

British Standards or standardised Britain?

In many ways the attention given to BS5750 far exceeds that which a reasoned analysis of its potential might indicate. It is, after all, both limited in scope (by design) and – with this being a matter of contention – limited in value (by virtue of both its form and its content).

That it has appeared as a discussion point at so many stages of the book is partly a response to circumstance. Whatever its level of usefulness, it is undeniably a talking point. The success of the (more or less formalised) marketing campaign which has built up around it has been to ensure that the vast majority of those involved at least know of its existence as an option. But there is further reason why the standard has been afforded such priority. For in full-bloodedly embracing the terminology of the market, and the ideology of narrow satisfaction of the needs of the source of finance (usually identified as the customer), it is representative of a trend. Therefore, partially, the debate surrounding BS5750 is a debate about whether the ideological baggage that accompanies such management systems is a welcome or useful influence on the development of CPE. Decisions made about the applicability of BS5750 can suggest implications which reach beyond the possible incorporation of one isolated system. Such decisions – and the reasons for those decisions – can provide constructive input for an alternative quality strategy.

Because exposure to BS5750 has been laden with hype, it is sometimes difficult to establish precisely what the system is all about. In offering a detailed review (in chapter 2) the intention was to get a feel for the assumptions, the expectations, and the fundamental driving forces behind the approach – as well as a knowledge of the practical requirements. The parallel introduction of existing evidence on its use in further education, and of the two new sources of information collated for this work, ensures that several angles exist from which to assess the value of the standard.

The lack of enthusiasm for the standard amongst providers indicates that it is unlikely to ever gain a universal welcome as the dominant feature of future policy. The exploration of the standard and its origins revealed solid enough foundations for such doubts. But where does a rejection of BS5750 leave us? Can the flirtation with national standards offer anything to be taken forward? It seems to me that it actually leaves us in a fairly strong position, and with some quite clear messages for future work. In many cases, an avoidance of those difficulties which were and are the downfall of BS5750 suggest more positive alternatives.

Selected examples can be used to make this point. One of the most debilitating of the system's defects was the co-existence of claims for objectivity with a persistent and implicit conservatism. An incorporation of explicit intentions and purposes would both allow the necessary re-introduction of a value-driven education, and an avoidance of falseness inherent in the above situation.

Problems with the bureaucratic, structured nature of activity, and difficulties with the inappropriate language of the standard, could be similarly discussed. But for a further illustration, a practical matter has been selected: money.

It does seem a little perverse that with the current emphasis on quality being flanked by (and quite possibly related to) public sector funding restrictions, an approach requiring such considerable sums of money should be so much in vogue. This seems particularly strange in view of the fact that much of the required money leaks (or gushes) away from education. External management consultants, assessors etc. are the prime beneficiaries. The extent to which such a transfer of resources can be supported is a topic that might well occupy those involved in policy formation.

While the case for the incorporation of BS5750 may be slight, the case for a detailed examination of it is anything but. A careful appraisal of the meaning and implications of the approach reveals issues, considered reflection on which can assist in the shaping of policy towards CPE-oriented concerns.

Provider contributions

This next theme – and the question relating to it – is probably the widest of all. It is also the one in which any relevance to decision making is at its most direct. Turning to the views of providers has the obvious advantage of offering judgements on what is likely to be favoured, and what is likely to be resisted. But the very act of placing value on the views of providers is important irrespective of outcome. For it serves to locate academics at the centre of QA, rather than at one stage removed, as is sometimes the implied, or indeed the actual, position.

How then do we go about using the available data? There is of course procedural detail to be assessed. Yet, if there is to be a continuity with the potential offered by context-specific and value-embracing approaches, a sense of prevailing motivations and of institutional realities are essential. Such a requirement is met by the evidence relating to the aims of provision, and to that on perceived barriers.

The sizeable levels of support for provision committed to social benefit revealed something about existing values. But the failure of this to translate into ideas of quality for the same provision complicates the situation. The tendency to reflect assumptions of a technical understanding of quality, and the consequent lack of association between the achievement of quality and the satisfaction of personal/departmental aims hinders the desired extension of quality discussions. QA was perceived as divorced from fundamental purpose. The (re)connection of purposes and goals (aims) with the means of achieving them (QA procedures) is a priority.

To defer scrutiny of matters identified as ongoing concerns about QA would – albeit at a more practical level – be as damaging as a denial of purpose. These included expressions of anxiety about the shape of the system, and of anxiety about demands that that same system would introduce. Issues such as the perceived threat to academic independence and the location of control for quality measures go to the centre of life in universities. Furthermore, they confirm the need to be sensitive to the demands of circumstance.

Retaining a sense of context-specificity, the consistently raised concerns with time consumption are hard to overlook. University CPE providers are not the only group to be so concerned, but that in no sense lessens the importance that should be ascribed to it. Evolving patterns of university life are intensifying such pressures; quality systems have to be developed with this in mind.

Evidence from the providers included details on other practical issues: on existing policies; on generally used procedures; and on those infrequently used. The availability of this detail provided a catalyst for the analysis of procedural options: the problems and possibilities of immediate and long-term evaluation are examples of individual mechanisms considered. Evidently, much of what will be included at the procedural level of a policy is already operational in some way or another. Thus, on this dimension appropriate selection and re-structuring – rather than starting from scratch – will be a policy's most salient features.

There were, of course, two data sets. The scarcity of moments of difference between the specialists and the non-specialists helped to confirm the validity of the evidence as a whole. One consequence of this is that while policy formulation must proceed from an awareness of differentiation amongst those providing CPE, the issue of a split between the centre and outlying departments need not be a concern.

Is the customer always right?

Casting doubt on the maxim buried in the above question is a contentious matter. Yet, it could be argued that this is a requirement for the emergence of a distinct CPE – one able to relate to the motivations of its own providers. Reflection on the case study material (from professional bodies and employers) gives rise to a questioning of whether quality CPE and customer satisfaction can ever be synonymous. More pointedly, it highlights the strains which exist between the aims of interest groups and those of a broadly based CPE. The orientation of policy is dependent upon the resolution of the issues raised.

The case examples gave an indication of the likely consequence of adopting a purely market-driven approach. For an air of pragmatism was constant. Not surprisingly, it was the direct (commercial or status) concerns of each vested interest which shaped the nature of involvement. And it was the content of CPE, as well as the reasons for participation, which came under this influence.

The nub of the problem is, then, that it is only ever likely to be through coincidence, rather than by design, that a course constructed to the absolute requirements of such interest groups will deal with the broader aims expressed by providers. It is not that the two emphases *cannot* co-exist. But it is the case that explicit attention is needed if this is to occur.

This is the kind of discussion which requires a return to aims and definitions. Customer satisfaction is eminently suited to an isolated and technicist conception of CPE; it is manifestly unsuited to a determining role within a socially located idea of the same subject. It brings with it a commercial reductionism: a concentration on just one aspect of provision.

Different implications, of varying sorts, can, therefore, be drawn from these four issues. These include the direct as well as the indirect; the practical and the conceptual; and those suitable for immediate application, alongside these needing considerable reflection. These are integrated with the identifiable characteristics of CPE to establish a strategy for quality provision.

A THREE-STRAND FRAMEWORK FOR QUALITY

The following proposal is a framework for action. It displays the imprint of the various phases of the work. It has a consistency with, and offers an extension of, both discussions of evidence, and positions outlined in relation to them. Above all, this approach looks to extend the understanding of quality beyond the merely mechanistic; it attempts to reinforce the notion of the need to link identifiable procedures with the reasons (aims, purposes) for undertaking that provision.

Although my own preferences will become (and in many instances already are) clear enough, this is not simply a prescriptive, report-like 'guide'. To determine outcome would be to remove the tie-up between practice and the achievement of aims. And these aims do, undoubtedly, vary. Thus, it is recognised that each dimension will be the subject of interpretation. But in each case the framework, as established, allows for the possibility of the development of QA in the broadest available terms. It allows for the integration of all manner of influences and objectives.

The framework is built on the assumption that quality assurance need not only be negative – a response, a legitimation task, the basis of a funding claim; but can be positive – formative, related to other than instrumental concerns. This ties in with a realisation that external pressures to introduce quality systems are not the only operating influence. For while the social and political pressures towards QA (as something 'new') are readily discernible, there is also an established interest amongst providers which pre-dates the present period. This confirms the positive potential which exists beneath the institutionalised necessity of QA. A staff commitment to extending standards – either through explicit procedures or by less tangible means – has existed independently of current trends. The task for an approach to QA is to work within the realm of realism set by the most visible forces of the former pressures (in this case the funding councils etc.), without letting this overshadow agendas established by the latter.

There are – as indicated above – three strands to the approach. The first is a consideration of quality as a socially and politically located process. This is all about establishing a sound foundation for policy making. It is here that we can begin to consider the feasibility of extending ideas on CPE into action. It is at this stage that questioning purpose is pivotal. It is also at the juncture that the examining of paths laid out for quality takes place. Here, as in other parts of the framework, a question-based format is employed. This is used to underline the expected role for value judgements and preferences within policy construction.

The second component of the framework also encourages explicit decision making. It relates to the selection of an appropriate form – or structure, or set of arrangements – by which QA can become established. This is, in itself, an important issue.

The third part is the consideration of procedural matters – the point at which the technical means of establishing and/or maintaining quality are decided upon. This is very much carried out in relation to strands one and two. In fact, at the time of actual practice, it is unlikely – and would probably be unhelpful – for each of these elements to be undertaken in rigid sequence. This is not unrelated to the fact that there are many connections between the phases: form relates closely with procedures; social considerations with defining aims etc. Separation into the three elements does though help to identify and tackle the matter systematically. The framework is represented diagrammatically in figure C.1, below.

Before going on to discuss each of these strands in more detail, a brief aside is perhaps appropriate. It is on the subject of proposing an approach with three strands (rather than say, one) despite evident concerns with time. Although I touched on this in chapter 5, in view of the priority given to this matter by providers, the following rationale is called for.

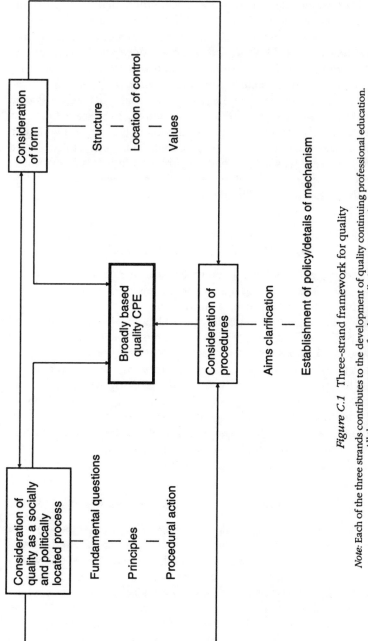

Figure C.1 Three-strand framework for quality

Note: Each of the three strands contributes to the development of quality continuing professional education. All the components are fundamentally interconnected.

My position rests on the following assertion: that the expenditure of time on some form of QA is virtually inevitable; that the issue then becomes one of *appropriate* and useful expenditure of time; and that this is most likely to be achieved once the principles and parameters of action have been established (in relation to exact locations) by those actually involved. Once purposes have been clarified, so practice can be effectively and positively directed towards them. One final point, there is nothing to indicate that when in place such a system would take any more time to deal with than the uncoordinated deployment of individual mechanisms. And there is every reason to expect that the requirements of externally imposed systems – geared to continual compliance for accreditation – would operate on a different scale entirely.

PART 1: QUALITY AS A SOCIALLY AND POLITICALLY LOCATED PROCESS

There are real problems when quality systems begin and end with the procedural. Throughout this text a range of these have been illuminated: the failure to consider the political agenda behind policy, the implicit values hiding behind the mask of objectivity, and the potential for a lack of fit between cross-sectional systems and eventual locations are just a selection. The inclusion of this phase in the approach is intended to provide a forum for the *explicit* consideration of these issues. It offers a means by which social and political objectives, if they are to have a bearing, do so on the basis of conscious decision making rather than implicit assumption. This opening strand is sub-divided into further areas which need attention in their own right. These are: the establishing of context, the clarification of principles, and the linking of these to action.

Establishing context, setting agenda

In this section the initial task is to bring on to the agenda – to raise as part of the decision-making process – a range of fundamental questions which are often overlooked. These are questions which are highly pertinent to the achievement of an understanding of quality. By association, they are also the kinds of questions which constitute the first phase of an examination of what is to be done about quality. They help to clarify the nature of the setting that is being engaged with; who or what constitutes its primary forces; and in what direction provision should be taken. The following questions are those which most readily suggest themselves as requiring the attention of those involved in CPE. It is not an exhaustive list. To some extent, just as values will impinge on the answers that are reached to these questions, so too (within inevitable limits) they will affect question formulation. This is a stage which should assist later decision making. It helps to establish a critical environment; it is not an end in itself.

At the broadest level, the following set of linked questions might well be asked: What has been the political process behind the quality initiative? What rationale was this based on? How do the objectives of the key players relate to those held at departmental level? And crucially, is there an assumed appropriate response (in the form of a favoured system or development pattern) to the quality agenda, and if so is this valid?

What this does is to permit the stripping-away of the gloss of isolationism and artificiality which can surround discussions of quality. It allows for local decisions to be made against an awareness of broader trends. So, for instance, it is possible to understand the simultaneous move towards quality in a range of diverse sectors as something other than miraculous coincidence. And, for example, when concepts such as the customer are introduced into discussions their appropriateness can be assessed with knowledge of all relevant factors. Implications – resulting from the history and contemporary deployment of concepts or themes – can be effectively anticipated. Research in several sectors has addressed the political component of quality. A failure to assess the relevance of such discussions will leave existing trends unchallenged. That can have serious consequences when looking to shape context-specific policies.

The process of context establishment, and question setting, can also be maintained at a rather more focused level. For instance, questions relating to the sector-specific institutions might be put in place. Indeed, it could be argued that these questions are vital for the development of educational policies. The most immediate of these would be: What precisely is required by external (funding, assessing etc.) bodies? How can these requirements be met within an approach designed to take account of local aims? And, how much freedom exists within which to work? Each one of these is geared towards the action determined by realism, and action suggested by professional interest.

Perhaps the most important of all the initial 'big' questions is concerned with the clarification of subject matter. These are the issues to which subsequent developments in practice will relate. They set the tone for the treatment of the topic as a whole. So, of relevance here are questions such as: What is the role and purpose of CPE? To what extent is technical updating the limit of its potential? What form should its social role take? What aims exist for it beyond income generation?

Once considered, corresponding questions about the identi-fication of the point at which 'quality' is achieved are necessarily introduced. Or, to be more specific, the question of what dimen-sions can be used to assess this is introduced; as is the issue of whether these 'indicators' need always be directly measurable. Thus it might be asked: Is the attending professional the final voice to be heard? And is primary influence to be retained by the paying client?

These are all issues which are absolutely fundamental in character. They are also those which a narrow conceptualisation of quality would by-pass. They are the kinds of matters which have a particular importance for a subject with such a precarious existence as CPE. In that sense, an engagement with quality offers CPE the opportunity to firmly establish an identity: one related to the import-ance of its provision.

Clarifying principles

This section relates closely to the above, but here concerns are taken one step further – to the formulation of principles. This is again undertaken by working towards answers to important questions.

A continuation of the review of the character of CPE can be used to illustrate the emphases here. And one of the ongoing issues of the book can be extended in this regard. For in an attempt to 'locate' CPE, a decision can be made about the point at which the legitimate responsibilities of CPE are seen to stop. So, as a matter of principle, as one of the means by which the parameters of quality concerns can be fixed, it can be asked: Does the customer – attending or paying – mark the end of the line for CPE? At once, several of the themes addressed in the text are seen to potentially influence policy.

It is here that the earliest theoretical concerns of the work re-surface as a matter of practical relevance. Abstract discussions about the nature of the client group can evolve into principles which take on a pivotal role in quality policy.

We can re-examine the central issue at this stage. As professionals (in however loose a conceptualisation as is appropriate), the deployment of skills in ways which impinge sharply on the lives of individuals is an essential part of occupational function. Although the acquisition of knowledge is in part about the confirmation or extension of position, its impact is actually more far reaching than that. This is because it is used or applied in real settings – it affects the life process of 'ultimate recipients' – the direct or indirect clients of (continuing professional education's) clients. The way in which this is manifested will vary, but the main point is that the continuing education of people in positions which affect the lives of others (for convenience grouped together by the term professionals) is not an isolated education, but directly links into the make-up of society.

The impact of those holding acknowledged expert labour is as extensive as it is varied. It relates to the nature of the built environment. Through the impact of engineers, architects and others, the very places in which people live and work are affected (even though a professional → ultimate client relationship may frequently be indirect). It relates to human health. Practitioners of orthodox medicine are the primary but by no means sole example of this. And it relates to the care and nurturing of that society, not least through teachers and welfare workers.

None of these applications is, or has been, without problems. Consequences of forms of urban structures (e.g. Castells 1977); and difficulties with welfare provision (see chapter 1) and the medical profession (see, for example Bochner 1983 on doctor–patient relationships) are all well documented. In these, and in many other instances, the learned expertise (or limited selection of that expertise, for instance in the bio-medical model of medical education which has frequently overlooked the importance of personal interaction) is inevitably implicated.

All this provides a complex – though potentially rewarding – environment for the practitioner of CPE. In terms of the clarification of principle, what it means is that matters dealing with the relationship between CPE and the ultimate recipient are there to be examined. Questions acting as a guide in this matter will, therefore, relate to occupational structure and pedagogic impact. Examples of such questions are: To what extent should an acknowledgement be made, in the formulation of provision, of the relative power and influence held by attending clients in post-course situations? And, similarly, can CPE address the potential consequences of provision for the ultimate recipient? The inclusion of such questions allows judgements to be made on the basis of eventual actions and societal locations of attending professionals, as well as in relation to their experience of provision. Such questions take discussion of quality on to a rather different level from that which shapes commercial systems. It is one marker on the way to an altogether wider definition of the area.

There is a logical corollary to the inclusion of non-professionals in the equation. It is to question the validity of a purely technical – that is to say, one grounded in information transfer – structure to courses. This sets out a further stage for the clarification of principle. It is also one with a very close affinity with decisions about course design. For a questioning of the bi-party model permits the inclusion of a much broader range of possible concerns against which the quality of professional education might be appraised.

The following is an example of how adopting a position in which the ultimate recipient is a reference point might link in with provision. It comes from an area which relies on the technical updating of practitioners: mainstream medicine. Within this field there is currently interest in the notion of empowerment – encouraging patients to take control of their own health. In the terms I have been employing this is a matter of the relationship between the client of CPE and the ultimate recipient. It is an example of the way in which professional action – in deciding to encourage or discourage the active patient – affects the wider community.

Under a bi-party model of judgements about quality, the mediated consequence of new CPE is only likely to be assessed from the perspective of the medic. So questions like: was the course enjoyable? Was new information imparted? Have new skills been effectively acquired? Will you attend another course? are measures of (customer) satisfaction and quality. What is all important is that such a two-way conceptualisation leaves no room for the ultimate recipient (and by implication, societal impact) to be included.

If we recall the positions of influence occupied by professionals, an attempt to gauge the value of provision (of say empowerment) by reference to customer criteria alone – value for money, enjoyment etc. – certainly seems to offer a rather skewed emphasis.

Of course, attention beyond the level of the customer is feasible. For instance, course content can be modified in line with need, and broadening the range of participants in planning and feedback – as discussed earlier – can directly influence quality. But there is another issue here. It is the acceptance that one feature of judgements about quality is how far its observable output equates with aimed for consequences. Thus, if CPE is to be consistently extended beyond the technical, assessment of the value of a given course – for example on empowerment (with all the complexities that it entails) – cannot be limited by frequently held assumptions of how to assess 'quality'. Feedback from primary participants contributes to an awareness of quality, but so too (quite legitimately) can an adjudication on the relationship between course orientation and explicitly identified aims for provision. For those original aims might well have been developed with a view to facilitating particular emphases in professional action. Consequently, broadening the terms of reference beyond a bi-party model means that input from, and in relation to, the ultimate recipient is feasible. The assessment of the quality of CPE, therefore, rests on rather more than customer satisfaction alone.

To take this one step further, the point has to be made that the notion of 'the ultimate client' does not refer to a homogeneous mass. Instead, professional activity feeds in to a system composed of individuals (and groups of individuals) with varying needs. And each of these are exposed to varying forms of injustice and inequality. Thus, once more at the level of principle we are faced with questions. One example of this might be: Does CPE need to consider its role within the complexities of a multi-cultural society, and, if so, how? There is a wide array of dimensions of inequality which could just as appropriately serve as the centre piece to such a question.

The clarification of the principles by which CPE is to be pursued can be argued to be a necessity in a period in which commentaries have blown apart the facade of professional altruism. The value vacuum characteristic of commercial systems equally encourages this. But the allegiance of providers to the offering of a CPE which has a positive impact on society (and/or parts thereof) is perhaps the most persuasive influence of all. Not only are the considerations of context and impact necessary as an intellectual exercise, they are also implied by the strategic need to address provider objectives.

Linking to action

Discussion of the third and final phase of this initial section need only be brief as it takes the process forward into a domain which is more fully the province of the final strand. It brings forward the need to link answers to the above questions, and the decided-upon principles, into policy formation and procedural action. The results would contribute to the overall process at several stages. For instance, they can have a direct bearing on the formulation and structuring of the formalised written policy. This is, of course, likely to have a central role in all approaches to QA. More specifically there is a contribution to be made in the clarification of the agreed-upon aims and purposes which will form the terms of reference for all ensuing work. Because this both constitutes the starting point, and serves as an ongoing source of information for departmental activity, decisions about the breadth of appropriate concerns have far-reaching influence.

The conclusions are also relevant to the planning of individual aspects of provision. How this is manifested depends on the nature of key variables: course type, selection of participants in planning process and the like. And, of absolute importance is that they allow for a measure of the achievement of quality. The tools used to judge this are many and various, and there is no reason why mechanisms should not continue to be independently generated to meet specific needs. The question of procedural selection will be returned to in strand three.

The first strand has been all about identifying quality in CPE as a socially and politically located process. It is both the notion of quality and the subject area of CPE that benefits from full contextualisation. For in working through questions relating to both, the potential for clear advance is evident. We can begin to see quality as influenced by process and, therefore, as something able to be influenced; and CPE as open to interpretation in ways which extend some way beyond the idea of a commercial short course provider.

PART 2: CONSIDERATION OF FORM

The systematic consideration of quality brings with it the need for some kind of formal arrangements for its institutionalisation. It requires a form. It requires an overall structure embracing an agreed-upon way of going about things. As with part 1, the inclusion of this strand permits a clearly thought-through basis to action. The form, as much as the content, can reveal an adherence to a particular way of going about the task.

Just as the explicit examination of the nature of CPE reduces the likelihood of a limited conceptualisation of it being embraced without challenge, so too a similar process is evident here. For assumptions about the working environment might also drift into policies. Take, for instance, the case of BS5750. Aside from the range of difficulties associated with its inappropriate content, one of its most problematic features was the form of quality system it assumed. It came as a package; the market-based rationale was sold, and sold hard, but the structures within which activity would take place were taken for granted. For example, we saw from an examination of the system that hierarchical working relationships were required; that clear authority structures had to be in place; and that the whole programme needed to be thoroughly and unswervingly pre-planned. Yet the appeal of the system was described in other terms. This is in part the problem of cross-sectoral transfer. But it is also in part related to the failure to treat each component (including structure) separately.

What follows are those dimensions which, it can be argued, require particular attention within the consideration of form. Each is developed from the analysis. In keeping with the nature of the framework, they are options, not a definitive list.

Of course, not every element of a discussion of form will be contentious. This is certainly the case with the first of these – the need to establish the approach to QA in a written, formalised manner. Indeed, rather than being a source of dissent, this surely provides one feature that is common to virtually all contributions to this field. This is frequently to do with the need to demonstrate that the issue is being addressed.

Yet, despite the fact that this might be able to be neatly thrown onto the 'obvious' pile, it equally needs to find its way on to the 'to be urgently considered' list. The widespread lack of such policies at the time of the research sees to that. But it would be wrong to limit the discussion of written policies to what needs – pragmatically – to be done. Certainly, written policies do offer a visible source of evidence of concern, and thereby a means of satisfying requirements of the moment. They do, though, perform a valid and recognisable function which is distinct from any presentational purpose. They provide the appropriate forum for the integration of all discussions pertinent to quality CPE: they provide the obvious point at which various strands can become interlinked. The form can be shaped to circumstance.

Where the explicit consideration of form really comes into its own is with the introduction of those decisions which have a direct impact on the style of activity, and with the inclusion of decisions on workload. It is of some importance that these should equate with the nuances and prevailing priorities of the setting involved.

A good example of this is the question of time, or rather its effective utilisation. On the basis of the new evidence it is not inappropriate to describe this broadly based concern as a dominant institutional feature of the 1990s. Though acknowledging the restrictions set by the need for some time expenditure, it is a problem which the consideration of form can work with.

For if – in line with my earlier argument – we take it that it is the *unnecessary* expenditure of time which is a major problem, the objective becomes the removal of that element from quality systems. There seem to be grounds for arguing that non-imposed systems would be better suited to avoiding this difficulty. After all, providers are hardly likely to devise approaches for themselves with built-in irrelevancies! While this consideration of non-imposed systems still has to take account of fixed sectoral requirements, there is undoubtedly substantial leeway involved. Rather than laying down systems to be complied with, the principle is of systems which evolve from requirements of practice with a structure to match. In this way, the frustrations of, and resistance to, 'bolted-on', time-consuming approaches are side-stepped. Moreover, this contributes to the quality issue becoming a regular concern; one built into provision. That is something for which there is wide support.

It is perhaps because quality is frequently described as a management issue that it is often accompanied by details of authority structures and responsibilities. While task demarcation is not specific to any sector or approach, it needs to be stressed that there is no single way of developing such responsibilities. Whether or not the introduction of QA should reflect, or change, the nature of the departmental and institutional responsibilities is a legitimate topic for debate. A part of many commercial systems is the expressed need to change institutional culture. Is this a necessary feature of arrangements in CPE? If so, how will this emerge, and with what organisational consequences? The emphasis on managerialism which can creep into the debate needs to be calmly examined. The point at which the form of a system is defined seems to be the obvious stage to do this.

One matter closely related to the style of a department, and to the way in which quality will relate to everyday practice, is the question of the flexibility of arrangements. This topic arises both from the evident limitations of systems which demand too great a degree of rigidity, and from their juxtaposition with practical alternatives (such as those from US continuing education). Only by ingraining the appropriateness of, and possibility for, flexibility can the (varying) aims of providers be met.

Sometimes the arrangements by which policies will be introduced are subjugated to the policies themselves. On occasion, this is reasonable enough. With the quality issue, it is not. For whether explicitly expressed or assumed, the forms of interactions and structures are implicated in the quality debate. As such, I am arguing for the examination of form alongside an examination of content. And, it seems that a strong case can be made for formalising these arrangements without recourse to context-neutral rigidity.

PART 3: CONSIDERATION OF POLICY AND PROCEDURE

This third and final part of the framework is the point at which the groundwork of parts 1 and 2 is developed into a practical strategy; one embracing the technical means of assuring quality. It is at this stage that individual mechanisms are decided upon; that existing activity is accepted, rejected or developed; and elements of the range available are integrated or dismissed.

But this is the continuation of a process, not a separate one. Decisions made at previous stages have a direct bearing here. As implied by the title of this strand, there are two elements involved here: policy creation, and procedural integration. Thus both clarification of purpose and the selection of individual mechanisms are a part of the process.

At the centre of these discussions is the creation of the written policy noted in the previous part of the framework. It will by now be clear that this will constitute rather more than a list of checks for course provision. This is the point at which the full range of comments, answers to questions, judgements and values needs to be brought together. For it is only once these objectives or indicators of valid activity are defined that mechanisms can be introduced.

Thus, decisions about the breadth of concerns to which CPE properly relates are introduced alongside decisions on the relationship to social and political context, and to the evolved nature of the issue. Questions about form are included, as are any specifically educational objectives, if these are not covered in the above. And so as not to lose sight of the full range of influences to which CPE is exposed, more practical first level objectives are integrated. These include reference to the requirements of immediate and visible clients, and the quality requirements of funding bodies and other influential groups.

In essence, the overall aim is to marry pragmatic realism with wider objectives. For the purposes of policy, what is needed on each of the dimensions is an understanding of how they relate to a shared understanding of quality CPE, and how that will be demonstrable. For instance, on the broader aims, a commitment (to be monitored) to a post-(or partially) technicist curricula may be in order. So, one measure of quality CPE might be the extent to which content can be shaped to equate with realities of modern professionalism. It could be subject to review, assessment and revision. On the more practical levels, client feedback might be defined as the only necessary measure of quality.

The inclusion or exclusion of particular objectives will be a matter for debate. However, once decided upon, the crucial thing is to ensure that they do not lie undeveloped in policies. They must be linked to practice.

From both the empirical and analytical reviews, a number of mechanisms/procedures can be identified as potentially useful in offering control over provision. Some of the more visible of these are already very widely used. There is no reason to change this. On the other hand, procedures need to be regarded as fairly neutral in themselves. They only achieve true effectiveness when employed in conjunction with clear objectives (at whatever level) in mind. As a consequence, although it is possible to describe a set of 'core' procedures which might well provide a sound base for QA in CPE, the way in which they are actually operationalised will depend in no small measure upon the stance taken towards issues detailed above.

The following is a list of some of the main options available. They are potential parts of a formalised written policy. They are the tools, not the sole answer. Experienced practitioners will rightly have their own variations of practice. Entirely different formulations will also exist. This is to be welcomed.

The preventive rather than corrective emphasis of QA sits comfortably alongside a priority of systematic course preparation. The use of formalised planning forums is already widely established. Indeed, where a single client exists, their use is virtually essential. But such pre-course activity need not be restricted to that circumstance. In fact, these groups provide one means by which the social basis of activity can come together with process. Course directors and key personnel can shape the composition of such groups in accordance with objectives. Participation may remain limited to the main (paying and providing) players, but it need not be. This will depend on course theme as well as the providers. But representatives of professional and/or community groups are obvious candidates for inclusion. In this way (pre-course) agenda setting becomes a concern of (participatory) QA procedures.

Despite the fact that it must in part exist at a point some way removed from the production of individual courses, the case for inclusion of staff development as a key, mainstream, ongoing procedure is a strong one. External tutors play an important role in CPE, yet their participation in training is not easily co-ordinated. There are, though, many levels of development, each of which might be used at different points. The evidence revealed that in many quarters staff development programmes are already regarded extremely positively. It is really a matter of personnel in individual contexts seeing how these can be most effectively utilised to meet local needs.

Included amongst possible options is the opportunity to examine lecturing and small group work in general. This may or may not be widely applicable. Focus on the specific requirements of working with adult audiences – and indeed post-qualification adult audiences – may be more directly relevant.

As the most visible, and 'image-friendly' of devices the use of on-the-day evaluation seems set to continue. However it is perhaps that perceived value – the fact that their very existence performs a (public relations) function – which might work against the achievement of their most effective deployment. It may act to prevent considered reflection on their value.

But such reflection should be promoted. It can lead to simple improvements which enhance the usefulness of the sheets substantially. One such straightforward measure which was discussed earlier is to ensure that their content is designed to produce usable information in relation to actual objectives. So, apart from the need to ensure sound design (lack of ambiguity in questions, for instance) the underlying priority is to structure questionnaires with a clear purpose in mind and to establish a means for results to influence practice. While this is in theory a standard enough idea, examples of actual practice seem to indicate a current failure to take it on board. The temptation to produce the bland and ill thought-out is real enough.

Another way of supporting the successful utilisation of this technique is by setting clear-cut limits on the role ascribed to it. Exit surveys can only ever produce information on the narrowest of dimensions. As a consequence, they should not be held out as *the* expression of a quality strategy. Their potential rests on the acceptance that they are but one component of a strategy – one linked to a defined level.

Despite the justifiable emphasis on preventive procedures, the above is far from the only form of monitoring which will find a legitimate place in quality strategies. For courses geared to practical applications or, indeed, for those having practical implications, the possibilities offered by longer-term forms of evaluation are substantial. Modes of post-course analysis, of greater or lesser complexity, can be, and in some cases already are, employed to examine the impact of provision in 'real-life' situations. With this type of procedure, the theoretically separable notions of quality of discrete forms of provision (courses); and quality CPE as a whole, come closer together. For broad objectives which may, for instance, require the consideration of the (changing) role of professionals in practice arenas are examined through a means which – as a matter of course – addresses the effectiveness of provision as a learning experience (a practical, tightly defined purpose).

The possibilities for forms of evaluation and modes of collecting feedback are seemingly endless. Short and long term; from tutors, from participants; formal and informal; oral, written; during, between (course components), and after the course.

It has been argued that 'Whatever technique of evaluation is employed, the most important thing is to ensure that positive steps are taken to analyse the information with a view to improving future performance' (Welsh and Woodward 1989: 34). While the point of making constructive use of feedback is certainly valid, the temptation of thinking that there is just one pool of information which any method of evaluation can equally well tap should be avoided. Verbal feedback and anonymous written feedback will not necessarily produce findings that concur; on-the-day and post-course evaluations have largely different purposes. An awareness of the most amenable circumstances for the use of each form is a necessary pre-condition of appropriate use. However, this certainly does not induce the necessity of being limited to one style per situation. The simultaneous use of more than one form is frequently effective over the period of a course.

Having paid attention to planning (both course specific and broadly based); the skills needed by practitioners; and the various means of collecting information on provision, it only remains to establish a means of identifying a link into future activity. Post-course meetings between core figures can provide just that. They offer an environment for assessing the degree to which objectives are being worked toward, or have been met. Related discussions – of the extent to which overall departmental practice is adhering to the quality strategy – need not, of course, be tied to meetings in the aftermath of a particular course.

Precisely which procedures are selected or developed depends on the contribution they can be seen to make to CPE, and, therefore, to the prevailing view of CPE. Decisions made with a view to public relations will limit possibilities. They may be viable in the short term; they certainly will not help to carve out an academic niche for CPE away from the periphery.

So to conclude, this is a framework which is dependent on each of its three strands. Each part is as potentially influential as the others. Without guiding aims and a sense of identity for the area, procedures are limited in their scope. Without explicit attention to the form and building blocks of a policy, implicit assumptions may work to undermine agreed-upon objectives. Thus, each stage is interconnected. And it is precisely because there is a role for each of these strands – and because each of these rely on value judgements – that the proposal takes the form of a framework, not an unalterable system. Ultimately, approaches to quality will depend on answers to the kinds of questions, and discussions on the kinds of issues, outlined. These can neither be systematically pre-determined, nor universally prescribed.

UNDERSTANDING CPE, PURSUING QUALITY

The framework is the culmination of a review which began by rejecting the trivialisation of the main concepts: quality (assurance) and CPE. While writings on quality assurance are frequently characterised by details of favoured systems from the outset, my approach has been different. Before moving to the practical level, I placed an emphasis on an examination of the area, one designed to establish a base of knowledge, and thereby to work towards an avoidance of the existing trivialisation.

This served to provide two reference points for the book. One was the pursuit of meaningful policy. The other was to provide a review of evidence of both direct and indirect relevance. Of course, the two were ultimately connected.

And it is that very connection which provides the answer to the question with which this concluding chapter was opened: whether anything has emerged from the wide-ranging review which has implications for policy. Quite simply, there is a necessary and valuable interaction between existing knowledge and future practice. Analyses of attitudes, experiences and systems have rounded out the understanding of quality (and matters pertaining to it) and CPE (and its location). The three-strand framework embodied those findings. The link between review and policy is thus established.

Policy initiatives which retain an affinity with commercially derivative conceptions of quality, and socially isolated, technicist, views of CPE, are bound and limited to incomplete, and unsuitable, outcomes. The alternative strategy inherent in the proposed model seeks to rid discussion of such inappropriate restrictions. It promotes the idea of engaging with quality in terms which are defined by the nature of CPE. While the possession of knowledge and expertise continues to be highly prized and influential, the role of CPE will remain a complex one. The value of that education will not be able to be satisfactorily assessed without reference to the context into which it fits.

It is the pursuit of an enduring conception of quality CPE minimally affected by transitory influences and restraints that the framework alludes to. 'Quality is in fashion' (Bell 1992: 128) a commentator recently announced. So it is. But the reality is that fashions change. While in time the nature of the fashionable terminology (and requirements) might well alter, the defining features of CPE are likely to be more resilient. Although the demands of the moment must – by necessity – be addressed, they should constitute a part of the deliberations, not be synonymous with them.

The unique position held by CPE – one in which financial, professional and social interests consistently co-exist – demands a context-specific approach to quality informed by the actual features of that situation. Developments on this basis would satisfy immediate material needs. They would also provide the basis for quality CPE in the longer term – quality meaningful in its broadest sense, irrespective of fashion.

BIBLIOGRAPHY

Alkin, M. (ed.) (1990) *Debate on Evaluation*, Newbury Park: Sage.

Allsop, A., Gate, S. and Woolgar, T. (1989) 'Swedish quality, but at a cost', *Health Service Journal* 9 February: 180.

Anthony, F. and Skinner, P. (1986) 'Ohio develops non credit continuing education standards for higher education', *Continuum* 50, 1: 49–57.

Apps, J. (1985) *Improving Practice in Continuing Education: Modern Approaches for Understanding the Field and Determining Priorities*, San Francisco: Jossey Bass.

Armstrong, J. (1991) *Quality Assurance in the Construction Industry* (Departmental Working Paper), Department of Continuing Professional Education, Leeds: University of Leeds.

Arnot, M. and Whitty, G. (1982) 'From reproduction to transformation: recent radical perspectives on the curriculum from the USA', *British Journal of Sociology of Education* 3, 1: 93–103.

Astin, W. (1985) *Achieving Educational Excellence: a Critical Assessment of Priorities and Practices in Higher Education*, San Francisco: Jossey Bass.

Bauer, M. (1992) 'Evaluation criteria and evaluation systems: reflections on developments in Sweden and other OECD countries', in A. Craft (ed.) (1992) *Quality Assurance in Higher Education, Proceedings of an International Conference, Hong Kong, 1991*, London: Falmer Press.

Bechard, R. and Harris, R. (1987) *Organisational Transition – Managing Complex Change*, Reading, Mass.: Addison Wesley.

Bell, D. (1973) *The Coming of Post Industrial Society*, New York: Basic Books.

Bell, J. (1992) 'Quality: the search for quality', in I. McNay (ed.) (1992) *Visions of Post-Compulsory Education*, Buckingham: SRHE/Open University Press.

Black, N. (1990) 'Quality assurance and medical care', *Journal of Public Health Medicine* 12, 2: 97–104.

Bochner, J. (1983) 'Doctors, patients and their cultures', in D. Pendleton and J. Hasler (eds) (1983) *Doctor and Patient Communication*, London: Academic Press.

British Standards Institution (1987) *BS5750/ISO 9000: 1987 A Positive Contribution to Better Business: an Executive's Guide to the Use of the UK*

National Standard and International Standard for Quality System, Milton Keynes: BSI.

—— (1990) *Guidance Notes for the Application of BS5750 Part 2/ISO 9002/EN 29002 to Education and Training*, Milton Keynes: BSI.

—— (1990a) *Draft British Standard Quality Management and Quality System Elements – Guidelines for Services* (ISO DP10004 amended) Milton Keynes: BSI.

—— (1991) *Guidance Notes for the Application of BS5750/ISO 9000/EN 2900*, Milton Keynes: BSI.

—— (1991a) *Guidance Notes for Application to Education and Training*, Milton Keynes: BSI.

—— (1992) *Annual Report 1991–92*, Milton Keynes: BSI.

—— (n.d.) *The Way to Capture New Markets: a Guide to BSI Quality Assurance*, Milton Keynes: BSI.

Brookman, J. (1992) 'Fears over quality test', *The Higher* 6 November 1992: 4.

Brooks, T. (1992) 'Total quality management in the NHS', *Health Services Management* April: 17–19.

Burrage, M. and Thorstendahl, R. (eds) (1990) *Professions in Theory and History*, London: Sage.

Carr-Hill, R. and Dalley, G. (1992) 'Assessing the effectiveness of quality', *Journal of Management in Medicine* 6, 1: 10–18.

Carr-Saunders, A. and Wilson, P. (1933) *The Professions*, London: Oxford University Press.

Castells, M. (1977) *The Urban Question*, London: Edward Arnold.

Cervero, R. (1988) *Effective Continuing Education for Professionals*, San Francisco: Jossey Bass.

Challis, L. (1991) 'Quality assurance in social services departments – new wine in old bottles?', *Research, Policy and Planning* 9, 1: 17–19.

Chandra, A. (1992) 'Towards an Indian accreditation system', in A. Craft (ed.) (1992) *Quality Assurance in Higher Education, Proceedings of an International Conference, Hong Kong, 1991*, London: Falmer Press.

Collins, D., Cockburn, M. and MacRobert, I. (n.d.) *The Applicability of BS5750 to College Operations, 1st Year Report*, Sandwell: Sandwell College of Further and Higher Education.

—— (1991) *The Applicability of BS5750 to College Operations, 2nd Year Report*, Sandwell: Sandwell College of Further and Higher Education.

Collins, R. (1990) 'Market closure and the conflict theory of the professions', in M. Burrage and R. Thorstendahl (eds) (1990) *Professions in Theory and History*, London: Sage.

Commission of the European Communities (1991) *Memorandum on Higher Education in the European Community*, Brussels: European Commission.

Committee of Vice Chancellors and Principals (1990) 'The CVCP Academic Audit Unit', *Trade In* 6: 1.

—— (1991) *Notes for the Guidance of Auditors*, Birmingham: CVCP.

—— (1992) *Annual Report of the Director 1990/1*, Birmingham: CVCP.

Constable, H. and Long, A. (1989) 'Creating professional vocabulary: issues in evaluating and running a short in-service course', *Studies in Science Education* 16: 195–208.

Craft, A. (ed.) (1992) *Quality Assurance in Higher Education, Proceedings of an International Conference, Hong Kong, 1991*, London: Falmer Press.

Crosby, P. (1975) *Quality is Free: the Art of Making Certain: How to Manage Quality So That It Becomes a Source of Profit for Your Business*, New York: McGraw-Hill.

de Wit, P. (1992) *Quality Assurance in University Continuing Vocational Education*, Birmingham: UCACE/Department of Employment.

Deming, W. (1986) *Out of the Crisis: Quality Productivity and Competitive Position*, Cambridge: Cambridge University Press.

Department of Education (1991) *Higher Education: a New Framework*, London: HMSO.

Deshler, D. (1984) 'Reflection on evaluation decision making', in D. Deshler (ed.) *Evaluation of Program Improvement*, San Francisco: Jossey Bass.

Dickens, P. (1990) 'Aiming for excellence in mental handicap services', *International Journal of Health Care Quality Assurance* 3, 1: 4–8.

—— and Horne, T. (1991) 'A quality status symbol', *Health Service Journal* 12 September: 25.

Donabedian, A. (1980) *The Definition of Quality and Approaches to Its Assessment*, Ann Arbor, Michigan: Health Administration Press.

—— (1989) 'Institutional and professional responsibilities in quality assurance', *Quality in Health Care* 1, 1: 3–11.

Economist (1992) 'The cracks in quality', *Economist* 323: 85–6.

Ellis, R. (1988) 'Quality assurance and care', in R. Ellis (ed.) (1988) *Professional Competence and Quality Assurance in the Caring Professions*, London: Croom Helm.

Ettinger, L. (1987) 'Collaboration as key to quality in continuing education programs', *Continuing Higher Education Review* 51, 1: 43–51.

Frackmann, E. (1992) 'The German experience', in A. Craft (ed.) (1992) *Quality Assurance in Higher Education, Proceedings on an International Conference, Hong Kong, 1991*, London: Falmer Press.

Freedman, L. (1987) *Quality in Continuing Education: Principles, Practices, and Standards for Colleges and Universities*, San Francisco: Jossey Bass.

Freemantle, N. (1992) 'Spot the flaw', *Health Service Journal* 9 July: 22–4.

Further Education Unit (1991) *Quality Matters: Business and Industry Quality Models and Further Education*, London: Further Education Unit.

Goodlad, S. (1984) 'Introduction', in S. Goodlad (ed.) (1984) *Education for the Professions*, Guildford: SRHE and NFER-Nelson.

Griffiths, R. (1983) *NHS Management Enquiry Report*, London: DHSS.

—— (1989) 'Quality held in trust?', *Health Service Journal* 30 November: 1466–7.

Hargreaves, A. (1982) 'Resistance and relative autonomy theories: problems of distortion and incoherence in recent Marxist sociology of education', *British Journal of Sociology of Education* 3, 2: 107–26.

Hartley, D. (1990) 'Beyond competency: a socio-technical approach to continuing professional education', *British Journal of In-Service Education* 16, 1: 66–70.

Health Service Journal (1992) 'Quality award', *Health Service Journal* 11 June: 39.

Her Majesty's Inspectorate (1991) *Aspects of Education in the USA: Quality and Its Assurance in Higher Education,* London: HMSO.

—— (1992) *Quality Assurance in Colleges of Further Education,* London: HMSO.

Higher Education Funding Council England (1992) *Quality Assessment,* Bristol: HEFCE.

Hodgson, F. and Whalley, G. (1990) 'Evaluating the effectiveness of in-service education', *British Journal of In-Service Education* 16, 1: 10–11.

Hopkinson, E. (1991) 'BS5750: quality system in ambulance services: part 1', *International Journal of Health Care Quality Assurance* 4, 6: 22–9.

Houle, C. (1980) *Continuing Learning in the Professions,* San Francisco: Jossey Bass.

—— (1983) 'Possible futures' in M. Stern (ed.) (1983) *Power and Conflict in Continuing Professional Education,* Belmont: Wadsworth.

—— (1984) 'Overview', in S. Goodlad (ed.) *Education for the Professions,* Guildford: SRHE and NFER-Nelson.

House, E. (ed.) (1986) *New Directions in Educational Evaluation,* Lewes: Falmer Press.

Hudson, B. (1991) 'Quality time', *Health Service Journal* 12 September: 22–3.

Hunt, J. (1989) 'Quality assurance at a time of cost curtailment', *Senior Nurse* 9, 8: 11–12.

Hurst, K. and Ball, J. (n.d.) 'Quality assurance', unpublished internal papers, Leeds: Nuffield Institute for Health.

—— (1990) 'Service with a smile', *Health Service Journal* 25 January: 120–1.

Jarratt, A. (1985) *Report of the Steering Committee for Efficiency Studies in Universities,* London: CVCP.

Jarvis, P. (1990) *An International Dictionary of Adult and Continuing Education,* London: Routledge.

Johnson, M. (1991) 'Health and social services', *New Community* 17, 4: 624–32.

Johnson, T. (1972) *Professions and Power,* London: MacMillan.

Kald, A. and Nilsson, E. (1991) 'Quality assessment in hernia surgery', *Quality Assurance in Health Care* 3, 3: 205–10.

Kalkwijk, J. (1992) 'The Netherlands: the inspectorate perspective', in A. Craft (ed.) (1992) *Quality Assurance in Higher Education, Proceedings of an International Conference, Hong Kong, 1991,* London: Falmer Press.

Knox, A. (1987) 'Strengthening continuing education instruction', *The Journal of Continuing Higher Education* 35, 3: 18–20.

Kwong Lee Dow (1992) 'Academic standards panels in Australia', in A. Craft (ed.) (1992) *Quality Assurance in Higher Education, Proceedings of an International Conference, Hong Kong, 1991,* London: Falmer Press.

Larsson, L. and Ötiman, S. (1992) 'Quality assurance in urine analysis', *Quality Assurance in Health Care* 4, 2: 141–50.

Lenn, M. (1992) 'The US accreditation system', in A. Craft (ed.) (1992) *Quality Assurance in Higher Education, Proceedings of an International Conference, Hong Kong, 1991,* London: Falmer Press.

Lewis, R. (1990) 'The current role of the Council for National Academic Awards', in C. Loder (ed.) (1990) *Quality Assurance and Accountability in Higher Education*, London: Kogan Page, Bedford Way Series.

Loder, C. (ed.) (1991) *Quality Assurance and Accountability in Higher Education*, London: Kogan Page.

Lynch, A. (1984) 'The personalised quality assurance program', *Health Management Forum* spring: 67–74.

Lynch, G. and Eastwood, A. (1991) 'The contribution of a quality assurance system to change within a social services department', *Research, Policy and Planning* 9, 1: 23–4.

Mason, R. (1985) 'International training in quality assurance', *World Hospitals* 21, 2: 6–7.

Maxwell, R. (1984) 'Quality assessment and health', *British Medical Journal* 288: 1470–2.

—— (1992) 'Dimensions of quality revisited: from thought to action', *Quality in Health Care* 1: 171–7.

McIlroy, J. (1988) 'A turning point in university adult and continuing education', *Adult Education* 61, 1: 7–14.

— and Spencer, B. (1988) *University Adult Education in Crisis*, Leeds: Leeds Studies in Adult and Continuing Education.

Mickevicius, V. and Stoughton, W. (1984) 'Management and quality assurance', *Health Management Forum* autumn: 4–9.

Mijnheer, B. (1992) 'Quality assurance in radiotherapy: physical and technical aspects', *Quality Assurance in Health Care* 4, 1: 9–18.

Muller, D. and Funnell, P. (1991) *Delivering Quality in Vocational Education*, London: Kogan Page.

Murphy, R. (1988) *Social Closure: The Theory of Monopolisation and Exclusion*, Oxford: Clarendon Press.

Øvretviet, J. (1990) 'What is quality in health services?', *Health Service Management* 86, 3: 132–3.

PA Consulting Group (1989) *How to Take Part in the Quality Revolution: a Management Guide*, London: PA Consulting Group.

Palumbo, D. (ed.) (1987) *The Politics of Program Evaluation*, Newbury Park: Sage.

Parkin, F. (1979) *Marxism and Class Theory: a Bourgeois Critique*, London: Tavistock.

Parsons, T. (1954) 'The professions and social structure', in T. Parsons (1954) *Essays in Sociological Theory*, New York: Free Press.

Perry, P. (1990) 'Is there a need for a higher education inspectorate', in C. Loder (ed.) (1991) *Quality Assurance and Accountability in Higher Education*, London: Kogan Page.

Peters, T. and Waterman, R. (1983) *In Search of Quality: Lessons from America's Best Run Companies*, New York: Harper & Row.

Pfeffer, N. (1992) 'Strings attached', *Health Service Journal* 2 April: 22–3.

—— and Coote, A. (1991) *Is Quality Good For You? A Critical Review of Quality Assurance in Welfare Services*, London: IPPR.

Pollitt, C. (1990) 'Doing business in the temple? managers and quality assurance in the public services', *Public Administration* 68, winter: 435–52.

Reerink, E. (1989) 'Editorial: quality assurance in health care of developing countries', *Quality Assurance in Health Care* 1, 4: 195–6.

Reynolds, P. (1986) *Academic Standards in Universities*, London: CVCP.

Rowntree, D. (1981) *Developing Courses for Students*, London: McGraw Hill.

Ruston, R. (1992) 'BS5750 and educational establishments', *Coombe Lodge Reports* 23: 85–94.

Saks, M. (1983) 'Removing the blinkers? a critique of recent contributions to the sociology of professions', *Sociological Review* 31, 1: 1–21.

Sallis, E. (1990) *The National Quality Survey*, Bristol: Staff College.

—— and Hingley, P. (1991) *College Quality Assurance Systems*, Bristol: Staff College.

Sensicle, A. (1992) 'The Hong Kong initiative', in A. Craft (ed.) (1992) *Quality Assurance in Higher Education, Proceedings of an International Conference, Hong Kong, 1991*, London: Falmer Press.

Shaw, C. (1986) *Introducing Quality Assurance*, London: Kings Fund.

Shimberg, B. (1983) 'What is competence? How can it be assessed?', in M. Stern (ed.) (1983) *Power and Conflict in Continuing Professional Education*, Belmont: Wadsworth.

Skinner, P. (1987) 'Ohio recognises critical components for quality off-campus programmes', *The Journal of Continuing Higher Education* 35, 1: 20–3.

Smylie, J., Calvert, B. and Gerber, G. (1991) 'Program evaluation as a measure of the quality of a new approach to community psychiatric care', *Quality Assurance in Health Care* 3, 4: 247–56.

Staropoli, A. (1992) 'The French comité national d'évaluation', in A. Craft (ed.) (1992) *Quality Assurance in Higher Education, Proceedings of an International Conference, Hong Kong, 1991*, London: Falmer Press.

Stern, M. (1982) 'Can you walk into the marketplace and keep your academic virtue?', *Mobius* 2: 54–65.

Todd, F. (1990) 'Comments on professional education', internal departmental paper, Department of Continuing Professional Education, Leeds: University of Leeds.

—— and Tovey, P. (1991) *Quality Assurance for Continuing Pro- fessional Education Course Development*, London: CNAA.

Touraine, A. (1974) *The Post Industrial Society: Tomorrow's Social History: Classes, Conflicts and Culture in the Programmed Society*, London: Random House.

Tovey, P. (1992) 'Assuring quality: current practice and future directions in continuing professional education', *Studies in the Education of Adults* 24, 2: 125–42.

Tucker, A. and Mautz, R. (1985) 'Queuing up for quality: the politics of graduate programming, *Educational Record* 66, 3: 11–14.

Volkwein, J. (1989) 'Changes in quality among public universities', *The Journal of Higher Education* 60, 2: 136–51.

Vroeijenstijn, T. (1992) 'External quality assessment: servant of two masters? the Netherlands university perspective', in A. Craft (ed.) (1992) *Quality Assurance in Higher Education, Proceedings of an International Conference, Hong Kong, 1991*, London: Falmer Press.

Vuori, H. (1992) 'Quality assurance in Finland', *British Medical Journal* 304: 162–4.

Welsh, L. and Woodward, P. (1989) *Continuing Professional Development: Towards a National Strategy*, London: FEU/PICKUP.

Westergaard, J. (1992) 'About and beyond the "underclass": some notes on influences of social climate on British sociology today', *Sociology* 26, 4: 575–87.

Williams, P. (1992) 'The UK academic audit unit', in A. Craft (ed.) (1992) *Quality Assurance in Higher Education, Proceedings of an International Conference, Hong Kong, 1991*, London: Falmer Press.

Williams, S. (1990) 'Assuring quality in community care', *International Journal of Health Care Quality Assurance* 3, 1: 9–15.

Wistow, G. (1991) 'Quality and research: the policy and legislative context', *Research, Policy and Planning* 9, 1: 9–12.

Witz, A. (1990) *Professions and Patriarchy*, London: Routledge.

Yin, R. (1989) *Case Study Research: design and methods*, Newbury Park: Sage.

NAME INDEX

Alkin, M. 85
Allsop, A. 32
Anthony, F. 90
Apps, J. 86
Armstrong, J. 11, 23, 24, 25, 28
Arnot, M. 68
Astin, W. 86

Ball, J. 32, 35
Bauer, M. 82, 83–4
Bechard, R. 39–40
Bell, D. 87
Bell, J. 202
Black, N. 31
Bochner, J. 191
British Standards Institution (BSI)
    40, 55–64 *passim*, 71–4 *passim*
Brookman, J. 85
Brooks, T. 41, 44
Burrage, M. 6

Carr-Hill, R. 31, 32–3, 44–5
Carr-Saunders, A. 6
Castells, M. 191
Cervero, R. 9
Challis, L. 49
Chandra, A. 82
Collins, D. 78
Collins, R. 6
Commission of the European
    Communities 10
Committee of Vice Chancellors
    and Principals (CVCP) 81, 81–2,
    85

Constable, H. 85
Coote, A. 49–52, 180
Craft, A. 82
Crosby, P. 44

Dalley, G. 31, 32–3, 44–5
De Wit, P. 85
Deming, W. 41
Department of Education 80
Deshler, D. 85, 89
Dickens, P. 40–1, 47
Donabedian, A. 36–7, 38, 47

Eastwood, A. 47
Ellis, R. 34, 41
Ettinger, L. 86

Frackmann, E. 82
Freedman, L. 86, 87, 88–90
Freemantle, N. 42–4
Funnell, P. 11, 12
Further Education Unit 77

Goodlad, S. 10
Griffiths, R. 33, 39–40

Harris, R. 39–40
Hartley, D. 10
Health Service Journal 40
Her Majesty's Inspectorate (HMI)
    77, 77–8, 79, 86
Hargreaves, A. 68
Higher Education Funding Council
    England (HEFCE) 80

210

SUBJECT INDEX

Academic Audit Unit (AAU) of the
    CVCP 81–2, 85
acceptability 35, 38
access to CPE 109–10, 163–4
access to services 35, 38
agenda setting 188–90
aims of CPE provision 146–7, 183;
    CPE specialists 98–100, 101–2;
    interest groups 153–9, 175, 176;
    non-CPE specialists 121–4
architects 26–7
audit, quality 80, 80–2, 84–5
authority system 71–3

barriers to QA 183–4; CPE
    specialists 111–13; non-CPE
    specialists 138–42; welfare 49
BS5750 15, 55–75, 178, 181–3, 195;
    achieving quality status 61;
    construction industry 23; CPE
    specialists 103–5, 112–13, 115;
    and education (assumptions
    and content 64–74; integration
    and transfer 62–4); further
    education and 63–4, 77, 78, 79,
    80; health 40–1; interest groups
    163; non-CPE specialists
    127–31, 144, 147; quality system
    requirements 59–62;
    requirements and structure
    58–9; system presentation 56–8
business needs see commercial
    viability
business studies 120

closed courses 109–10
closure, social 6–7
collegial interaction 89
commercial organisations 39–40,
    150, 151; aims of CPE 153–6;
    criticism of TQM 163–4;
    in-house provision 160–4; links
    to universities 169–71
commercial viability: BS5750 56–8,
    67–8; construction industry
    28–30; interest groups 153–4,
    155, 163, 175–6
community care 47
competitiveness 56–8
constituency representation 89
construction industry 22, 22–30,
    102, 178–9; nature of 23–5;
    participants, professionals and
    QA 25–8;technical accuracy and
    commercial viability 28–30
consumerism 33, 51
context 54; BS5750 and 65–6;
    construction industry 30;
    context-specific QA models and
    health 34–8; establishing 160–1,
    188–90; transfer of systems and
    178–81; UK continuing
    education 84–6
continuing professional
    development (CPD) 156–7
continuing professional education
    (CPE): characteristics of 5–6;
    extent of provision 96–7;
    professions and 3–11; quality

212